BECOMING AN EFFECTIVE THERAPIST

LEN SPERRY

Barry University and Medical College of Wisconsin

JON CARLSON

Governors State University

DIANE KJOS

Governors State University

Boston ■ New York ■ San Francisco
Mexico City ■ Montreal ■ Toronto ■ London ■ Madrid
Munich ■ Paris ■ Hong Kong ■ Singapore ■ Tokyo
Cape Town ■ Sydney

Executive Editor: *Virginia Lanigan*
Series Editorial Assistant: *Robert Champagne*
Marketing Manager: *Taryn Wahlquist*
Production Editor: *Michael Granger*
Editorial Production Service: *Modern Graphics, Inc.*
Composition Buyer: *Linda Cox*
Manufacturing Buyer: *JoAnne Sweeney*
Cover Administrator: *Kristina Mose-Libon*
Electronic Composition: *Modern Graphics, Inc.*

For related titles and support materials, visit our online catalog at www.ablongman.com.

Between the time Website information is gathered and then published, it is not unusual for some sites to have closed. Also, the transcription of URLs can result in unintended typographical errors. The publisher would appreciate notification where these errors occur so that they may be corrected in subsequent editions.

Library of Congress Cataloging-in-Publication Data

Becoming an effective therapist / Len Sperry, Jon Carlson, Diane Kjos.
   p. cm.
   ISBN 0-205-32207-7
   1. Psychotherapy.   2. counseling.   3. Psychotherapists—Training of.   4.
Counselors—Training of.

RC480.5 .B378 2003
616.89′14—dc21

                                                            2002071679

Printed in the United States of America
10   9   8   7   6   5   10   09   08

CONTENTS

Preface   v

Acknowledgments   ix

PART I   OVERVIEW: BECOMING AN EFFECTIVE THERAPIST   1

CHAPTER ONE
The Effective Therapist: An Overview   1

PART II. ENGAGEMENT   23

CHAPTER TWO
Initiating the Therapeutic Process   23

CHAPTER THREE
Establishing the Therapeutic Relationship   36

PART III. ASSESSMENT   55

CHAPTER FOUR
Diagnostic Assessment   55

CHAPTER FIVE
From Diagnostic Assessment to Formulation
and Intervention   70

CHAPTER SIX
Focused and Ongoing Assessment   86

PART IV. INTERVENTIONS   99

CHAPTER SEVEN
Cognitive and Behavioral Interventions   99

CHAPTER EIGHT
Psychodynamic Interventions   110

CHAPTER NINE
Interventive and Solution-Focused Interventions   131

CHAPTER TEN
Systemic and Psychoeducational Interventions   148

PART V. MAINTENANCE AND TERMINATION   159

CHAPTER ELEVEN
Maintaining Clinical Gains, Preventing Relapse, and
Terminating Treatment   159

PART VI. THE PRACTICE OF EFFECTIVE COUNSELING
AND PSYCHOTHERAPY   177

CHAPTER TWELVE
Practical Issues and Ethical Dilemmas   177

CHAPTER THIRTEEN
The Effective Therapist in Action   195

Index   209

Practicing effective counseling and psychotherapy involves both skill and experience. This text is part of a unique learning system—consisting of a text, video and workbook—that is designed to develop and enhance the core skills and strategies necessary to become an effective therapist. The text describes and illustrates the skills and strategies that experienced, effective therapists use in everyday therapeutic encounters with individuals, couples, and families. While some background information, such as the theory supporting specific skills and some historical and contextual information, is included, it is kept to a minimum. The key focus, however, is on developing competency in the core of skills of counseling and psychotherapy which contribute to the learner's effectiveness as a therapist. These core skills reflect the four phases of effective psychotherapy, for example, engagement, assessment, intervention, and maintenance and termination, and recent research on the curative factors in psychotherapy, i.e., therapeutic relationship, specific strategies and interventions, client resources, and the expectancy effect. Each core skill is briefly introduced, described, and illustrated before the learner is guided through a series of skill development exercises which provide them the experience of actually practicing these skills.

What makes *Becoming an Effective Therapist* unique is a focus on the core skills of effective counseling and psychotherapy within the frameworks of the four curative factors in psychotherapy and the four phases of psychotherapy. This book provides the learner with highly effective skill development exercises to master the core skills and assistance in integrating these skills and strategies for working with individuals, couples and families. Besides contextualizing these skills in today's environment of accountability, i.e., managed care, and multiculturalism, the book provides a conceptual "compass" which indicates the most appropriate skills to use in each of the four phases of psychotherapy. Finally, as noted earlier, this book is part of an extraordinarily effective learning system which includes a video and workbook. The video depicts a real life, in-session portrayal of the core psychotherapeutic skill. Each of these skills is demonstrated by master clinicians. The video provides expert instruction to facilitate skill development. The accompanying workbook provides a series of exercises to further enhance your mastery of the content and skills both conceptually and experientially. The workbook contains a series of role-play scenarios, instructions on maximizing the use of the video, as well as case material to help you apply what you have learned.

The text is divided into six parts and consists of 13 chapters. Part I is an introduction and overview of the book. It consists of the initial chapter. Chapter 1 briefly describes the rapid changes and the paradigm shift that is occurring in the practice of counseling and psychotherapy. It emphasizes three current trends that are impacting psychotherapy practice: movement from traditional psychotherapy systems to an integrative perspective; focused awareness on multicultural factors; and, increasing demands for accountability. These trends are referred to as the *integrative-multicultural-accountability* perspective. The chapter then conceptualizes the practice of effective psychotherapy in the midst of this paradigm shift by blending theory, best practices, and psychotherapy research. This leads to a discussion of the basic curative factors in psychotherapy and the four stages of the treatment process, which serve as an outline for subsequent chapters. Readers are also introduced to the total learning system consisting of textbook, instructional videos, practice video, and workbook, and we suggest a learning strategy to optimize understanding of therapeutic concepts and the development of basic and intermediate level therapeutic skills.

Part II consists of two chapters and focuses on engagement, the first of the four phases of psychotherapy. Chapter 2 emphasizes that effective therapy requires that clients become fully engaged in the treatment process. The chapter describes the differences between high and low levels of engagement in therapy and the various ways in which therapists tend to misinterpret clients' motivation for therapy. It then emphasizes six strategies for facilitating the engagement process. These include fostering the client's level of readiness for change, eliciting the client's expectations for treatment, aligning goals, and establishing a collaborative relationship between client and therapist. Chapter 3 describes and illustrates a number of standard, traditional concepts and skills about therapeutic relationships. It emphasizes basic and intermediate-level attending and joining skills, active listening, and empathic responding skills.

Part III focuses on the second phase of psychotherapy, assessment, and consists of three chapters. The demands of contemporary practice require that therapists conceptualize and perform an assessment that is functionally-focused. This means that the therapists must develop competence in several areas including: assessing client motivation and readiness for therapy; observing client emotional, cognitive, and behavioral functioning; monitoring client behavior, thoughts, and feeling states, and so on. Chapter 4 emphasizes functional assessment skills. Current practice requires that therapists perform an appropriate diagnostic evaluation in terms of DSM criteria. This means assessing a client's symptoms and levels of functioning; developing sufficient interviewing skills to conduct a mental status exam and evaluate for dangerousness and self-harm; specifying personality pattern and style; and, establishing a DSM diagnosis. Chapter 5 emphasizes these diagnostic assessment skills. While a DSM-IV diagnosis is usually required by third-party payors, it may have only limited value in understanding the client and in planning treatment. Chapter 6 focuses on the value and clinical utility of developing a clinical formulation. It describes how to utilize the formulation in developing a treatment plan and making decisions about treatment duration, frequency, and focus as well in choosing treatment modalities and methods.

Part IV focuses on the third phase of psychotherapy, intervention. It consists of four chapters. Chapter 7 looks at the broad landscape of cognitive and behavioral therapies. It emphasizes key skills in both areas: cognitive restructuring skills; clinically useful desensitization and exposure skills; social skills training skills; and, behavioral rehearsal skills. Chapter 8 begins with a brief overview of psychodynamic theory and strategy and emphasizes insight and the role of insight in counseling and psychotherapy. It then describes the process of interpretation in clinical practice. It also describes the importance of recognizing and dealing with transference and countertransference dynamics. Much of the chapter focuses on developing basic psychodynamically-oriented skills. Chapter 9 distinguishes diagnostic interviewing from therapeutic interviewing and then describes interventive interviewing and its value in briefer therapies and managed care contexts. It then illustrates interventive interviewing strategies which have their origins in several orientations, including solution-focused therapy, and are useful in working in both an individual and couples context. Ten intervention skills are emphasized. Chapter 10 describes various systemic and psychoeducational interventions that are useful in individual, couple, and family therapeutic contexts. The skills emphasized in this chapter include reframing, paradoxical interventions, enactment and expressive skills, as well as various psychoeducational methods.

Part V consists of one chapter and focuses on the fourth phase of psychotherapy, maintenance and termination, as well as some common therapeutic and ethical dilemmas in the practice of counseling and psychotherapy, and concludes with an extended case example. Effective therapists are skilled in fostering change in their clients as well as maintaining that change. Since relapse is inevitable therapists must also utilize relapse prevention skills. And, they must know how to effectively plan for termination and follow-up, should it be indicated. Chapter 11 emphasizes these specific skills.

Part VI consists of two chapters and focuses on the actual practice of counseling and psychotherapy. Beginning therapists quickly find themselves faced with many practical predicaments. Chapter 12 focuses on the legal and ethical issues that frequently arise in therapy, and the skills involved with managing boundaries both inside and outside of sessions. Other skills include the effective use of supervision and referral resources. In addition, the use of the Internet as a resource in counseling and psychotherapy practice is explored. Finally, Chapter 13 pulls together the various understandings and skills learned in previous chapters into a composite whole. In this chapter, a full-length case study provides an overview of the entire therapy process: engagement, assessment, intervention, and maintenance/termination, from beginning to end.

ACKNOWLEDGMENTS

Several individuals have been quite instrumental in bringing closure to this writing project. We particularly want to express our heartfelt thanks to Virginia Lanigan, Robert Champagne, and Marty Tenney and the rest of the Allyn & Bacon crew for helping us launch this ship that seemed to have lost power and direction at times. Several professional reviewers such as Tim Melchert, Marquette University; as well as Lillian M. Range, University of Southern Mississippi; Joe S. Bean, Shorter College; Patricia A. Markes, University of Nevada, Las Vegas; Matt Carlson, Penn State University; William V. Fassbender, The College of New Jersey; Doris Moore, Methodist College; and Laurie Rokutani, College of William and Mary; offered valuable feedback for which we are grateful. Likewise we wish to recognize Maureen Duffy, Bill Nicoll, Scott Gillig, and Richard Tureen for their ongoing friendship and colleagueship. Finally, we wish to acknowledge our students—past, present, and future—who provide us the opportunity to develop and implement many of the skill-development strategies and exercises that constitute this book.

PART I OVERVIEW: BECOMING AN EFFECTIVE THERAPIST

- - - - -

CHAPTER 1

THE EFFECTIVE THERAPIST: AN OVERVIEW

PSYCHOTHERAPY FOR A NEW MILLENNIUM

Living today involves experiencing the unrelenting pace of change in society, the uncertainties of a global economy, the reconfiguration of private corporations and social institutions, the increasing privatization of public services, and the unimaginable changes in the delivery of health care services. All these factors have impacted, and continue to impact, the practice of counseling and psychotherapy.

In particular, managed behavioral health care, with its focus on accountability and cost containment, has profoundly influenced the way therapists think and act. Another significant factor impacting practice is the pressing demand for therapist sensitivity and competence with cultural factors such as ethnicity, race, language, gender, sexual orientation, disability, and social economic level. A legitimate question raised by all these changes is, Can counseling and psychotherapy approaches that were instituted 20 to 90 years ago effectively speak to and respond to today's rapidly changing world?

The answer appears to be a qualified *yes*. As psychotherapy approaches have developed and matured over the past two decades, there are indications that some common themes and integrative mechanisms are emerging. These common and integrating themes and mechanisms will be highlighted in this section, as we believe they represent a paradigm shift in the field of counseling and psychotherapy. We describe this emerging paradigm shift as the *integrative-multicultural-accountability perspective.* Before addressing this perspective directly, we look at the learning objectives for this chapter followed by several integrative developments that are enlivening the field of counseling and psychotherapy.

WHAT YOU WILL LEARN IN THIS CHAPTER

1. An integrative review of the four traditional orientations or perspectives in counseling and psychotherapy: psychodynamic, cognitive-behavioral, humanistic, and systemic

2. A clinical description of the four basic curative factors in psychotherapy: client resources; therapeutic relationship; therapeutic intervention; and faith, hope and expectancy

3. A brief overview of the four phases of the counseling and psychotherapy process: engagement, pattern assessment, pattern change, and maintenance/termination, which serves as a model for the remaining chapters of this text

4. A quick introduction to the emerging integrative/multicultural/accountability perspective which will inform psychotherapeutic practice in the coming millennium

5. A user-friendly orientation to the *Effective Therapist* learning system

FOUR TRADITIONAL PERSPECTIVES IN PSYCHOTHERAPY

Clarkin, Frances and Perry (1985) indicate that is possible to categorize the three hundred or more psychotherapy approaches in terms of four major perspectives: psychodynamic, cognitive-behavioral, systems or family, and humanistic. They also contend that these perspectives can be succinctly described and compared in terms of three basic distinguishing factors: therapeutic focus, therapeutic relationship, and therapeutic change process.

We briefly describe these four major perspectives and compare them in terms of the three basic factors. To help focus your understanding of the following discussion, think of the three factors as providing answers to three questions—what, who, and how—regarding each of the four major perspectives. Accordingly, therapeutic focus answers the "what" question, therapeutic relationship answers the "who" question, and therapeutic change process answers the "how" question. You will come to understand that therapeutic focus refers to what the therapist emphasizes, for example, defenses, maladaptive behavior, schemas, etc.; while therapeutic relationship refers to the nature of therapist–client relation or bond, for example, expert–novice, superior–inferior, or mutual collaborators; and, therapeutic change refers to the mechanisms of change that underlie the psychotherapeutic process. You should note that this discussion is not intended to fully describe the history and theory of each of these psychotherapy approaches. You are referred to a standard textbook on theories of counseling and psychotherapy for such a discussion. This section selectively surveys integrating developments in each of these major approaches.

Some of the common and integrating themes and mechanisms from the three perspectives are (1) the therapeutic focus is tending to an emphasis on *schemas;* (2) therapeutic relationships are tending to being *collaborative;* and (3) the common mechanism of therapeutic change appears to be *desensitization.* Desensitization is a process of extinguishing an emotional response, such as anxiety, dysphoria, existential despair, and so on, to a stimuli that formerly induced it (Beitman & Mooney, 1991).

Psychodynamic Perspective

The psychodynamic perspective encompasses a wide range of therapeutic approaches that emphasize the concept that thoughts, feelings, and behaviors are manifestations of inner drives, such as the unconscious. Psychodynamics is a broad category that includes both traditional and contemporary orientations of psychoanalysis, for example, individual or Adlerian psychotherapy, and Jungian analysis, to name a few.

Therapeutic Focus. Traditional psychoanalysts focused on the inner drives of id, ego, and superego. Modern analysts are more likely to focus on relational themes, emphasizing the self, love objects and their interaction. Recently, some object-relations theorists have emphasized schema theory. Slap and Slap-Shelton (1991) describe a schema model of psychoanalysis which they contrast with the structural model devised by Freud. These authors contend that Freud's structural model, the tripartite model of id, ego, and superego, is a theoretical and clinical *cul de sac.* They contend that the schema model is a more parsimonious way of conceptualizing mental functioning and psychopathology that better fits the clinical data of psychoanalysis than the structural model.

The schema model they propose is a two-part model consisting of the ego and sequestered schema. The ego consists of many schemas, which are loosely linked and integrated with one another and relatively accessible to consciousness. These schemas are based on past experience but are modified by new experience and form the basis of adaptive behavior. Sequestered schemas are organized around traumatic events and situations in childhood that were not mastered or integrated by the immature psyche of the child. These schema remain latent and repressed. To the extent these sequestered or pathological schemas are active, current relationships are cognitively processed according to these schemas rather than being treated objectively by the more adaptive schemas of the ego. Essentially, current situations cannot be perceived and processed in accord with the reality of the present event but rather as replications of unmastered childhood conflict.

Another variation of ego psychology is the approach described by Weiss (1993). Weiss contends that in his later writings Freud espoused the "higher mental functioning hypothesis" in which psychopathology is a function of pathogenic beliefs. For Weiss, psychotherapy is a process in which the client is helped by the therapist to change these beliefs. These pathogenic beliefs involve self view, world view, and the moral and ethical assumptions of others. These beliefs, which are to varying degrees unconscious, organize the individual's personality and psychopathology. The individual's personality reflects his attempt at mastery and adaptation. These beliefs warn the individual about the dangerous consequences of pursuing certain goals or experiencing certain wishes, affects, or ideas.

Horowitz (1988) offers another view of schemas within the psychoanalytic perspective. He proposes that everyone has a repertoire of multiple schemas of self and other. Self-schemas include ways to gain pleasure or avoid displeasure, also called innovational schemas; relating to other people and the world, or role schemas; and, ways of helping an individual decide which of two motives to choose, called value schemas. Finally, there are superordinate schemas which articulate the self to the other schemas.

Self-schema develop from the interaction of genetic and environmental factors. Role relationship models develop in the context of interpersonal behavioral patterns. In psychotherapy, the client's schemas become manifest in the role-relationship modes between therapist and client. The therapeutic relationship allows the client to develop insight into these schemas. During the process of working through, the client is assisted in gradually replacing or modifying these schemas.

Therapeutic Relationship. Among classical psychoanalytic writers the terms *therapeutic alliance* and *working alliance* had strong overtones of the therapist's role of expert and healer (Horowitz, et al., 1984). More recently, proponents of ego psychology and object relations viewpoints are more likely to endorse a more collaborative and cooperative relationship. Strupp and Binder (1984) describe it this way: "The therapeutic stance should be that of a reasonable, mature and trustworthy adult who fosters a symmetrical relationship between equals" (p. 46). Luborsky (1984) uses the designation *helping alliance* to reflect this respectful, cooperative stance. Similarly, the Adlerian approach emphasizes a cooperative and collaborative relationship (Dinkmeyer & Sperry, 2000).

In Weiss' approach (1993) the therapist and client have the same purpose: the disconfirmation of pathogenic beliefs. When clients perceive their therapist to be sympathetic to their plans, they typically react by feeling less anxious, more secure, and more confident in their therapist. Accordingly, the therapist does not take a neutral stance, as does the traditional psychoanalyst, but rather becomes the client's ally in their efforts to disprove pathogenic beliefs and pursue more adaptive goals. Therapists' interventions are most helpful to clients when they are compatible with the client's plan or strategy. This contrasts with the traditional psychoanalytic view that the therapist's task was to help the client make the unconscious conscious by interpreting the client's resistances. Like self-psychology, Weiss recognized the curative role of a therapist's warmth and empathy as opposed to the stance of neutrality.

In self-psychology, the therapist's role is not neutral. Rather, the therapist's role is to become a *participant observer* in therapeutic process. In this process, empathy is essentially strengthening the self-structure. Kohut (1984) considered empathy to be a form of vicarious introspection and saw it as having two functions: understanding and interpretation. While understanding is an immediate apprehension of the client's subjective world, interpretation is utilized to assist clients to see that their current reactions are based on empathic failure of significant others in childhood. Thus, empathy serves to validate and help clients organize their subjective world. Eventually, this results in a cohesive sense of self.

Therapeutic Change. In traditional psychoanalysis, neuroses develop when defense mechanisms protect the ego from/against instinctual drives and the remittent anxiety. The change procedure in traditional psychoanalysis consists of four distinct procedures: confrontation, clarification, interpretation, and working through (Greenson, 1967). During confrontation the issue or concern is made evident and explicit, such as a resistance. In clarification, the concern is brought into sharper focus pointing to several instances that exemplify it. In interpretation, the unconscious meaning or cause is made conscious. Finally, working through refers to the repetitive and incremental process of exploring resistances that prevent insight from leading to change. The theory is that the unconscious keeps forbidden and terrifying fantasies, impulses, thought, and feeling from consciousness. Psychoanalytic therapy attempts to minimize and desensitize anxiety by moving in small increments toward the feared object while Adlerian therapy uncovers and removes the neurotic 'safeguard' in an incremental fashion.

In a schema-based approach, such as described by Slap and Slap-Shelton (1991), treatment consists of helping the client to describe, clarify, and work through these sequestered, pathological schema. These schemas are exposed to the client's mature, adaptive ego in order to achieve integration. Clients are helped to recognize how they create and recreate scenarios that reopen their pathologic schemas. The repeated demonstration and working through of the traumatic events which gave rise to the pathological schemas engenders a greater degree of self-observation, understanding, and emotional growth. Psychotherapy for Weiss (1993) is a process in which the therapist helps the client to change these beliefs through interpretation, but interpretation is not the only mechanism of change. In fact, Weiss trusts that clients may be helped to disconfirm these pathogenic beliefs and pursue healthier goals, primarily, by their experiences with their therapists. After accomplishing this, clients may feel safe enough to develop insight on their own without the benefit of interpretation.

Cognitive-Behavioral Perspective

The cognitive-behavioral perspective includes various approaches that emphasize the primacy of maladaptive behaviors or faulty cognitions, or a combination of both maladaptive behaviors and cognitions as the basis for psychopathology. These range from classical behavioral conditioning to contemporary cognitive therapy.

Therapeutic Focus. There was little room in classical behaviorism for any discussion of structure of the mind. However, Beck and his coworkers have pioneered schema theory within the cognitive-behavioral perspective. Beck (1964) introduced the schema concept with reference to depression and more recently (Beck & Freeman, 1990) to the treatment of personality disorders. Early developments in cognitive therapy focused on cognitive distortion and dysfunctional beliefs as they related to depressive and anxiety disorders. However, cognitive therapists pursued a third level of analysis, schemas, to aid in the understanding and treatment of personality disorders which proved to be impervious to the treatment methods based on the first two levels of analysis. Thirty years ago, Beck first described the cognitive triad of depression as negative views of the self, the world, and the future. More recently he has proposed other schemas and subschemas in a manner very similar to lifestyle convictions. He has described various types of schemas: cognitive, affective, motivational, instrumental, and control schemas. Most well-developed, however, are the cognitive schemas regarding self-evaluation and world view, or evaluation of others. Some cognitive therapists (Young, 1990) have described early maladaptive schemas and triggering schemas that are strikingly similar to Adlerian formulations of various personality disorders. Finally, Bandura (1978), a social learning theorist, described self systems, and Kelly (1955), whom many regard as a crypto-Adlerian, described personal constructs in a manner reminiscent of lifestyle convictions.

Therapeutic Relationship. Perhaps the most outspoken proponent of collaboration is the cognitive therapist, Aaron Beck. He uses the term *collaborative empiricism* to refer to a therapeutic relationship that is "collaborative and requires jointly determining the goals for treatment . . . and where the therapist and patient become co-investigators . . ." (Beck & Weishaar, 1989, p. 301). Beck also believes that the therapist's role is that of a guide and catalyst who promotes corrective experiences in addition to utilizing warmth, accurate empathy, and genuineness to appreciate the patient's personal worldview.

Several other behavioral and cognitive-therapists endorse the collaborative perspective (Fishman, 1988; Schwartz, 1988; Woolford, 1988). Meichenbaum (Turk & Meichenbaum, 1983) accentuates the clinical value of a collaborative relationship when he advocates the importance of "entering the patient's perspective." In so doing, ". . . the patient and therapist can work together to establish a similar understanding and common expectations (of treatment)" (p. 7).

Therapeutic Change. Wolpe (1983) and Marks (1987) describe systematic desensitization as a step-by-step procedure for replacing anxiety with relaxation while gradually increasing the client's exposure to an anxiety-producing situation or object. Thus, exposure, in varying degrees, leads to or produces desensitization. These various exposure treatments ranging from desensitization in fantasy, to desensitization in vitro, from implosion or flooding in fantasy to real-life flooding, modeling, operant conditioning, and cognitive rehearsal. In the process, desensitization and extinction clients must redeploy their attention away from negative self-evaluations and toward either the feared object itself or helpful environmental aspects. As a result, they learn a greater degree of self-control or mastery (Beitman & Mooney, 1991). Similarly, more cognitively oriented therapy approaches such as cognitive therapy and rational-emotive therapy target cognition to be desensitized through cognitive restructuring or disputation.

Humanistic Perspective

The humanistic perspective includes a variety of approaches that emphasize experience and meaning rather than drives, behavior, or cognitions. These include Rogers' client-centered therapy, existential analysis, and a variety of experiential approaches.

Therapeutic Focus. Carl Rogers (Raskin & Rogers, 1989) described the self concept, the self ideal and the self-structure as the perception of the relationship of the I or me to others and to various aspects of life (p. 169). Kohutian's self-psychology articulates the self and its development from the selfobject, with reference to the object that represents Gestalt Schools (May & Yalom, 1989) but also emphasizes I-Thou relations (Yontef & Simkin, 1989, p. 339). Although not formally labeled as lifestyle convictions or schemas, the experiential perspective clearly allows for this therapeutic focus.

Therapeutic Relationship. Carl Rogers (1951), who developed person (client) centered therapy, emphasized the importance of the therapist's utilization of warmth, accurate empathy, and genuineness to appreciate the client's inner world, as well as to effect change. Existentialist psychotherapists believe that a collaborative relationship of equals is fundamental to good therapeutic work (May & Yalom, 1988). Kohutian's self-psychology clearly emphasizes the importance of collaboration, with its emphasis on the therapist's empathic mirroring to connect with the patient's inner world from the vantage point of the experiencing insider (Kohut, 1977; 1984).

Therapeutic Change. Yalom (1980) contends that existential psychodynamics are similar to the psychoanalytic view of neurosis and desensitization. While the psychoanalytic formula has instinctual drives arousing anxiety which is then contained by defense mechanisms, the existential formula has awareness of ultimate concerns arousing anxiety which is contained by defense mechanisms. Ultimate existential concerns are death, meaninglessness, isolation, and freedom. The therapeutic strategy utilized in the experiential and existential approaches involves helping the client face the feared awareness of each ultimate concerns. Common to these various therapeutic approaches is helping the client gradually face their fears and stay with them. For example, Havens (1974) proposes that direct human-emotional contact by the therapist desensitizes isolation. Exposure via human contact can extinguish the fear that led the individual to become isolated from others. Havens describes that in the process of facing their fears the phenomena of phenomenological reduction occurs. This means that attitudes are reframed or reconfigured based more totally on experiencing the other people. In "staying with" the other the therapist remains in the phenomenological world of the other to expose the client to an ultimate human connection. Beitman and Mooney (1991) suggest that other experiential approaches, such as the gestalt therapies, and by extension client-centered therapies that target affects, effect change through the same mechanism of desensitization.

System Perspective

Therapeutic Focus. Psychoanalytically oriented family therapists, particularly the object-relations approaches, and cognitive behaviorally oriented family therapy systems that reflect the schema-based perspective with individual patients also utilize schema formulations with couples and families. This is particularly evident in Beck's book on marital therapy (1988), and Wachtel and Wachtel's book on combining individual and family therapy (1986).

Therapeutic Relationship. A comparison of family therapy systems approaches suggests that the communications approach of Satir, the strategic approach, the structural approach, and the MRI Interactional approach (Watzlawick, Weakland, & Fisch, 1974), all place a premium on collaboration between therapist and the client, couple, or family, particularly with regard to cooperation and realigning roles and relationships (Sherman & Dinkmeyer, 1987, pp. 106–107). In addition, Bowen's Family Systems approach (1978) thus endorses a collaborative relationship, wherein the therapist's role is largely that of a coach. Foley (1989) concludes that in the object relations family system (Bowen), structural, and strategic perspectives concludes that the therapist's role is that of teacher and a role model of positive healthy behavior rather than that of expert.

Therapeutic Change. Reframing is a classic curative mechanism in systemic and family therapeutic approaches. Reframing of the client's reality changes the conceptual or emotional context of the problem so that its meaning can be reconstrued in a more manageable and acceptable way. While the concrete facts remain unchanged, the client's perception of the facts is changed. Reframing is often utilized early in the course of strategic therapy and structured family therapy to enable the client to take some initial steps toward the therapeutic perspectives; the mechanism of exposure and desensitization occurs in an incremental fashion (Watzlawick, 1974).

The Integrative-Multicultural-Accountability Perspective

The practice of psychotherapy at the onset of the twenty-first century will be significantly different than it was during most of the twentieth century. This is largely due to the paradigm shift in behavioral health practice, including psychotherapy, that has been underway since the late 1980s. This paradigm shift involves every facet of behavioral health practice including the role of the clinician, the cultural context of therapy, the nature of the relationship between clinician and client, as well as clinical practice patterns. This shift has already resulted in the demystification of some basic tenets and sacred cows of clinical lore. There are three aspects to this paradigm shift: (1) a focus on accountability, (2) a greater sensitivity to cultural factors, and (3) the trend toward integration.

The first and most tangible aspect of this paradigm shift has been what can be called the outcomes revolution (Sperry, 1997). Clinicians find it the most tangible of the three aspects because it has immediate economic consequences. This revolution refers to the increasing emphasis, and even demand, that clinicians selectively provide only the kind of cost-effective therapeutic interventions that result in positive outcomes. That is, if they want to be reimbursed, and possibly even remain in a given provider network, for the psychotherapeutic services they provide. Although the outcomes revolution began prior to the recent explosion of managed behavioral health care, the managed behavioral health care movement has dramatically demonstrated the necessity for outcomes and has accelerated developments in the technology associated with outcomes. Furthermore, managed behavioral health care has sharpened the focus and direction of outcomes research. Essentially, managed behavioral health care involves the utilization of accountability methods in the provision of cost-effective, medically necessary treatment with the goal of removing *medical necessity*. Medical necessity, also called treatment necessity, is the basis for the authorization of behavioral health care, such as psychotherapy. In terms of psychotherapy, medical necessity refers to the determination that psychotherapeutic treatment is "appropriate (and) necessary to meet a person's health needs, and consistent with the diagnosis and clinical standards of care" (NCQA, 1998).

Outcomes measures and outcomes systems are basically accountability methods, while medical necessity has become central to any contemporary discussion of outcomes. Cost-effectiveness and treatment efficiency have become the norm for the provisions of behavioral health services. *Treatment efficiency* refers to the clinical utility of a course of treatment provided by a given provider in a given clinical setting. It answers the question, Is the treatment working for this particular client? Treatment efficiency should not be confused with treatment efficacy or treatment effectiveness. *Treatment efficacy* refers to a research protocol that psychotherapy researchers use to study how well a treatment performs when provided under optimal research conditions, for example, double-blind, crossover study design. It answers the question, Does a new treatment intervention produce better outcomes than commonly used interventions or a placebo treatment? *Treatment effectiveness* refers to a research protocol that health services researchers use to study how well a treatment intervention performs with clients in a clinical setting. It answers the question, Generally speaking, does a given treatment intervention produce beneficial results in actual clinical practice? (Howard, Moras, Brill, Martinovich, & Lutz, 1996). For the practicing clinician the concepts of treatment efficacy or effectiveness are not clinically useful; only treatment efficiency is clinically useful.

This norm of cost-effectiveness and treatment efficiency is radically different from that in which most behavioral health professionals were trained. The result is that many are confused and concerned about the meaning and implications of this paradigm shift imposed on the profession. Some view managed behavioral health care's emphasis on accountability as an intrusion into their practice style or as actually or potentially unethical. While some have embraced managed behavioral health care wholeheartedly, others have come to accept it as inevitable. Whatever their perspective on managed behavioral health care, psychotherapists-in-training will, no doubt, practice in an environment that requires accountability in terms of the quality and outcomes of treatment, as well as the cost-effectiveness of the treatment they provide. One of the emphases of this book and learning system is to introduce you to the type of skills that are consistent with this accountability-focus.

The second dimension of this paradigm shift is the cultural or multicultural aspect. The rapidly changing demographics of America is reshaping its cultural landscape from a Caucasian-majority society to one in which Caucasians may become a minority by the year 2050. Today, terms such as *ethnic minority* are being replaced by *multiculturalism* and *diversity*. Multiculturalism refers to more than ethnicity; it includes language, customs, social beliefs and values, norms, religious practices, gender role expectations, and so on. Why are such cultural factors important in counseling and psychotherapy?

Cultural factors are important in therapy since these factors impact an individual's basic personality and identity structure. "Cultural factors interact with and are molded by the specific historical experiences of the patient as well as by his or her race, gender, age, values and belief systems, country of origin, family migration events, language, and social and ethnic favors, with their resulting degrees of discrimination and disenfranchisement . . . (T)hese variables interact to shape what ultimately becomes a personal identity" (GAP, 2002, p. 19).

In its broadest sense, multiculturalism is generic to all counseling relationships (Pedersen, 1991), and impacts countless aspects of the psychotherapy process. For example, consider the influence of language on one aspect of the therapy process—assessment. It is common for therapists to assess the level of severity of symptoms reported by clients at the beginning and throughout the course of treatment. Usually, this is done by verbal report on a simple 1 (low distress) to 5 (high distress) rating scale. A recent study found that first generation Hispanic clients reported different levels of symptomatic distress to Hispanic or Anglo therapists depending on language usage. When Hispanic clients were interviewed by Hispanic therapists symptom severity was lowest when interviewed in English, higher in Spanish, and greatest in bilingual interviews. Interestingly, Anglo therapists rated symptoms as less severe and assigned higher global assessment of functioning scores (GAF) than did Hispanic therapists. The researchers suggest that bilingual clients often experience greater cognitive difficulty in their second language but express more emotional difficulty in their first. Accordingly, they recommend that because of the shortage of bilingual therapists, therapists need to be trained "to provide competent services to their growing minority clientele" (Malgady & Costantino, 1998, p. 127).

Clinicians who speak and write about standards and competencies in multicultural counseling and psychotherapy indicate that training of counselors and psychotherapists must foster cultural sensitivity and competence in attitudes and beliefs, knowledge, and skills. Since cultural sensitivity assumes a recognition of the cultural dimension, assessment of this dimension is emphasized in this book, particularly in Chapters 4 and 5.

Finally, the third aspect of this paradigm shift is the trend toward integration in clinical practice. There are two ways of achieving integration: (1) integrating theory and techniques from several approaches into clinical practice; and, (2) integrating the findings of relevant clinical research into clinical practice. Table 1.1 compares this integrative perspective to the four traditional perspectives.

This book and learning system is commited to integration in both ways rather than a narrow, sectarian approach to training therapists. The first section of this chapter described integration in terms of four traditional perspectives: psychodynamic, cognitive-behavioral, humanistic, and systemic. The next two sections of this chapter describe the second way of integration.

CURATIVE FACTORS AND DYNAMICS
IN PSYCHOTHERAPY

Based on his review of several psychotherapy outcome research studies, Michael Lambert proposed that there are four common curative elements central to all forms of psychotherapy irrespective of the therapists' theoretical orientation; modality of treatment, individual, group, family; or dosage, i.e., the frequency, duration, and number of sessions (Lambert, 1992). Some would argue that these four elements represent a common, unifying language for the practice of psychotherapy (Miller, Duncan, & Hubble, 1997). The four factors are: (1) client resources; (2) therapeutic relationship; (3) intervention strategies and tactics; and, (4) faith, hope, and expectancy (Lambert, 1992) (Table 1.2).

Client Resources

As we suggest throughout this text, clients do not come for treatment in a vacuum. They come with symptoms, worries, conflicts, and predicaments. They come with a unique

TABLE 1.1 A Comparison of Five Psychotherapy Perspectives

PERSPECTIVE	THERAPEUTIC FOCUS	THERAPEUTIC RELATIONSHIP	THERAPEUTIC CHANGE PROCESS
Psychodynamic	Psychopathology is the result of defensive reactions to anxiety, faulty object representations, or pathogenic schema. Hence, one of these should be the focus of therapy.	Classical psychoanalytic approaches: therapeutic alliance where therapist is neutral but an expert, while the client is submissive. Self-psychology: participant observer Adlerian: cooperative	Clarification Confrontation Interpretation Mirroring Desensitization strategy working through

Cognitive-Behavioral	Psychopathology is the result of maladaptive behavior patterns (behavioral) and/or dysfunctional cognitions or schemas (cognitive). Hence, one or both of these should be the focus of therapy.	Traditional behavioral therapy approach: therapist is expert/client is learner
		Contemporary cognitive therapy approach: collaborative empiricism
			Cognitive restructuring
			Desensitization strategies
			   Systematic desensitization
			   Exposure
			   Cognitive and behavioral rehearsal
			Skill training
			Modeling and reinforcement

Experiential	Psychopathology is the result of discrepancy between real and ideal self (schemas), and/or disturbance in boundary between self and others so that one is not centered in the here and now. Hence, one or more of these should be the focus of therapy.	Therapist–client relationship is collaborative	Empathic listening and responding
			Desensitization strategies
			   Phenomenological reduction
			   Staying with
			   Empty chair technique
			   Guided fantasy
			   Enactment

Systems	Psychopathology is the result of dysfunctional patterns of family boundaries, schemas, power, intimacy, or skill deficits. Hence, one or more of these should be the focus of therapy.	Varies from expert–novice to collaborative depending on the specific approach	Joining
			Skill training (i.e., parenting skills)
			Boundary restructuring
			Desensitization strategies
			   Paradox
			   Reframing
			   Enactment

Integrative-multicultural-accountability	Psychopathology is the result of intrapersonal, interpersonal and/or system dynamics in a given cultural context. Hence, focus therapy on the factors relevant to the cultural context in a cost-effective, efficient manner.	Varies from expert–novice to collaborative depending on client need and cultural context	Tailored integration of above interventions that are culturally sensitive, cost-effective, and efficacious

TABLE 1.2   Four Basic Curative Factors in Psychotherapy

THERAPEUTIC FACTORS	DESCRIPTION
Client Resources	Client resources refer to those resources—both inner and outer—that the client brings to therapy, that aid in recovery *irrespective* of participation in the treatment process. Inner resources include the client's readiness for change, coping and personal/social skills, motivation, ego-strength, intelligence, achievements, psychological-mindedness, courage, and past history of success in change efforts. Outer resources are specific environmental resources that impact the client. These include the client's social support system, financial resources, and even fortuitous events called spontaneous remission factors by Lambert.
Relationship	These include the common or core conditions of effective treatment described by Carl Rogers and others as empathy, respect, genuineness, and unconditional regard. It also includes other factors such as congruency, warmth, concreteness, and acceptance. These dynamics typify a therapeutic relationship in which clients believe they are understood, safe, and encouraged to disclose painful and intimate material, as well as to think, feel, and act in healthier and more adaptive ways. These factors transcend the therapist's theoretical orientation called common factors by Lambert.
Intervention strategies and tactics	These include factors that are unique to specific therapy approaches and range from psychoanalytic to cognitive-behavioral to humanistic to systems as well as to the integrative: clinical interpretation, free-association, confrontation, cognitive restructuring, medication, empty chair technique, biofeedback, systematic desensitization, reframing, family sculpting, miracle questions, or other solution-focused techniques. Called techniques by Lambert.
Faith/hope/expectancy	That proportion of treatment outcomes related to clients' belief in their therapist or provider of care, as well their belief in and hopefulness about the efficacy of the specific treatment to make a difference in their lives. Related to this belief are specific expectations about how, when, and why change will occur. Called placebo effect by Lambert; the opposite of the negative placebo or nocebo effect.

developmental history and cultural roots that define them. And, they come with certain resources, both personal and environmental, that significantly contribute to the outcome of therapy. In medical and psychological research literature, the client's contribution to outcome is related to the phenomenon called spontaneous remission. Similar to the spontaneous remission of a cancerous tumor or the debilitating symptoms of multiple sclerosis, the client in psychotherapy can experience a remission of their depressive or anxious symptoms. Some experience this remission after making their first therapy appointment, but not before keeping that appointment. On the other hand, some clients may be in therapy for months or years with little or no discernible change. What accounts for this difference? It is a matter of the absence or presence of certain kinds of client resources.

Are client resources that important? The presence of such client resources is estimated to account for about 40 percent of improvement that occurs in any treatment (Lambert, 1992). Client resources refer to those resources, both inner and outer, which the client brings to therapy, that aid in recovery *irrespective* of participation in the treatment process. Inner resources include the client's readiness for change, coping and personal/social skills, motivation, ego-strength, intelligence, achievements, psychological-mindedness, courage, and past history of success in change efforts. Outer resources are specific environmental resources that impact the client. These include the client's social support system, financial resources, and even fortuitous events.

Therapeutic Relationship

The therapeutic relationship is the context in which the process of therapy is experienced and enacted. While there are notable differences in the way this relationship is described among the various psychotherapy approaches, most acknowledge the importance of this relationship. A correlation has been found between the therapeutic relationship and psychotherapy outcome, across these various approaches. It is estimated that about 30 percent of the variance in psychotherapy outcome is due to relationship factors as compared to 40 percent which is attributed to client resources or spontaneous remission factors (Lambert, 1992). Based on his analysis of psychotherapy research, Strupp (1995) concludes that the therapeutic relationship is "the sine qua non in all forms of psychotherapy" (p. 70). Furthermore, the research of Orlinsky, Grawe, and Parks (1994) suggests that the quality of the client's participation in the therapeutic relationship is the essential determinant of outcome. In short, clients who are motivated, engaged, and collaborate in the work with the therapist benefit the most from the experience.

Important to the formation of a strong therapeutic alliance is what Carl Rogers called the core conditions of effective counseling and psychotherapy: empathy, respect, and genuineness (Rogers, 1951). It appears that when clients feel understood, safe, and hopeful, they are more likely to risk disclosing painful affects and intimate details of their lives, as well as risk thinking, feeling, and acting in more adaptive and healthier ways. However, these core conditions must actually be felt by the client, and these core conditions will be experienced differently by clients depending on their internal dynamics and cultural matrix. Duncan, Solovey, and Rusk (1992) contend that the most helpful alliances are likely to develop when the therapist establishes a therapeutic relationship that matches the client's definition of empathy, respect, and genuineness.

Intervention Strategies and Tactics

One of the defining features of psychotherapeutic approaches is a unique set of constructs for explaining the change process and socializing clients to become receptive and responsive to various technical intervention strategies and tactics. Such strategies and tactics include clinical interpretation, free-association, confrontation, cognitive restructuring, medication, empty chair technique, biofeedback, systematic desensitization, reframing, family sculpting, miracle questions, or other solution-focused techniques. The content and process of therapeutic sessions are ostensibly different depending on the therapist's theoretical perspective and orientation.

Despite the field's fascination, and near obsession, with specific intervention strategies and tactics, the overall impact of specific intervention on the outcome of treatment is rather minimal. In a seminal review of psychotherapy outcome research, Lambert (1992) estimates that a clinician's therapeutic perspective and intervention strategies and tactics contribute only about 15 percent of the variance in psychotherapy outcome. Miller, Duncan and Hubble (1997) observe that, by and large, clients are much less impressed with their therapists' interventions than are their therapists. They contend that an immediate implication of Lambert's research finding is "that therapists spend less time trying to figure out the right intervention or practicing the right brand of therapy and spend more time doing what they do best: understanding, listening, building relationships, and encouraging clients to find ways to help themselves" (p. 30).

Faith, Hope, and Expectancy

Lambert (1992) notes that the remaining 15 percent of the variance of psychotherapy is attributed to the phenomenon known as the placebo effect. The placebo effect is that proportion of treatment outcomes related to clients' belief in their therapist or provider of care, as well their belief in and hopefulness about the efficacy of the specific treatment to make a difference in their lives. Much continues to be written about the dynamics of the placebo effect and the negative placebo, or nocebo effect, which can actually diminish or neutralize the effect of a powerful treatment (Harrington, 1997). Benson (1996) and Mathews and Clark (1998) recently described the placebo effect as the faith factor suggesting that an individual's belief in the cure or in the clinician who provides the cure has healing or curative power. Related to this belief are specific expectations about how, when, and why change will occur. Research indicates that simply expecting therapy to be helpful somehow reverses demoralization and mobilizes hope, and facilitates improvement (Frank & Frank, 1991). Presumably, the creation of such hope is strongly influenced by the therapist's attitude toward the client at the very outset of treatment. When doubt about positive outcomes, because of the severity or chronicity of the condition or limitations in client or treatment resources are conveyed, even in subtle ways, the placebo effect is unlikely to be triggered nor will the client's sense of hopelessness be easily reversed. However, when the clinician instills hope and the belief that the treatment will likely work, verbally and nonverbally, improvement and positive treatment outcomes tend to occur.

In other words, fostering a positive expectation for change appears to be a prerequisite for successful treatment (Snyder, Irving, & Anderson, 1991).

FOUR PHASES OF THE PSYCHOTHERAPY PROCESS

The course of psychotherapy can be understood as having a beginning point, a middle, and an ending point. Various efforts to describe the course and process of psychotherapy have yielded various formats, such as relationship, assessment, insight and reorientation

(Dinkmeyer & Sperry, 2000). Since this text advocates a multicultural understanding of the therapy process, we sought a model that was culture-sensitive. The phase model adapted from the research of Beitman (1987) consists of four stages of individual psychotherapy that reflect commonalities among both eastern and western therapy systems and approaches (Table 1.3). The four phases described here have been described by Sperry (1999) and serve as a model and advanced organizer for the remaining chapters of this text. The next ten chapters describe the requisite therapeutic skills associated with the four phases that characterize an effective therapist. The four essential phases are as follows.

Phase 1: Engagement

Engagement is the first and most important stage of treatment. Effective treatment outcomes require that the client be sufficiently engaged, for example, commited to and actively involved in, the treatment process. In other words, engagement is required for any therapeutic change to occur. Typically, therapists assume that a client who shows up for sessions and talks about their concerns is engaged in treatment. However, it only takes an instance or two of nonadherence with treatment activities, such as homework, for the ther-

TABLE 1.3   Phases of the Psychotherapy Process

STAGE	GOAL	THERAPEUTIC METHODS
Engagement	To develop a working therapeutic relationship and maximize the client's readiness and motivation for change.	■ Manifest empathic listening ■ Trigger the placebo effect ■ Reverse the client's demoralization ■ Provide effective suggestions and socialization to therapy
Assessment	To specify the client's maladaptive pattern, including behavioral, effective and cognitive (i.e., schema) components, which if changed, lead to more adaptive functioning.	■ Utilize diagnostic questioning strategies ■ Utilize interventive questioning strategies ■ Assess by means of psychological inventories or other Questionnaires ■ Utilize role playing and enactment to elicit and/or clarify pattern
Intervention	To modify or transform the client's maladaptive pattern into a more adaptive pattern.	■ Utilize pattern interruption strategies ■ Utilize cognitive restructuring, interpretation, and/or reframing methods ■ Elicit and support client change factors
Maintenance/termination	To maintain the new adaptive pattern and reduce/eliminate the client's reliance on the treatment relationship.	■ Employ relapse prevention strategies ■ Set or negotiate a termination date ■ Schedule weaning sessions, when indicated ■ Increasingly space medication or therapeutic maintenance sessions when continued use is warranted

apist to question the client's degree of engagement. A general rule is that until an optimal degree of engagement is achieved formal treatment should not proceed. Optimal engagement is indicated by:

1. the client's active involvement in negotiating treatment goals, and realistic expectations for their role, and the therapist's role, in the change process.
2. the client's willingness to follow the ground rules of therapy.
3. the negotiation of a formal or informal treatment contract.
4. high level of client readiness for change, for example, the action level.

A high level of client readiness for change predicts collaboration, compliance, positive changes, while a low readiness predicts resistance, noncompliance, and no change.

The goal of the engagement phase is to develop a working therapeutic relationship and to maximize the client's readiness for change. There are many therapeutic strategies to facilitate optimal engagement. They include: manifest empathic listening; trigger the placebo effect; reverse the client's demoralization; and, provide effective suggestions and socialization to therapy. These are described in detail in Chapter 3.

Phase 2: Assessment

We use the term *assessment* in a very focused fashion: assessment of the client's maladaptive patterns. Pattern refers to the predictable and consistent style or manner in which a person thinks, feels, acts, copes, and defends the self both in stressful and nonstressful circumstances. It reflects the individual's baseline functioning. This pattern has physical, psychological, and social features, such as a sedentary and coronary-prone lifestyle, dependent personality style or disorder, or collusion in a relative's marital problems. The pattern also includes the individual's functional strengths, which counterbalance dysfunction. Patterns include a predictable manner of behavior and thinking. One way of specifying the behavioral component of a pattern is with DSM-IV Axis II personality traits or disorder terms, while *schema* is a specific way of describing the content and style of the thinking component. The goal of the assessment phase of treatment is to specify the client's maladaptive pattern, including behavioral, effective, and cognitive (i.e., *schema*) components, which, if changed, lead to more adaptive functioning. Commonly used therapeutic methods useful in pattern assessment are diagnostic questioning protocols or strategies, interventive questioning strategies, as well as assessment by means of psychological inventories or other questionnaires. In addition, the therapist also may use role playing or other forms of in-session enactment to elicit and/or clarify client patterns.

Phase 3: Intervention

The goal of the intervention phase is straightforward: to modify or transform the client's maladaptive pattern into a more adaptive pattern. Intervention methods potentially include all therapeutic intervention strategies and tactics. For example, these methods include focused pattern interruption strategies, cognitive restructuring, interpretation, and/or reframing methods. A significant intervention method that is so obvious that it is often overlooked is eliciting and supporting internal and external client resources.

In clinical settings, maladaptive patterns often manifest themselves with symptomatic distress and functional impairment. Thus, decreasing symptomatology and/or increasing life functioning are typical treatment goals. Individuals and couples who present for psychological treatment in symptomatic distress are seeking relief from symptoms they have not been able to reduce by their own efforts. Thus, symptom reduction or removal is one of the first goals of treatment. Usually, this goal is achieved with medication and/or behavioral interventions. Research indicates that as symptoms increase one or more areas of life functioning decrease; and therapeutic efforts to increase functional capacity tend to be thwarted until symptomatology is decreased (Sperry, Brill, Howard, & Grissom, 1996).

Phase 4: Maintenance and Termination

The goals of the maintenance/termination phase of treatment are to maintain the newly acquired adaptive pattern, to prevent relapse, and to reduce/eliminate the client's reliance on the treatment relationship. Technically, relapse refers to a continuation of the original episode, while recurrence is the instigation of a new episode. In this text, both terms are used synonymously. In order to prevent relapse, therapists must assess the client's risk factors and potential for relapse, and incorporate relapse prevention strategies into the treatment process.

Therapeutic methods to accomplish these goals are: to employ relapse prevention strategies; to set or negotiate a termination date; to schedule weaning sessions; and, when indicated, to increasingly space medication maintenance sessions when continued use is warranted.

THE EFFECTIVE THERAPIST LEARNING SYSTEM

This textbook is just one part of a total learning system for becoming an effective therapist. Here is a brief overview and orientation to the Effective Therapist Learning System.

Becoming an Effective Therapist (text). This text has been designed to briefly introduce you to the skills sets that experienced, effective therapists utilize in everyday therapeutic encounters with clients. While some background information is included, specifically, the theory supporting the specific skills and some historical and contextual information, it has been kept to a minimum. We have intentionally done this because we believe that while such information might be interesting, it will not, in and of itself, make you a better therapist. Rather, competency in a given set of skills, all the various therapeutic strategies and tactics such as engaging the client (strategy) by making empathic responses (tactic), and a lot of experience learning to perfect these skills will contribute to your effectiveness as a therapist.

Becoming an Effective Therapist (video). This learning system includes a video that has been designed to provide you with a real-life, in-session portrayal of a specific psychotherapeutic skill. Each of these skills is demonstrated by a master clinician. The purpose of the video is to facilitate your understanding and skill development through the learning process called modeling or imitation learning. When a learner observes an expert performing a specific action, the learner is more likely to accurately imitate or reproduce that action, rather than if the learner read or was given a detailed description of the action. By observing a correct and effective use of a given skill and practicing it in a similar context, the learner can be expected to learn that skill with a reasonable degree of accuracy.

Becoming an Effective Therapist (learning guide). This learning guide, or workbook, provides a series of exercises to learn the material both conceptually and experientially. The guide contains a series of role-play scenarios and accompanying instructions that assist you in developing skill, or experiential competence. It also contains case material to help you apply what you have learned (conceptually).

Using the *Becoming an Effective Therapist* Learning System

Here is the learning method that we have found to be extremely valuable in our years of training psychotherapists. We believe that it can maximize your effort to understand and develop skill-competence.

1. Read the specified section in the text. The assigned reading segment will describe the specific skill, provide several examples, usually, case material or transcripts, as well as background material, for example, who developed the technique or skill, for what purpose, and its clinical value.
2. Watch the specified video clip with your learning group or on your own. The text indicates what you should be watching for.
3. Complete the specified Learning Guide exercise and/or reread and study the text section. These exercises should increase your familiarity with the concept/skill and prepare you for the next step.
4. Practice the specified psychotherapeutic skill(s). Usually this involves role-playing a specified scenario (cf. Learning Guide) with your study partner. If you have access to video equipment, you might tape the role-played scenario and then review it looking for areas of strength and potential areas of improvement.

An Important Note to the Learner

To avoid misunderstanding, and to keep matters in perspective, we need to say that we do not believe that skill-learning equals effective psychotherapy. Rather, successful therapeutic work is embedded in a helping relationship between two individuals, a client and a therapist. Relationship dynamics are among the most important. While it is true that being an effective therapist involves more than skill competence, there is a certain degree of skill involved in establishing and maintaining a helping relationship. We hope that you validate this conclusion in the course of your reading, viewing, practicing, and working through the learning exercises in this learning system.

SUMMARY: A CONVERGENCE OF PERSPECTIVES, SKILLS, AND PROCESSES

We conclude this discussion with the following observations.

1. The practice of psychotherapy has been viewed from three distinct vantage points: (1) from the therapist's stance (the five perspectives—the four traditional perspectives plus the integrative perspective), (2) from the stance of the outcomes of treatment (the four common curative factors), and (3) from the process of psychotherapy itself (the four phases). Not only are there actual or emerging integrative themes *within* each vantage point, there are also emerging integrative themes *among* these vantage points. Integration occurs in two ways: integrating theory and technique from several approaches into clinical practice, and integrating the finding of clinical research into clinical practice.

2. From the vantage point of the four traditional psychotherapy perspectives there are clear trends. For instance, with regard to the dimension of therapeutic focus there is a common theme of schema and pattern across all four perspectives.

3. With regard to the dimension of therapeutic relationship there is an emerging consensus that collaboration replaces the earlier emphasis on the therapist as an expert or director of change.

4. With regard to the dimension of therapeutic change process, it appears that desensitization is a common mechanism to explain the various intervention strategies and tactics.

5. Furthermore, it is interesting to note that while treatment intervention methods remain quite distinct, despite all the integrative developments within the four traditional perspectives, experience therapists, who ascribe to one of the traditional perspectives, tend to be quite eclectic in their clinical practice. That is to say, the more experienced they become, the more likely therapists are to use a variety of interventions strategies and/or tactics and techniques from one or more other perspectives than their own.

6. From the vantage point of treatment outcomes research on the curative factors of psychotherapy, we can also note some integrative themes that relate to the four perspectives and phases/processes. The most obvious is that relationship is common to both perspective and curative factors. Outcomes research suggests that the more collaborative the relationship, the more involved the client becomes in the therapy process which tends to promote positive outcomes. Furthermore, relationship is considered to be the second most important factor in accounting for therapeutic change or outcomes according to Lambert's research. Of course, engagement is a particular way of describing an effective relationship.

8. When clients achieve an adequate level of engagement in therapy, it can be assumed that sufficient client resources are available and operative in the therapy process. Again, this should significantly impact treatment outcomes.

9. From a multicultural perspective, it can be assumed that a client who is adequately engaged in treatment is very likely to experience the therapeutic relationship as culturally sensitive and competent.

10. Pattern identification involves patterns and has a cognitive and a behavioral component. One effective way of classifying patterns cognitively is in terms of schemas.

11. From the vantage point of curative factors, relationship refers to the way in which the therapist establishes an environment that promotes the client's risk-taking and action, while faith-hope-expectancy refer to self-curative energy that is elicited from the client. To the extent to which the therapist is also able to engage the client's inner and outer client resources, the stage is set for change to occur.

12. Finally, the therapist's role is to facilitate, orchestrate, and coach the process of change which results not only from various intervention strategies and tactics but from the self-healing energies within and around the client and from the healing energy emerging from the therapeutic relationship itself.

REFERENCES

Bandura, A. (1978). The self-system in reciprocal determinism. *American Psychologist, 33:* 343–358.

Beck, A. (1964). Thinking and depression: II: Theory and therapy. *Archives of General Psychiatry, 10:* 561–571.

Beck, A. (1988). *Love is never enough.* New York: Harper and Row.

Beck, A. & Freeman, A. (1990). *Cognitive therapy of personality disorders.* New York: Guilford.

Beck, A. & Weishaar, T. (1989). Cognitive therapy. In R. Corsini & D. Wedding (Eds.) *Current psychotherapies* (pp. 285–322). Itasca, IL: F.E. Peacock.

Beitman, B. (1987). *The structure of individual psychotherapy.* New York: Guilford.

Beitman, B., & Mooney, J. (1991). Exposure and desensitization as common change processes in pharmacotherapy and psychotherapy. In B. Beitman & G. Klerman (Eds.). *Integrating pharmacotherapy and psychotherapy* (pp. 435–446). Washington, DC: American Psychiatric Association.

Benson, H. (1996). *Timeless healing: The power and biology of belief.* New York: Scribners.

Bowen, M. (1978). *Family therapy in clinical practice.* New York: Jason Aronson.

Clarkin, J., Frances, A. & Perry, S. (1985). The psychosocial treatments. In R. Michaels, A. Cooper, S. Guze, et al. (Eds.) *Psychiatry.* Philadelphia: J.B. Lippincott.

Dinkmeyer, D. & Sperry, L (2000). *Counseling and psychotherapy: An integrated, individual psychology approach (3rd ed.).* Upper Saddle River, NJ: Prentice-Hall.

Duncan, B., Solovey, A. & Rusk G. (1992). *Changing the rules: A client-directed approach to therapy.* New York: Guilford.

Fishman, D. (1988). Paradigmatic decisions in behavior therapy: A provisional roadmap. In D. Fishman, C. Franks, & E. Rotgers (Eds.) *Paradigms in behavior therapy: Present and promise* (pp. 277–291). New York: Springer.

Foley, V. (1989). Family therapy. In R. Corsini & D. Wedding. (Eds.). *Current psychotherapies.* Itasca, IL: F.E. Peacock, pp. 455–502.

Frank, J. & Frank, J. (1993). *Persuasion and healing: A comparative study of psychotherapy (3rd ed.).* Baltimore: Johns Hopkins Press.

Greenson, R. (1967). *The Technique and Practice of Psychoanalysis, Volume 1.* New York: International Universities Press.

Group for the Advancement of Psychiatry (GAP) (2002). *Cultural assessment in clinical psychiatry.* Washington, DC: American Psychiatric Press.

Harrington, A. (Ed.) (1997). *The placebo effect: An interdisciplinary investigation.* Cambridge: Harvard University Press.

Havens, L. (1974). Existential use of the self. *American Journal of Psychiatry, 131:* 1–10.

Horowitz, M. (1988). *Introduction to psychodynamics: A new synthesis.* New York: Basic Books.

Horowitz, M., Marmat, C., Krupnick, J. et al. (1984). *Personality styles and brief psychotherapy.* New York: Basic Books.

Howard, K., Moras, K., Brill, P., Martinovich, Z., & Lutz, W. (1996). Evaluation of psychotherapy: Efficacy, effectiveness, and patient progress. *American Psychology, 51,* 1059–1064.

Kelly, G. (1955). *The psychology of personal constructs.* New York: Norton.

Kohut, H. (1977). *The restoration of the self.* New York: International Universities Press.

Kohut, H. (1984). *How does analysis cure?* Chicago: University of Chicago Press.

Lambert, M. (1992). Implication of psychotherapy outcome research for eclectic psychotherapy. In J. Norcross (Ed.). *Handbook of eclectic psychotherapy* (pp. 436–462). New York: Brunner/Mazel.

Luborsky, L. (1984). *Principles of psychoanalytic psychotherapy: A manual for supportive-expressive treatment.* New York: Basic Books.

Malgady, R. & Costantino, G. (1998). Symptom severity in bilingual Hispanics as a function of clinician ethnicity and language of interview. *Psychological Assessment, 10,* 120–127.

Marks, I. (1987). *Fears, phobias and rituals.* New York: Oxford University Press.

Mathews, D. & Clark, C. (1998). *The faith factor.* New York: Viking.

May, R. & Yalom, I. (1989). *Existential psychotherapy.* In R. Corsini & D. Wedding (Eds.) Current psychotherapies (4th ed., pp. 363–404). Itasca, IL: F.E. Peacock.

Miller, S., Duncan, B., & Hubble, M. (1997). *Escape from babel: Toward a unifying language for psychotherapy practice.* New York: Norton.

National Committee for Quality Assurance (NCQA) (1998). *MBHO surveyor guidelines for the accreditation of managed behavioral healthcare organizations.* Washington, DC: Author.

Orlinsky, D., Grawe, K. & Parks, B. (1994). Process and outcome in psychotherapy. In Bergin, A. & Garfield, S. (Eds.). *Handbook of psychotherapy and behavior change* (4th ed., pp. 270–376). New York: Wiley.

Pederson, P. (1991). Multiculturalism as a generic approach to counseling. *Journal of Counseling and Human Development, 70,* 6–12.

Raskin, N. & Rogers, C. (1989). Person-centered therapy. In R. Corsini & D. Wedding (Eds.) *Current psychotherapies* (4th ed., pp. 155–196). Itasca, IL: F.E. Peacock.

Rogers, C. (1951). *Client-centered therapy.* Boston: Houghton Mifflin.

Schwartz, G. (1988). Cognitive behavioral therapy and health psychology. In D. Fishman, C. Franks, and E. Rotgers (Eds.) *Paradigms in behavior therapy: Present and promise* (pp. 197–231). New York: Springer.

Sherman, R. & Dinkmeyer, D. (1987). *Systems of family therapy: An Adlerian integration.* New York: Brunner/Mazel.

Slap, J. & Slap-Shelton, L. (1981). *The schema in clinical psychoanalysis.* Hillsdale, NJ: The Analytic Press.

Snyder, C., Irving, L., & Anderson, J. (1991). Hope and health. In Snyder, C. & Forsyth, D. (Eds.). *Handbook of social and clinical psychology.* New York: Pergamon.

Sperry, L. (1997). Treatment outcomes: An overview. *Psychiatric Annals 27:* 95–99.

Sperry, L., Brill, P., Howard, K. & Grissom, G. (1996). *Treatment outcomes in psychotherapy and psychiatric interventions.* New York: Brunner/Mazel.

Strupp, H. (1995). The psychotherapist's skills revisited. *Clinical Psychology, 2:* 70–74.

Strupp, H. & Binder, J. (1984). *Psychotherapy in a new key: A guide to time-limited dynamic psychotherapy.* New York: Basic Books.

Turk, I. & Meichenbaum, D. (1983). *Pain and behavioral medicine: A cognitive-behavioral approach.* New York: Guilford.

Wachtel, P. & Wachtel, E. (1986). *Family dynamics in individual psychotherapy.* New York: Guilford.

Watzlawick, P., Weakland, J., & Fisch, R. (1974). *Change: Principles of problem formation and problem resolution.* New York: Norton.

Weiss, J (1993). *How psychotherapy works: Process and technique.* New York: Guilford.

Wolpe, J. (1983). *The practice of behavior therapy (3rd ed.).* New York: Pergamon.

Woolford, R. (1988). The self in cognitive behavior therapy. In D. Fishman, C. Franks and E. Rotgers (Eds.) *Paradigms in behavior therapy: Present and promise* (pp. 132–162). New York: Springer.

Yalom, I. (1980). *Existential psychotherapy.* New York: Basic Books.

Yontef, G. & Simkin, J. (1989). Gestalt therapy. In R. Corsini & D. Wedding (Eds.) *Current psychotherapies* (4th ed., pp. 323–362). Itasca, IL: F.E. Peacock.

Young, J. (1990). *Cognitive therapy for personality disorders: A schema-focused approach.* Sarasota, FL: Professional Resource Exchange.

PART II ENGAGEMENT

CHAPTER 2

INITIATING THE THERAPEUTIC PROCESS

If you were to pick clients who were most likely to benefit from therapy what would you look for? Would they be younger rather than older? Articulate and able to identify feelings? Intelligent or well-educated? Have minimal symptoms and impairment? Or, have similar values to yours? Three decades of research efforts have not demonstrated the predictive value of any of these characteristics. Rather, recent research suggests that a client's motivation, or more specifically their stage of readiness for change, is a better predictor of treatment outcome than age, problem severity, socioeconomic status, self-esteem, or social support network (Prochaska, DiClementi, & Norcross, 1992). As you will learn, stage of readiness for change is a key factor of the engagement phase of therapy.

The engagement phase was briefly introduced in Chapter 1. It was noted that engagement is the first and most important stage of treatment. While it includes the client's motivation for change it is much broader than motivation. The client's level of engagement can be significantly increased by the therapist, and by the nature and quality of the therapeutic relationship process, early in the course of treatment. We also pointed out that unless the client is sufficiently engaged in the treatment process, effective treatment outcomes are unlikely. In short, engagement is essential for therapeutic change to occur. It is all too common for therapists to assume that a client is engaged in therapy if they merely show up for sessions and disclose feelings and concerns. The result is predictable: premature termination, lack of progress, or negative therapeutic reaction, that is, the client regresses. Furthermore, we suggested in Chapter 1 that it is a strategic error to proceed with the other phases of therapy, assessment, intervention, and maintenance/termination, until engagement was sufficiently achieved. In Chapter 2 and Chapter 3 we develop these themes and introduce you to a number of powerful therapeutic skills for fostering the engagement process.

WHAT YOU WILL LEARN IN THIS CHAPTER

1. What characterizes clients who are sufficiently engaged in the treatment process.
2. Seven therapeutic intervention skills for fostering client engagement in therapy.
3. Five stages of readiness for change and methods of optimizing readiness for change; and the origins of this approach to motivation for treatment.
4. The meaning and value of the client's explanatory model and expectations for treatment—particularly cultural expectations—in fostering engagement and in planning treatment.
5. The value and methods for negotiating the focus and goals of treatment.
6. The importance of reversing demoralization and triggering the placebo effect in the early phase of treatment.

CHARACTERISTICS OF CLIENT ENGAGEMENT

Two clients begin treatment with you at roughly the same time. Both are single, female college graduates in their late 20s. You are pleasantly surprised to find that, although they do not know each other, they share some similarities. Both meet DSM-IV criteria for the diagnosis of Adjustment Disorder with Anxiety, and both experienced symptoms following the break-up of long-term intimate relationships. Furthermore, both work full-time, one for a newspaper and the other for an advertising agency. However, after four sessions with each client, the similarities stop. The first client is now basically asymptomatic and able to face life without the security of the relationship with her former boyfriend. The second client remains symptomatic and is becoming increasing socially isolated, missing work, and even coming late for three of her sessions. Additionally, she seems resistant to most of your intervention efforts. Why such differences between these two clients? A very likely explanation is engagement. The first client appears not only to have a high level of readiness for change, but also is engaged in the treatment process. Table 2.1 summarizes several differences between clients with a high level of engagement and those with a low level.

The main differences between these two sets of characteristics involve empathy, treatment goals and focus, treatment outcomes, hopefulness, and confidence in treatment in addition to level of readiness for change. These factors, with the exception of empathy which is described in Chapter 3, are detailed in subsequent sections of this chapter. Readiness for change is described in greater detail than the other factors because it is a significant engagement factor.

TABLE 2.1   Characteristics of Client Engagement or Lack of Engagement in the Process of Therapy

CHARACTERISTICS OF ENGAGED CLIENTS	CHARACTERISTICS OF NONENGAGED CLIENTS	POSSIBLE REASONS FOR NONENGAGEMENT
Feels adequately understood and accepted by therapist	Does not feel adequately understood and accepted by therapist	Insufficient empathy manifested by therapist to client
Attends sessions, actively participates, takes therapeutic risks, and makes changes	May show up for sessions but makes little or no progress or seems resistant to change	Suboptimal level of client readiness for change
Appears to share a common view of the causes of their problem with the therapist	Does not share the therapist's views of the causes of their problem, which were probably not discussed	Discrepancy between client's explanatory model and therapist's case formulation
Appears to share a common view of treatment outcomes and client–therapist roles with the therapist	Does not share the therapist's views about the outcomes of treatment and client responsibilities, which were probably not discussed	Discrepancy between client's and therapist's expectations for treatment outcome/roles
Appears to share a common view about treatment focus and goals with the therapist	Does not share the therapist's views about treatment focus and goals with the therapist, which were probably not discussed	Discrepancy between client and therapist on focus and goals of treatment
Hopeful about problem resolution	Little or not hopeful about problem resolution	Client remains demoralized
Is sufficiently confident that therapy will be helpful and effective	Is not sufficiently confident that therapy will be helpful and effective	Placebo-effect is insufficient

Motivation for Therapy: Some Background Information

Motivation for therapy has been an idea that therapists have valued for decades. While most agree that motivation is essential for effective treatment, few have been able to effectively define and operationalize this global and somewhat elusive construct. In 1964 Schofield published a book entitled: *Psychotherapy: The Purchase of Friendship.* In it he reports his research on client variables in psychotherapy predictive of positive treatment outcomes, and, introduces the acronym "YAVIS" to the mental health community. YAVIS is shorthand for Young, Attractive, Verbal, Intelligent, and Successful. With this acronym, Schofield summarized what he and others interpreted their research on client motivation and treatment outcomes to mean: that young clients—particularly those under age 40, who were attractive—meaning they subscribed similar (middle class) values as their therapists, who were verbal—meaning they were articulate and willing to talk about themselves especially in identifying and discussing feelings and fantasies, who were, likewise, intelligent—which usually meant they were reasonably well-educated, and who were successful—meaning that they were able hold a job for a reasonable period of time and foster intimate relationships, were most likely to be both motivated and successful in therapy. Over the years, as students become acquainted with YAVIS, they have two distinct reactions. First, YAVIS individuals do not seem like they need therapy, since they appear to have so much going for them. And second, that therapists with a bias for YAVIS clients would probably not value multicultural clients.

There is extensive literature on client variables that impact treatment outcomes, just as there is a broad and rich literature on client-therapist matching. The reader is referred to respective chapters on these topics in Garfield and Bergin's classic text (1994) (3rd ed.), to learn more about these lines of research and their implications for the practice of psychotherapy. For our purposes, we focus on the seminal research on readiness for change. This line of research is quite different from previous efforts on motivation for treatment in which motivation has been dichotomized, that is, either clients are motivated for treatment or they are resistant to treatment, and has been considered a stable personality feature or trait. Rather, readiness for change was conceptualized as a changeable, dynamic process in which motivation was as much a product of the therapeutic context as it was of the client's personality and history (Miller, Duncan, & Hubble, 1997).

In the 1980s, James Prochaska and Carlo DiClementi (1982) began describing their research on readiness for change. This research and concomitant clinical applications may well be one of the most important breakthroughs in understanding, motivation for treatment, but more importantly, how individuals change during the treatment process. As noted above, stage of readiness for change has been shown to be a better predictor of treatment outcome than age, problem severity, socioeconomic status, self-esteem, or social support network (Prochaska, DiClementi, & Norcross, 1992).

EMPATHIC UNDERSTANDING AND RESPONDING

Empathy is a powerful factor in achieving engagement. Fifty years ago, Carl Rogers championed empathy as a core condition for effecting change in therapy. Empathy was understood as requiring a therapist to view and experience reality from a client's subjective perspective while still maintaining the perspective of an objective observer. In short, empathy was framed as a therapist's attitude and behavior. As a result, therapist training programs emphasized the therapist skill of empathic responding. Unfortunately, recent research has indicated that therapist-provided empathy (and other core conditions) is not sufficient to effect change. It seems that because core conditions such as empathy, warmth, respect and genuineness are, in part, culturally determined, it should not be reasonable to expect that the same empathic response of a therapist will have varying effects on different clients. Rather, current research suggests that therapists are most likely to facilitate engagement when they intentionally tailor the provision of empathic and the other core conditions to the client's definition of these variables (Miller, Duncan, & Hubble, 1997). This expanded notion of emphatic understanding and responding is described and illustrated as a basic clinical skill in considerable detail in Chapter 3.

CLIENT'S READINESS FOR CHANGE

Readiness is conceptualized as having a number of identified stages that clients move through during the process of change. These stages are: precontemplation, contemplation, preparation, action, and maintenance. This stage model is particularly attractive in that it appears to be quite useful in understanding and predicting client change across a wide array of client concerns beyond psychotherapy such as smoking cessation, weight management, alcohol and substance treatment, and so on. Furthermore, this model is applicable across all theoretical orientations, appears to be culture-neutral, and can provide some quantitative measure of both motivation and change dynamics.

A preliminary assessment of readiness for change can be extremely valuable and useful in treatment planning. Since most clients cycle in and out of these stages several times before achieving their goals, it is helpful to gauge the current status of each problem during the initial session, and to monitor movement of these stages. Ideally, the client enters therapy at the preparation or action stage which means that treatment outcomes will be predictably positive. When the client enters at the precontemplative or contemplative stage, the therapist's primary task is to tailor treatment in order to move the client toward the action stage. Prochaska and his colleagues outline these five stages (Table 2.2).

Stages of Readiness for Change

Precontemplation. In this stage the client simply considers the possibility of change, and may not have formulated their concerns as a problem to be solved or actions to be taken. Often clients who remain in this stage for more than a few sessions are in treatment involuntarily. That is, their treatment may be court-mandated or prescribed by a family member, particularly a spouse, that is, "If you don't get therapy our relationship is over." Or, they may come to therapy to complain about someone else, or to blame others for their problems such as a work supervisor, teacher, or coach. Whatever the cir-

TABLE 2.2   Stages of Readiness for Change

STAGE	DESCRIPTION OF STAGE
Precontemplation	Client denies both the presence of a problem and the need for any treatment.
Contemplation	Client admits the presence of a problem and possibly needing treatment, but not at the current time.
Preparation	Client expresses the intention to work in treatment, including willingness to assume responsibility and collaborate with treatment.
Action	Client expresses, by word and action, efforts to work on making change in treatment.
Maintenance	Client continues to work on the process of change both inside and outside the treatment context.

Source: Adapted from Prochaska & DiClementi, 1984.

cumstance, they do not believe they have a problem or a need to change. In fact, when some clients enter therapy, they may only be seeking reassurance that there is, in fact, no serious illness, such as a severe mood disorder or psychosis. The therapist's role is to assess the client's perception of his or her concerns. At this stage, a clinician's perception and conclusion that a treatable condition exists, such as alcohol abuse or some other destructive behavior, is both inconsistent with the client's perception and his belief that any change is needed.

Contemplation. At this stage, clients are aware that they have problems. In other words, the client's perception begins to match the therapist's perception. However, the client is not yet convinced that change is needed. They may agree that change may be necessary, but have some awareness that making those changes will be difficult. Since clients at this stage are not particularly clear about what changes are needed, the therapist's role is to help them consider both their options as well as the consequences of their choices.

Preparation. During this phase clients know that change is in order and begin to take steps to make those changes. At this stage most clients are considering the best way to proceed. Therapists can help them evaluate their plans with such questions as: What changes can you imagine yourself making? What have you tried that worked in the past? As therapy proceeds, What do you envision yourself doing? What might hold you back? Who would notice these changes? In what ways might this affect you? What are the some advantages for making changes now?

Action. In this stage, the client is ready to act. The advantages of changing outweigh the advantages of not changing. The client is clear about some course of action and is actively engaged in trying out solutions. Therapists can help by providing support, fine-tuning strategies, assessing the outcome, and offering encouragement. Most therapists function very well when clients are at this stage.

Maintenance. Once clients have made changes, they must practice and manage any setbacks. This is the time for figuring out how to preserve what seems to be working and to revise whatever is not quite going as well as expected, but the overall goal is to keep the changes in place. Sometimes, after a period of time, clients come back for a tune-up. They may have made changes in the past but are now fearful of losing ground.

THE CLINICAL UTILITY OF MOTIVATION AND READINESS FOR CHANGE: IMPLICATIONS FOR PSYCHOTHERAPY PRACTICE

In their research, Prochaska and his colleagues found that individuals who move from one stage to the next, such as from contemplation to preparation, during the initial sessions of treatment approximately doubled their chances of making changes and solving their problems within a period six months than those who did not move stages. Interestingly, when individuals moved up two stages, such as from contemplation to action, for example, during the initial sessions they were four times more likely to succeed at making change than those who did not (Prochaska, Velicer, Fava, et al., 1997).

On the other hand, the failure of individuals to make some movement in the initial sessions is highly predictive of limited change, no change, or even negative therapeutic outcomes in the overall course of treatment (Sperry, Brill, Howard, & Grissom, 1996). One study found that, on the average, individuals who showed no movement by the third session showed no improvement over the entire course of therapy irrespective of the type of treatment employed (Brown, Dreis, & Nace, 1999). It appears that stage of readiness for change is a strong predictor of change even when medication is the main treatment intervention. In a study of drug treatment for anxiety disorders, it was noted that stage of readiness measures were more predictive of symptom reduction than whether study participants were assigned to either the drug or the placebo condition. In short, stage of readiness had considerably more predictive power than the pharmacokinetics of the antianxiety medication (Beitman, Beck, Deuser, et al., 1994).

There is growing evidence that therapists can improve the likelihood of successful treatment outcomes by tailoring treatment to the client's stage of readiness for change. This has important clinical and health policy implications, especially with regard to cost-effectiveness and efficacy. For instance, premature termination, when the client leaves treatment before a planned termination occurs, indicates a low level of engagement in treatment and continues to be a clinical embarrassment for many therapists. Research by Prochaska (1999) reports that when therapists plan and implement stage-appropriate treatment interventions, clients are more likely to remain in and progress in treatment than when therapists are either unaware of levels of readiness or do not plan and implement appropriate interventions. Studies have also shown that stage-appropriate interventions are also cost-effective. (Prochaska et al., 1997)

How can a therapist tailor stage-appropriate treatment interventions to facilitate client movement toward the action stage? In addition to some suggestions earlier, Table 2.3 indicates interventions for each of the five stages of readiness.

Client's Explanatory Models

Different cultures provide varying explanations for illnesses as well as normal versus abnormal behavior (Kleinman, 1988). For example, a syndrome that includes pseudo-hallucinations, anxiety, hyperventilations, and seizure-like behavior among a young Hispanic female would likely be diagnosed by an American psychiatrist as a psychotic disorder and treated with hospitalization and medication. It is more likely that this presentation is not a psychosis at all, but rather a transient condition called *ataque* (Harwood, 1977; Patcher, 1993). In Hispanic folk culture, this and other psychological presentations may be better understood in terms of hot–cold theory of disease (Harwood, 1971). Even in white, middle-class America, individuals can have varying explanations for the symptoms and problems they experience. With depression, for example, some clients will be quite convinced that their depressed feelings are caused by a chemical imbalance in their brain, while others are equally convinced that the basis of their symptoms lies in early sexual abuse or because they were separated from their mother when they were young children. These

TABLE 2.3   Interventions to Optimize Stage of Readiness for Change

STAGE	INTERVENTIONS
Precontemplation	1. Explore the client's explanatory model 2. Suggest the client think about the situation from another perspective 3. Provide education and information
Contemplation	1. Encourage the client to think about making changes 2. Suggest an observational task (i.e., what happens to make the situation better or worse) 3. Join with the client's ambivalence to action with a go slow directive
Preparation	1. Offer several viable treatment options 2. Invite client to choose from among these options
Action	1. Elicit details of the client's successful efforts 2. Reinforce those efforts and encourage other efforts
Maintenance	1. Support the client's successful efforts 2. Predict relapse and setbacks 3. Help client plan contingency plans

Source: Adapted from Miller, Duncan, & Hubble, 1997.

differing explanations about the cause of etiology or a medical or psychiatric illness is called *explanatory model* (Kleinman, 1988).

An explanatory model is the client's personal interpretation or explanation of disease and symptoms. In other words, these models are the client's own personal clinical formulation of the symptoms and problems they are experiencing, akin to the professional clinical case formulation the therapist will develop to understand the diagnostic features of client's situation. While the therapist's case formulation is typically based on one of the traditional psychotherapy perspectives, the client's is based on their own personal perceptions, knowledge base, and cultural heritage. These models provide an important diagnostic window into the client's personal meaning, values, and cultural heritage. They are also powerful predictors of the client's adherence to the treatment process, including whether a client will follow through on intersession activities, such as homework, and compliance or noncompliance with medication. To the extent to which there is wide discrepancy between the explanatory model and the therapist's case formulation, treatment problems ranging from nonadherence or standstill to premature termination, can be expected.

The effective therapist carefully considers explanatory models in formulating diagnoses and treatment plans. Often, the client's explanatory mode is fraught with misinformation or misattribution, and it is then imperative to discuss, educate, and modify the client's model so that a mutually agreed upon explanation emerges. For instance, a client with a bipolar disorder who believes that their illness was caused by insomnia and can be cured by a good night's sleep needs to have their explanation modified with reality-based information on the etiology, symptom picture, treatment alternatives, and course of the illness. Similarly, the client who explains the experience of generalized anxiety in terms of a single early life trauma should hear the therapist describe a more complete model of the illness, including biological basis and current psychosocial precipitants, which also allows for these particular concerns about the early trauma. Specific irrational beliefs about illness or treatment also must be elicited and addressed.

Helping clients understand their illness is best done in a biopsychosocial context, particularly for those clients seeking some magic solution to their problems. Negotiated explanations that are tailored to the client's experience are particularly valuable. Such an explanation should be simple, integrate biological and psychosocial mechanisms, while incorporating appropriate elements of the client's explanation. For example, the client who insists that hypoglycemia is the basis for her panic disorder might be offered a treatment plan in which blood glucose would be checked immediately and re-evaluated if a four week trial of medication is not successful. Chapter 4 describes and illustrates the skill of assessing explanatory models.

EXPECTATIONS FOR TREATMENT: PERSONAL AND CULTURAL

Personal. Generally, clients expect that they will receive help from the therapist and that therapy will somehow solve their concerns. Before the first session even begins, clients already are developing expectations of therapy and for the therapist, and so are therapists about clients. Clients' expectations of therapy come from the media, for example, movies, TV or stories in weekly news magazines, from friends and colleagues that have been in therapy, or from previous experience with psychotherapists, psychiatrists, pastoral counselors, or other behavioral health providers. To the extent to which there is a reasonable degree of similarity between client and therapist expectations, the changes of successful treatment outcomes increase.

Clients tend to have specific expectations for the outcome of treatment, the length of treatment, and the occurrence of change in therapy. Generally speaking, patients with high and realistic expectations of change do change more than clients with low or unrealistic expectations. Research confirms the clinical observation that clients with moderate to high levels of expectation for treatment do in fact respond better than those clients with minimal or no expectations of improvement (Sotsky, Gaiss, Shea, et al., 1991). In a review of studies on client expectations for treatment, Garfield and Bergin (1994) note that most clients expect therapy to be relatively short, no more than 10 sessions, and that they expect to experience some improvement earlier in the course of the sessions rather than later. The client's perceptions and expectations about roles and responsibilities in therapy are also important (Sperry, 1995). The matter of role and responsibilities, for example, how active or passive the client and therapists will be, and what type and how much responsibility the client and the therapist will take, are essential items for discussion and negotiation early in the course treatment, typically in the first session. For instance, if a client expects that only medication will cure a relationship problem without the need for any individual change, the therapist should not be surprised when the client is ambivalent about inviting her significant other to a therapy session or does not follow up on some therapist assigned homework. Unless expectations about client role and responsibilities are clarified, and modified if need be, the type of change expected by the therapist is unlikely.

Cultural. Treatment expectations can also be influenced by cultural factors and norms. Among some Hispanics, for example, it is commonplace for family members to accompany the designated client to sessions. Since there may be the unspoken expectation that family members will be included in the treatment process, the culturally sensitive and effective therapist will inquire about such expectations. Similarly, there may be silent expectations about the type of intervention utilized. Clients of some cultural groups may prefer action-oriented approaches over strictly talk-oriented therapies. In other cultures, the expectation may be that healing requires some measure of touch or contact. I vividly recall a psychological consultation with a hospitalized elderly woman of middle-eastern descent who was diagnosed by the nursing staff as agitated and depressed. As I read the medical chart, the attending physician came into the room, spoke briefly with the woman, and immediately ordered a topical form of the medication she had been prescribed by an internal medicine resident. The attending physician then caringly applied the nitroglycerin ointment over her heart region. Immediately, the woman relaxed and smiled. Outside the room I asked the wise physician about what I had witnessed. He pointed out that traditional middle-eastern patients believe that healing only comes by touch and that the only medications that really work for them are those that are applied topically, rubbed on the skin, for example.

Insoo Berg indicates the importance of cultural sensitivity regarding treatment expectations when making specific therapeutic recommendations involving children and adolescents. She notes that the oft given therapeutic advice to ground older children and adolescents for violating family rules or behavior issues is confusing to some Asian families. Berg explains that parental expectations about disciplining children in Asian cultures may be the exact opposite of parental expectations in mainline American culture. For example, in Korea where family unity and closeness is a core value, misbehaving adolescents are disciplined by being distanced from the family rather than grounded or forced to stay at home and away from their friends (Berg, Sperry, & Carlson, 1999). The point here is that effective therapists are sensitive to cultural values, norms, and mores when approaching treatment expectations.

Accordingly, the effective therapist will elicit the client's expectations for treatment, including expectations about objectives, outcomes, methods, and therapist and client roles and responsibilities. Unrealistically high or low client expectations need to be noted and discussed. The client needs to be queried about what they expect from treatment: symptom relief, improvement in functioning, personality change, and so on, as well as about expected modalities, for example, individual therapy, medication, couple, group or family session, and treatment methods, such as psychodynamic interpretation, behavioral interventions, etc. Chapter 4 describes and illustrates the skill of assessing both client and therapist expectations.

Treatment Focus and Goals

It is useful and sometimes absolutely necessary to orient clients to the treatment process. Because much of the process and outcome of psychotherapy is affected by the client's perceptions and attitudes at the start of therapy, the therapist should describe the treatment process, its outcomes, and the roles and responsibilities that the therapist will take. Presumably, the therapist has already elicited the client's expectations for treatment and can evaluate how realistic they are. The therapist can then begin negotiating a mutually agreeable and realistic treatment plan. This process is called role induction (Frank, 1984) and research indicates that this effort to socialize clients about psychotherapy results in fewer premature terminations as well as increased treatment outcomes.

Reversing Demoralization

Demoralization is the subjective sense of alienation, loss of self-esteem, hopelessness, or the feeling that no one can help, and sometimes even helplessness, or the feeling that others could help but will not. Demoralization often accompanies the symptoms and distress that individuals seeking counseling and psychotherapy experience. Basically, these clients feel hopeless and demoralized. Jerome Frank, the author of the classic book *Persuasion and Healing* (1993) which first appeared in 1958, contends that psychotherapy is effective primarily because it reverses demoralization and restores the client's hope that their life will improve. Typically, clients experience an increased sense of hopefulness days prior to a
reduction in symptoms and impaired functioning. Beginning therapists often find this observation counterintuitive, believing instead that clients would only experience hopefulness and optimism after their symptoms of depression or anxiety were significantly relieved or reduced. What accounts for this change, and how does it happen? No one really understand this mechanism of remoralization, but it has been hypothesized that therapists somehow lend their own sense of hopefulness to clients. This is one of the most powerful elements of the psychotherapeutic relationship (Frank, 1984).

The degree to which clients are demoralized is a function of their basic view of life, optimistic versus pessimistic, as well as their specific expectations of what the future holds for them. Seligman (1998) has described the processes of learned helplessness and learned optimism and his research indicates that individuals can alter their basic view of life from pessimistic to optimistic. He offers a number of suggestions which have applicability in psychotherapy.

Generally speaking, the presence of an empathic and confident therapist who listens attentively and offers basic reassurance is usually sufficient to foster remoralization in most clients. For those clients who are habitually pessimistic and are unduly demoralized by their present circumstances and distress, additional efforts are usually needed. For instance, the therapist may need to reach out enthusiastically to such clients and utilize nonverbal pacing, that is, match the patient's rate and style of speech, which increases a sense of connection and identification. The therapist may need to positively reframe or normalize the client's complaints or fears whenever possible from the beginning moments of the first session. Furthermore, the therapist might engender early therapeutic successes with focused symptom reduction techniques and by suggesting easily accomplishable intersession activities, such as homework that sets the stage for more success. Finally, the therapist may want to involve family or others in the client's social support network whenever feasible.

Triggering the Placebo Effect

Somewhat similar to remoralization is the placebo effect. It refers to that part of improvement from treatment that results from nonspecific factors such as faith, suggestions, expectancy, or a certain kind of explanation of their problems that reassures the patient. While remoralization is basically related to the phenomenon of hope, the placebo effect is essentially a reflection of the client's faith in the clinician and/or the treatment process or medication.

The impact of the placebo effect seems to vary depending on diagnosis, for example, placebo effect response is much higher in patients with depression, panic disorder, and generalized anxiety disorder than with patients with obsessive-compulsive disorder or schizophrenia. The placebo effect not only enhances the relationship between client and clinician, it can also increase treatment compliance.

There are several ways of triggering or enhancing the placebo effect. These include the clinician's attentiveness to the client shown by active listening and clarification or reflection of what the client has said; the clinician's expression of interest and concern for the client; the clinician's confident, professional manner; as well as the clinician's expression of confidence in the treatment plan and outcomes of treatment. In the initial phase of treatment the placebo effect is enhanced by more frequent face-to-face meetings. It is then sustained as the client improves and less frequent sessions are scheduled and framed to the client as opportunities to monitor continued progress.

SUMMARY

This chapter focused on the engagement process: what it is, its importance in the overall treatment process, and how to foster it. We began by contrasting the seven characteristics that distinguish clients who are engaged in the treatment process from those who are not sufficiently engaged in the process of treatment. The rest of the chapter focused on the skills for fostering client engagement in therapy. Table 2.4 lists these seven skills.

TABLE 2.4   Seven Skills for Fostering Client Engagement in Therapy

1. Providing empathic listening and responding
2. Optimizing client's level of readiness for change
3. Exploring client's explanatory model
4. Eliciting client's expectation for treatment outcomes and involvement in the treatment process
5. Negotiating a mutual agreeable treatment focus, goals, and outcomes
6. Reversing client's demoralization
7. Triggering placebo effect in client

REFERENCES

Beitman, B., Beck, M., Deuser, W., Carler, C., Davidson, J. & Maddock, R. (1994). Patient stages of change predicts outcomes in a panic disorder medication trial. *Anxiety, 1,* 64–69.

Berg, I., Sperry, L. & Carlson, J. (1999). Intimacy and culture: A solution-focused perspective: An interview. In J. Carlson & L. Sperry (Eds.). *The intimate couple* (pp. 41–54). New York: Brunner/Mazel.

Brown, J., Dreis, S., & Nace, D. (1999). What makes a difference in psychotherapy outcome and why does managed care want to know? In M. Hubble, D. Duncan, & S. Miller (Eds.). *The heart and soul of change.* Washington, DC: APA Books.

Frank, J. (1984). Therapeutic components of all psychotherapies. In J. Myers (Ed.). *Cures by psychotherapy: What affects change?* New York: Praeger.

Frank, J. & Frank, J. (1993). *Persuasion and healing: A comparative study of psychotherapy (3rd ed.).* Baltimore: Johns Hopkins Press.

Garfield, S. & Bergin, A. (1994). *Handbook of psychotherapy and behavior change (3rd ed.).* New York: Wiley.

Harwood, A. (1971). The hot-cold theory of disease: Implications for the treatment of Puerto Rican patients. *Journal of the American Medical Association, 216,* 1153–1158.

Harwood, A. (1977). *Rx—Spiritist as needed: A study of a Puerto-Rican mental health resource.* New York: Wiley.

Kleinman, A. (1988). *The illness narratives.* New York: Basic Books.

Miller, S., Duncan, B., & Hubble, M. (1997). *Escape from Babel: Toward a unifying language for psychotherapy practice.* New York: Norton.

Patcher, L. (1993). Latino folk illness. *Medical Anthropology, 15,* 2, 137–148.

Prochaska, J. (1999). How do people change and how can we change to help many more people? In M. Hubble, D. Duncan & S. Miller (Eds.). *The heart and soul of change.* Washington, DC: APA Books.

Prochaska, J. & DiClementi, C. (1982). Transtheoretical therapy: Toward a more integrative model of change. *Psychotherapy, 19,* 276–288.

Prochaska, J., DiClementi, C. & Norcross, J. (1992). In search of how people change. *American Psychologist, 47,* 1102–1114.

Prochaska, J., Velicer, W., Fava, D., Ruggerio, L., Laforge, R. & Rossi, E. (1997). Counselor and stimulus-control enhancement of a stage-matched expert system for smokers in a managed care setting. Unpublished manuscript.

Schofield, W. (1964). *Psychotherapy: The purchase of friendship.* Englewood Cliffs, NJ: Prentice-Hall.

Seligman, M. (1998). *Learned optimism (reissued edition).* New York: Pocket Books.

Sotsky, S., Galss, D., Shea, M. et al. (1991). Patient Predictors of Response to Psychotherapy and Pharmacotherapy: Findings in the NIMH Treatment of Depression Collaborative Research Program. *American Journal of Psychiatry, 148:* 997–1008.

Sperry, L. (1995). *Psychopharmacology and psychotherapy: Strategies for maximzing treatment outcomes.* New York: Brunner/Mazel.

Sperry, I., Brill, P., Howard, K. & Grissom, G. (1996). *Treatment outcomes in psychotherapy and psychiatric interventions.* New York: Brunner/Mazel.

CHAPTER 3

ESTABLISHING THE THERAPEUTIC RELATIONSHIP

WHAT YOU WILL LEARN IN THIS CHAPTER

1. Why engagement skills are vital to counseling effectiveness.
2. Attending and joining skills including internal attending, physical attending, and verbal attending and how these skills are effectively used.
3. Active listening skills including minimal prompts, reflecting content, and reflecting feelings and when and how these skills contribute to the engagement process.
4. Empathic responding skills and how they are used in the engagement process.
5. Encouragement skills and their contribution to a positive outcome in therapy.

ENGAGEMENT SKILLS: OVERVIEW

The first step in counseling or psychotherapy is to develop a therapeutic relationship with the client. The process of developing this relationship is engagement which "refers to the ongoing development of a sense of safety and respect from which patients feel increasingly free to share their problems, while gaining an increased confidence in the clinician's potential to understand them" (Shea, 1998, p. 10). No doubt, you will find that you are already using many of these skills in your daily life as they are basic to forming and maintaining good relationships in any setting. As you learn to identify these skills, observe them in action, and purposefully practice them; you will begin to develop the ability to use them intentionally and strategically in therapeutic settings. Suggested practice activities let you try them out for yourself. Examples taken from actual counseling sessions and video clips of these sessions give you an opportunity to observe some of these skills in action.

ENGAGEMENT SKILLS—UTILITY AND VALUE

Psychotherapy is based on a relationship between the therapist and the client. One of the first tasks in therapy is to form that relationship or alliance with the client. "The quality of the relationship is a central contributor to therapeutic progress. Its significance transcends the most respected models and research-validated techniques" (Duncan, Hubble, & Miller, 1997, p. 27). The goal is to develop a rapport with the client that leads to the desired therapeutic change. Effectiveness in counseling is related to the client and counselor's ability to like, respect, and trust each other. In engagement we begin to develop a mutual caring, respect and trust that allows our clients the sense of safety needed to feel comfortable enough to share their deepest concerns, the good and bad they see in themselves, and their triumphs and tragedies. This engagement forms the basis of the client's motivation for change and willingness to do the work necessary to achieve a positive outcome. In some client/therapist relationships, this alliance comes about relatively easily; for others, it may take time and hard work on the part of both the therapist and the client. While there are identified skills and interventions related to forming a therapeutic relationship, each individual, couple, or family is unique and how we work with each depends on the needs and responses of the client.

The optimal therapeutic relationship according to Mahoney (1991) ". . . creates a special and intimate human context—a context in and from which the client can safely experiment with and explore familiar and novel ways of experiencing self, world (especially the interpersonal), and possible relationships" (p. 267). The personhood of the therapist is fundamental to the quality of the relationship and thus a significant factor in the ultimate outcome of therapy. Carl Rogers is probably the individual most closely associated with the idea that the counselor or therapist's attitude toward the client is one of the most important components of good therapy. He held that, in order to work effectively with a client, the therapist must be empathic and genuine and hold unconditional positive regard for the client. These qualities are communicated both verbally and nonverbally. The existentialist Martin Buber (Gould, 1993) is credited with characterizing the effective therapeutic relationship as an I-Thou relationship where the therapist holds the client in high regard and behaves in a manner that communicates this regard.

In order to develop the therapeutic relationship the counselor uses a specific set of skills which, while central to the engagement process, are employed throughout the counseling relationship. These include attending and joining behaviors, active listening, empathic responding, and encouragement. While these are fundamental skills, often called "beginning skills" in counseling, they are vital in not only forming a therapeutic relationship but in setting a pattern for ongoing therapy. Bugental (1987, p. 49) defines the therapeutic alliance as ". . . the powerful joining of forces which energizes and supports the long, difficult, and frequently painful work of life-changing psychotherapy." Throughout the chapter, you will see how these skills influence the expectations and behavior of the client.

ATTENDING AND JOINING SKILLS

The counselor begins using the attending and joining skills of internal, physical, and verbal attending in the first contact with a client. These skills are basic to effective engagement and are active throughout the therapeutic process. Attending and joining skills contribute not only to engagement in a therapeutic setting but also to our skills used in social and business contacts as well. And, because these are basic relational skills, they are skills we may well have learned and use on a daily basis. As you read this chapter, think of ways you use these skills in everyday life and how you respond when others attend or do not attend to you. What are some clues that others are not attending? What keeps you from fully attending to another?

Internal Attending

Counselors become specialists in attending to their clients. That is, they give their clients their attention in a way that allows clients to feel heard and respected. Our internal attending to clients can give them a sense of safety and space to pay attention to themselves. Attending is, more than anything else, a state of mind on the part of the counselor. Thus, the first step in engagement starts before the client enters the room. The counselor who is in a bad mood, worried, or anxious will have difficulty fully attending to the client. The counselor needs to put aside personal concerns including any physical discomfort or immediate worries before beginning the counseling session and be present for the client.

Marge had a sinus infection and overslept. She really wanted to stay home but knew she could not afford to miss any more work this month. When she got to work, all the parking spaces were taken and so she quickly parked on the street, knowing that she would need to move her car as soon as possible to avoid a parking ticket. Her first client of the day was waiting for her. He immediately let Marge know that he was upset because he had been on time and she was late. As the client made his complaint, Marge realized that her head really ached and wondered if she had any aspirin in her desk. How does Marge attend to herself and her disgruntled client? Should she have come to work at all?

ACTIVITY I: **ATTENDING**

1. Recall a time you felt attended to and a time that you did not feel attended to.
2. Recall a time you attended to someone else. What happened?

Much of what constitutes internal attending comes from how the counselor prepares and practices over time as well as how well the counselor takes care of themself. Part of that preparation, practice, and self care may include the counselor receiving personal counseling as well as paying attention to factors such as physical health, diet, and exercise. Through practice and self care, the counselor is able to make a shift from personal issues to the client's issues and be fully present for the client. There are many ways to do this and what works for one may not work for another. Self-talk, paying attention to your breathing, and positioning your body in a specific way are some ways you can begin to adopt the stance of attending.

In the following excerpt (Carlson & Kjos, 2000d), James Bugental suggests a centering activity for both himself and Gina.

TH 1:   Gina, I find it best when starting something like this to make a transition.
CL 1:   Okay.

TH 2:   And what I am going to do and encourage you to try is just to breathe inside and, and get quiet inside.

CL 2:   Okay.

TH 3:   So we start from a level playing ground or whatever that means.

CL 3:   Okay. Neutrality, okay. All right.

ACTIVITY II: TRY THIS BEFORE BEGINNING A SESSION

Sit comfortably with both feet on the floor, your hands on your knees, and pay attention to your breathing. Breath in and out several times until you feel calm and relaxed.

Counselors also attend to their own internal feelings and responses during a session as these can provide valuable information about the client and what is happening in the session. The counselor might begin to feel confused, anxious, or want to rescue the client. Are these feelings related to the client's issues, the counselor's issues, or both? The counselor's internal responses may serve as guides for future interventions as well as important topics for supervision. Jane was working with a client who had been charged with physically abusing his wife. She found herself liking the client and enjoyed working with him. Then, during a session, she realized that she was feeling anxious and somewhat afraid of the client. "What's different?" she asked herself. "What's bringing on these feelings?" Jane took a risk and said to the client, "I'm having a sense of some feelings of anxiety or being upset today." The client paused and then begin to relate an upsetting interchange he had with his daughter just that morning and how he had been so anxious to get a chance to talk about it but he was really afraid of what Jane would think of him if she heard what his daughter had said about him.

Physical Attending

Physical attending has two perspectives. The first is attending to the counselor's body positioning, body shifts, hand movements, eye movement, facial expressions, and nods. The second is attending to the client's body positioning, body shifts, hand movements, eye movement, facial expressions, and nods. Clients listen more to what we do than what we say and physical attending begins with greeting the client. At the first meeting, many counselors seek to shake hands with the client in a formal greeting. This begins the formation of a relationship that has the ingredients of formality and respect.

One key factor in physical attending is how we are positioned in relationship to the client. Should you face the client? What about having a desk or table between you and the client? How close should you be? Some counselors prefer to sit facing the client. Others prefer an angled seating arrangement. It is generally thought to be less helpful for the counselor to be sitting behind a desk or other barrier or right next to the client as these arrangements allow for less visual information. The seating should allow both the counselor and the client to comfortably look at each another as much information is shared through visual cues. Needs for distance or proximity may be influenced by culture as well as psychological factors. Some clients need more distance than others, so it is important to allow for both distance and closeness by offering alternative seating arrangements or providing chairs that are easily moved.

Counselors often shift their bodies to subtly mirror the client. That is, if the client leans forward, the counselor might lean forward a bit too. If the client crosses his arms, the counselor might cross his arms too. Mirroring is probably one of the most powerful resources counselors can use in joining or being present with a client. In family counseling, the counselor may choose one family member to mirror while paying attention to another. Often the client that is chosen is the one who seems separate from the rest of the family. Mirroring is a nonverbal way of communication that can show understanding and can often do so with more impact than a verbal response. However, it must be done carefully and subtly so clients do not feel they are being mimicked. Some counselors find it helpful to pace their breathing with the client from time to time, and may use that to join with one member of a family group. Both mirroring and pacing one's breath to that of the client can give the counselor important nonverbal information as well. What is it like to sit like this? What am I feeling when I breathe at this rate?

A key component of physical attending is that of taking in visual information and eye contact. Subtle client behaviors such as body shifts, hand movements, color changes in the face or neck, head nods, and facial expressions are all clues the counselor pays attention to in visual attending. What do they mean? Does the client appear to be becoming more relaxed or more uncomfortable? Is there interest or withdrawal? While we can usually trust our intuition, counselors should be careful to not prematurely assign meaning to this information as there are cultural differences in the meaning of nonverbal behaviors. For example, in some countries a no is indicated by an upward movement of the head. In other cultures this would be interpreted as a yes, and a downward look is meant as a sign of respect.

In some cultures, eye contact is thought to communicate our interest and attention. Different clients tolerate different levels of eye contact and clients tolerate different amounts of eye contact at different times. Thus eye contact can provide important information for the counselor if both cultural and clinical factors are considered. Does the client have difficulty maintaining eye contact? Is this a cultural factor or is there another reason? Are there times when the client looks away? What precipitates the client's looking away? Is the client looking inward or upward or downward? Again, the counselor needs to be aware of the cultural differences related to eye contact. For some, looking downward is a sign of respect, for others it indicates a discomfort with direct eye contact. If you are not sure, check it out with the client. Consider the following exchange.

TH: I notice you look mostly at your hands. I'm curious about that.

CL: I guess I do that a lot.

TH: With everyone?

CL: Well, not everyone. This is hard, you know, being here.

TH: And looking at your hands makes it easier.

A client's tears are sometimes hard for beginning counselors to deal with. Think about the times you have cried. Sometimes tears come as a relief, sometimes they represent a feeling we cannot quite verbalize. While we often relate tears to sorrow, they also come with laughter. While you will want to be aware of your client's tears, how you respond to these tears should be guided by what is going on in the session. Some people cry more easily than others and it is useful to remember to have tissues available for your clients as a sign of permission for them to cry. However, you do not need to hand a client a tissue if they appear to be getting tearful. It is better to just have them available and let the client decide whether to use them or not.

Hand movements, facial expressions, and head nods are ways of expressing ideas without words. Thus the counselor can use hand movements to indicate "Tell me more" or to suggest that the client slow down or stop speaking. A frown or a smile, an affirmative or negative nod are all forms of communication and can be therapeutic or counter-therapeutic. Consider the counselor whose says to the client "You're feeling a real sense of accomplishment" coupled with a nonverbal message of disapproval.

ACTIVITY III: USING NONVERBAL SKILLS

Choose a partner and arrange your chairs in a way that seems most comfortable to both of you. Take turns being the counselor and the client. If you are the counselor, note what information you get from simply using nonverbal attending skills. After a few minutes stop, and change roles, then stop again and share with your partner how you experienced this activity.

Note taking is also a form of physical attending. Some counselors prefer to have a pad of paper available to write brief notes about what the client is saying. As with other forms of attending, note taking influences what the client thinks, feels, and says. Thus, if the counselor is selective about what is recorded, note taking becomes a form of nonverbal encouragement. "This is important. My counselor is writing it down" may be the thought that crosses the mind of the client. Because of this, note taking can serve to encourage certain types of statements. Notes should be brief, just a word or phrase that is important. Before taking notes, it is important to inform the client that you plan to do some note taking and offer to give the client a copy of the notes at the end of the session. Thus, in his interview with Ollie and his mother (Carlson & Kjos, 2000e), Stephen Madigan asks if they would mind if he takes some notes and says, "And if you'd like to take them home with you tonight, you can." (p. 6).

Verbal Attending

Verbal attending is the words, phrases, and times of silence counselors use to indicate they are attending to the client. How the counselor verbally attends to the client in the engagement process influences the client's responses during this process as well as later in the relationship. It is important, therefore, to pay attention to the client's pace and vocabulary and be able to join the client in a way that is both genuine and helpful. For example if a client speaks slowly and hesitantly, the counselor may want to respond at a slower pace. In the same manner, the counselor will use a vocabulary that meets that of the client rather than talk down to the client or attempt to be overly familiar. Effective verbal attending also allows for silence.

What the counselor says or does not say during the engagement process is important as it sets expectations for further dialog. Thus, if the counselor asks a series of questions, the client will wait for another question and may strive to find the right answers for the counselor. If the counselor's verbal responses focus on the problem, the client may believe that the counselor is interested in hearing about the problem. In like manner, if the counselor's verbal responses focus on how the client is dealing with the problem, the client may see that how the client handles problems is more important than the problem itself. As counselors, we shape and guide the client's communication by what we choose to pay attention to, what we choose to ignore, and by how we craft our responses to the client.

ACTIVE LISTENING SKILLS

Another term often associated with verbal attending is *active listening.* Use of the word active in this case suggests that the counselor plays an active part in the verbal interchange. This may mean interrupting the client who seems to have an unending flow of words. In fact, during the engagement process, the counselor may be somewhat more active than later in the counseling relationship to provide the client with the sense of holding or security that gives the client a feeling of comfort and trust. At the same time, it helps the client maintain focus. At this point in the client-therapist relationship, long periods of silence may be threatening. A client who talks on and on without any direction, may go away feeling lost and confused.

Sue, a young mother, drove a car pool for nursery school for her son and three friends. One of the boys had attention deficit hyperactivity disorder and when he got out of the car, he would run toward whatever his eyes saw. Sue was afraid he would run out on a busy highway. She tried placing him in the backseat directly behind her. When she stopped the car, she would jump out, open the back door of the car, and, as he got out, gently put her hand on his head and turn his face toward the door of the nursery school. This would direct his focus and he would move toward the door rather than dash into the street or across the parking lot.

Active listening is that gentle guide that holds clients in a way that allows them to tell their story without getting into trouble. It provides security and direction for clients. The focus of active listening is on the client, not the counselor. It may be comforting to the counselor but it is not helpful to the client to respond with statements such as "I know just how you feel" or "I had a problem like that once" or "I've had a lot of clients with problems like yours."

The skills associated with active listening are minimal prompts, reflecting content, reflecting feeling, and the appropriate use of silence. These skills serve to let clients know that the counselor is listening and hearing what is being said, to acknowledge feelings attached to the clients' statements, to encourage clients to continue in a particular vein, and to respect the client's need to think through what they want to say or have said. When used appropriately and deliberately, active listening is a way of being with the client and serves to facilitate the client's story and guide clients to focus on the issues that are of concern.

Minimal Prompts

Minimal prompts are sounds the counselor makes such as *Mmm* or *Uh huh,* one or two word responses such as *Yes* or *Go on* or the simple restating of the last one or two words the client says. Depending on their use, minimal prompts can play a number of roles. First, they let clients know that the counselor is listening and interested in what they are saying and can serve to encourage clients to go on or continue on a particular subject. Second, they can shape the client's dialogue in that the counselor can use them to help the client maintain focus or provide direction to the client. Finally, they can keep the client talking, and in that way, they may help a client who is lost or confused stay lost and confused.

When a client is talking about difficult issues or feelings, the counselor can use minimal prompts to express empathy or concern without breaking into the client's train of thought. By restating the last word or words of the client's statement, the counselor might ask for more information or clarification. Minimal prompts can also amplify or emphasize what the client is saying. In the following dialog (Carlson & Kjos, 2000b), note how Lenore Walker uses minimal prompts to help Gina tell a difficult story.

> **CL 41:**   We had disagreed on something, [uh huh] and he wouldn't actually hear me through, [mhm] which at the time was very frustrating for me. And I don't even remember what I did. I don't know if I like pushed him or just to get his attention, but he hit me, in my face.
>
> **TH 42:**   Slapped you?
>
> **CL 42:**   Yeah.
>
> **TH 43:**   Open hand?
>
> **CL 43:**   Um, yeah, it was open hand, but it wasn't as hard as the second time he did it, so . . . (pp. 10–11)

With the first minimal prompt (uh huh), Walker lets Gina know she is interested in what Gina is saying. The second prompt (mhm) may be seen as an empathic response, and the next two responses amplify Gina's story.

Reflecting Content

During the engagement process and throughout the therapy process, counselors selectively reflect content to let the client know that they hear what is being said, to clarify, and serve to encourage the client to move deeper. Like minimal prompts, reflection of content also signals to the client areas of interest or importance to the therapeutic outcome. Reflection of content can range in length from a few words to a full sentence. One form of reflecting content is to simply restate what the client has said.

> **CL:**   I had a fight with my father last night.
>
> **TH:**   You fought with your father.

Another form of reflecting content is to focus on a key part of what the client has said.

CL: I had a fight with my father last night and I got so upset I really didn't sleep. I just wish I knew what to do about him.

TH: You don't know what to do about your father.

Reflection of content can also help to clarify what the client is saying.

CL: I got terminated yesterday.

TH: You got terminated.

CL: Yeah, I got into an argument with the foreman and the boss walked in and just fired me on the spot.

What might the client's response have been if the counselor had asked, "Why did you get terminated?", instead of simply reflecting content? Note the therapist's reflection of content in the following exchange between John Krumboltz and Robin (Carlson & Kjos, 2000c).

CL 21: She talks specifically to my husband, Ed, and says, "Oh, thank you for that card," or "Oh, thank you for that gift. You picked it out so well," and my husband will immediately say, "Well what did you get? I don't know what you got because Robin bought it," (TH yeahm, yeahm) you know, that type of thing. But she never acknowledges.

TH 22: She won't acknowledge that you did it.

CL 22: No, no. (TH Mhm, mhm) Everything comes from her son. (p. 8)

Here Krumboltz chooses to use minimal prompts and then reflects the content of what Robin is saying by paraphrasing her statement concerning being acknowledged. The choice Krumboltz made to focus on the mother-in-law not acknowledging Robin sets a direction for the therapy session. He might have chosen, instead, to focus on Robin's relationship with her husband by asking a question such as, "Your husband doesn't buy presents for his mother?"

Reflecting Feeling

The third component of active listening is reflecting feeling. The simplest form of reflecting feeling is to simply repeat back the feeling word the client reports. Because clients often have few words to use to describe their feelings, counselors need to become experts in both identifying and labeling feelings. There are many words that can be used to describe the various aspects of such feelings as mad, sad, glad, or bad. When your client says, "I am so mad at her," does he mean that he is irritated or livid, annoyed or incensed, furious or irate? When counselors reflect feelings, they help clients clarify their feelings. What if the client had simply said "I'm really mad at her" or "I'm upset with her."

ACTIVITY IV

Stop a minute and jot down all the words you can think of that describe *mad*. Be sure to include the gradients of the word as well. Then look up mad in a thesaurus. Can you add to your list? Now that you have become an expert on mad, try the same exercise with glad or sad or bad or another feeling word that comes to mind.

If clients do not say how they are feeling or how they felt about a particular situation, the counselor strives to identify the feelings that are attached to what the client does say. This may be more difficult than reflecting content. What we hear, see, feel, and know from experience contribute to our ability to accurately reflect feelings. Often, the client's facial expressions and gestures, or tone will suggest a feeling. At other times, the counselor may think "Someone in this situation would be upset" or, "If I were in this situation, I might be upset" and then proceed to reflect that feeling in a statement such as "I'm wondering if you found yourself getting upset when that happened." The accurate reflection of feelings also includes checking out our impressions with the client. At times, the client will not be ready to hear what we have to say. Notice how Guerin explores and clarifies feelings with Pam's mother in the following exchange (Carlson & Kjos, 2000a).

TH 56: Now, does it upset you Judy to remember those times or that the relationship with you and Pam isn't better?

M 11: I've just grown to adjust to it, you know.

TH 57: I understand, but it seems like something we are talking about is upsetting you, and what I am trying to get clear about is it the state of the relationship between you or is it some of that old stuff and reflecting back.

M 12: Oh, no. It, I just wish that she was the daughter I always wanted, that we could be closer, yes.

TH 58: Okay, so you get kind of melancholy about that. Wishing it could be so.

M 13: Yeah. But I says she doesn't so . . . (p. 15).

Pam's mother is not quite ready to say she is upset but she will admit to being kind of melancholy about her relationship with Pam. Napier bases his initial statement on what he is observing in Pam's mother—in his opinion, she looks upset.

There are some ways of reflecting feeling that can be counterproductive such as telling clients how they should or should not feel, or suggesting that others control their feelings. Clients may take umbrage at being told "You must feel . . ." no matter what tone is used in delivering the message. Nor is it a good idea to say, "If I were you, I would feel . . ." or "I know just how you feel." Obviously you are not the client and the client is not you. If the client is really upset or angry or hurt, the counselor might be tempted to say "Don't feel that way" or "It will get better." Such responses reflect the counselor's difficulty with negative feelings, minimize or negate the client's feelings, and serve to hinder the therapeutic relationship. The use of the phrase "makes you feel" as in "He makes you so angry" may be an accurate reflection of how someone sees a situation, but it may also communicate to clients that they have no choice in the matter of how they feel and are at the mercy of others who control their feelings.

As you become adept at hearing feelings and helping clients clearly define these feelings, you will become more able to truly understand what is happening for the client and develop an empathy with the client. This ability serves not only as a base for joining with the client, but, as you will read later on in this chapter, starts you on a path to building more advanced therapeutic skills.

Silence

You may wonder what role silence has in active listening. After all, this seems such a passive activity. Beginning counselors often fear silence, possibly believing that if nothing is being said, nothing is happening. However, knowing when to speak and when to maintain silence is an important skill in listening to our clients. Langs (1992) suggests a number of characteristics of, or roles for, appropriate silence in the therapeutic relationship. Silence can provide a sense of security and serve as a way of communicating relatedness. It can show acceptance of the client's need to not talk and provide "a sense of presence awaiting for further development" (p. 110). Silence can be both confrontational and nonconfrontational, comforting or threatening. It gives the client room to think and decide what to say and how to say it and it challenges the client to internal exploration.

Effective use of silence is largely based on our visual attending. What can you learn from watching the client? Are there changes in the client's physical stance? What about facial color or expression? Is the client looking at you expectantly or looking away as if thinking about something? Do you need to stay out of the way? Is the client waiting for you to say something? Do you need to speak at this time? Have you said something that has pushed the client away or caused the client to lose trust in you? Is the client confused? Sometimes silence is a form of resistance on the part of the client.

How long should we allow silence to continue? It depends on what we perceive, or what seems to be going on with the client. At times clients need time to think something through. At other times, they may be confused. Depending on what the client seems to need at the time the counselor can reflect on the silence. Thus, if the client appears confused the counselor might say, "I get the sense that you are confused about this." When the client appears to be thinking something through, the reflection might be, "You seem to need some time to think about this."

ACTIVITY V

How comfortable are you with silence? What happens to you when there is a long silence? Are you someone who needs to fill up that space? Or do you find silence a friend? During the next few days, notice your responses to silence.

EMPATHIC RESPONDING SKILLS

"The most direct route to trust in psychotherapy is empathy" (Welch, 1998). All of the skills we have discussed to this point form a basis for empathic responding, which is the ability to hear and communicate to the client the feelings and the underlying meaning of what the client is saying and what the client is not saying in a way that the client feels deeply understood. True empathy is an attitude that comes from within the individual and, while it can be refined and enhanced, it cannot be manufactured. In order to be empathic, we need to be able to feel with the client, as if what is happening to the client may be happening or have happened to us and in order to do that, we need to put our own concerns and needs aside.

Empathy is not sympathy or feeling sorry for the client or needing to take up the client's cause. The word empathic implies the ability to feel *with* another; the word sympathetic implies the ability to feel *for* another. Empathy is built on a deep respect for the client and the client's strengths and abilities even in the face of adversity. It is not identifying with the client in a way that causes us to lose our separateness or objectivity.

Empathy is more than simply reflecting feelings, and a truly empathic response may not even include a feeling word. Empathic responses add to the feeling and meaning of what the client is verbally and nonverbally communicating. There are indications that the counselor is attuned to what the client is experiencing, both in the session and in the world at large. These responses reflect a deep level of respect and caring and begin to tap into the client's emotions, thoughts, and beliefs concerning the problem that is brought to counseling. Empathy creates in the client a deeper sense of being heard and understood; of being valued as someone who has something worthwhile to offer. This, in turn, leads to a richer level of self-exploration and self-understanding on the part of the client and allows for even deeper levels of affect.

We cannot be truly empathic until we hear and understand the client. Duncan, Hubble, and Miller (1997) tell us that "Being empathic begins by giving undivided attention to what the client is saying, attempting to understand the client's experience, and then sharing that understanding with the client." In the following excerpt, Carlson & Kjos, 2000e, a white therapist (TH), opens the door for a black mother (M) to talk about racism and her concern about her son in this environment. We can assume that this is not something that Madigan, a white man from Canada, has experienced in his life. Notice how he attempts to understand her experience and shares that understanding with her.

TH 96:   Would you mind, would that be a good place to go here and tell me your hunch about what's going on?

M 49:   Okay, I had experience with schools . . . another district school that I didn't have, never had this type of problem. This school district out here, ah, it just seem like the least little anything, things that could be straightened out, they the district make a big thing out of it.

TH 97:   Yeah

M 50:   And that, and if the kids get to high school and he doesn't watch what he's doing. I mean real careful, be real careful they're out.

TH 98:   I see. Do you have a sense as to why the school district here is structured this way and the one you used to be in is not?

M 51:   Ah, yes. I know why.

TH 99:   Why is that?

M 52:   Ah, I was told that they hadn't got used to the, ah black kids goin' to his school.

TH 100:   Mmm, As a mother, what is it like to have that told to you. That the school is operating in certain ways because black kids are now in the school.

M 53:   Well, I didn't like it. I've never had anyone to bother me. I mean, no matter what color they were. I never had no one to bother me. But it seem like once the boys get in that school district they really have to be careful. The girls can get out pretty good if they, if they don't get to be bad girls, but the boys have to really watch their selves real careful in everything they do.

TH 101:   Mmhm, So do you think that race had something to do with how Ollie was treated?

M 54:   I think so because if it hadda been a white boy, it was a white boy, but if it hadda been two white boys I don't think they woulda, they wouldn't have went to court.

At the end of this session with Ollie and his mother, the mother says to Madigan "I'd, I'd like to say I didn't know we would get to tell this story but it's a true story." Madigans effort to truly understand the mother and her concerns demonstrates his empathy with a situation that he might find difficulty identifying with. As a result, the mother feels truly heard.

Premature attempts at empathy—reflecting a feeling that may be inaccurate—can inhibit the process of engagement. When we act on the assumption that we know how someone is feeling or should feel, we communicate a lack of respect.

Clients have varying abilities to deal with empathy and different ways of responding to our empathic statements. Because of this, the client's response to our use of empathy provides us information that may be useful in the further development of our relationship with the client and contribute to the diagnosis and thus to more effective treatment planning. True empathy is built on our hearing and understanding the client and true empathy, in turn, enhances our understanding of the client and strengthens the client/counselor relationship.

ACTIVITY VI

1. Watch for examples of verbal and nonverbal empathy in your day-to-day encounters.
2. Experiment with empathy in your day-to-day encounters. How would you express empathy to the checker in the grocery store on a very busy day?

ENCOURAGEMENT SKILLS

Clients often seek counseling because they are discouraged and have difficulty seeing themselves in a positive light. They bring their problems and failures to the counselor, possibly hoping that someone can tell them what to do so that everything will be all right. The decision to seek counseling may have taken courage but it may also have represented a de-celeration of failure—"I just can't handle this."

Therapy itself takes courage. Building a therapeutic relationship, dealing with painful issues, and initiating life changes all take a certain amount of determination and tenacity. Encouragement empowers clients keep going and striving for change. Without encouragement, the client may have low expectations of the effectiveness of therapy or feel that therapy will just be an exercise in futility. Clients, who in the first session, simply re-late one problem after another to an empathic and caring counselor, may, in considering all of the negatives, decide that counseling is not going to help at all and seek some other remedy. Clients who are discouraged are more apt to miss sessions and, when they do come, to continue to focus on the problem rather than be willing to consider ways of cop-ing with their problems.

We encourage our clients both verbally and nonverbally. We encourage our clients to talk more about something, to share more information, and to trust us because we un-derstand them. We can also encourage our clients to do more of what works, and to rec-ognize and own their own strengths. Our encouragement provides the motivation, optimism, support, and confidence clients need to persevere.

It is important to differentiate between courage and praise. While many of us bask in praise, especially when we feel we have earned it, praise may condition us to look to others for validation rather than use self-validation. Praise, when seen as flattery, can ac-tually hinder the client–counselor relationship. The client may react to praise by hiding true thoughts or feelings so as not to disappoint the counselor who has been so approving. Praise is not encouragement.

In addition to encouraging clients to share particular information by our attending to what they say, we can encourage the client's productive behavior by marking or paying at-tention to that behavior and linking positive feelings and thoughts to the behavior. Clients are also encouraged when the counselor elicits and notes the client's strengths and positive characteristics.

Marking Behaviors

From behavior theory we have learned that, if we get positive attention for our behavior, we are apt to do more of it. By marking or reflecting productive client behaviors, we help our clients see themselves as able and encourage more productive behavior. Conversely, by focusing on negative behaviors, we may actually encourage our clients to see themselves in a more negative light. Note how Insoo Kim Berg (Carlson & Kjos, 2000g). encourages Robin in the following interaction.

> **CL 45:**   Well, I guess it was that I didn't want to fight. I didn't want to get into an argument about it. It was not worth it. Um, so, therefore, I just wasn't going to do it. No matter what he said, I wasn't going to let it bother me. Because I didn't want to, um . . .
>
> **TH 46:**   And you knew that.
>
> **CL 46:**   Yeah.

TH 47:   You knew.

CL 47:   Right.

TH 48:   Wow. [CL Right] How did you know that?

CL 48:   (laughter) I don't know. That's a good question.

TH 49:   How did you decide that?

CL 49:   I don't know, um. I was tired for one. [TH Okay] Um, well, and, plus it's a repeat pattern.

What do you think Robin is saying to herself at this point? Berg has paid special attention to the fact that Robin knew that, to avoid a fight, she needed to not let what was said or done bother her and that she could make a choice about it. Robin is so pleased to realize this that she laughs. Berg pays attention to both Robin's knowing (cognition) and doing (behavior) and, by so doing, suggests that Robin is able to manage difficult situations.

What if Berg had, instead, chosen to use praise in an attempt to encourage Robin. After all, Berg is an expert. Would that have helped Robin feel good about herself and raised her self-esteem? By refraining from praise, and, instead, marking Robin's positive behaviors, Berg allows Robin to realize that she has already demonstrated the ability to solve her problems. Robin is encouraged to do more of what works, to repeat behaviors that are productive. In encouragement, we help clients appreciate what they have done or said and thus teach them to encourage themselves.

Eliciting Positives

We also encourage clients by helping them define their own strengths and positive characteristics. Again, we can do that by simply marking or reflecting back what the client says.

CL: I'm fairly dependable.

TH: You're someone people can depend on.

Initial sessions are often litanies of problems and positive characteristics can give balance to the therapist's view of clients and help clients feel less discouraged about what is not so positive. For some clients, the counselor may need to be more proactive. One way of doing this is to elicit and reflect the client's positive characteristics by asking the client to report what another might say.

Karen, 22 years old, was referred for counseling after a brief hospitalization for depression with psychotic features. During the first session, Karen reported a number of things that were wrong with her. She could not drive, she was not very smart, her mother got impatient with her, and she was having all kinds of ideas about dying and about her mother dying. The counselor asked, "What about friends?" Karen responded, "I have one friend, he's always asking me to do things—he's not a boyfriend, he's gay, but he likes me."

"If I were to ask him why he likes you, what would he say?" the counselor asked.

After some thought, Karen began to list the things her friend might say about her. "He'd say I'm a good friend, I keep secrets, I'm fun to be with, and he thinks I'm beautiful. He says I look like Roseanne when I smile." Then Karen smiled.

"You do look a bit like Roseanne when you smile," the counselor responded. "Now let's see—you're fun to be with, and you must be dependable because you're a good friend and keep secrets. And, you are here because you want to take care of yourself."

Another way we encourage our clients is by empowering them to take charge of their own therapy and direction in their lives. Our ability to empower our clients is rooted in our respect for them. Empowerment may mean asking permission before touching a client or, as mentioned earlier, taking notes during the session. We empower our clients when we offer a choice of where they will sit and when we wait in silence, without interrupting, for them to process a new idea, to struggle to get something said just right, or during a time of tears.

Encouragement is helping clients gain more control over their lives by learning to praise themselves for what they do rather than looking to others for that praise. Encouragement gives clients the incentive to continue to work in counseling and helps them realize that they do have the strength and, indeed, the courage to make changes in their lives.

SUMMARY

The first steps in counseling are toward engagement. The therapeutic relationship forms the basis for change. Effective engagement starts with the counselor and involves a number of skills and interventions that help the client move toward a readiness for and commitment to change. We have seen that the skills of engagement are not restricted to the engagement stage of counseling nor are they restricted to the counseling process. These are skills that are used in everyday life and are found to be helpful in sales, management, and teaching. Note how they are used by the people around you and pay attention to how you use them in your daily life. As you become aware of these skills and how you use them or do not use them in your life, you will move toward becoming an effective therapist.

ACTIVITY VI: INVESTIGATING

View the first ten minutes of two different therapy sessions from either *Psychotherapy with the Experts* or *Family Therapy with the Experts*. Take note of the skills the counselors use during the first part of the session. What nonverbal skills do you observe? What do you hear the therapist saying? How many engagement skills can you identify?

REFERENCES

Bugental, J. F. T. (1987). *The art of the psychotherapist*. New York: Jossey Bass.

Carlson, J. & Kjos, D. (2000a). *Bowenian therapy with Dr. Phil Guerin* (reprint): Family therapy with the experts video. Boston: Allyn & Bacon.

Carlson, J. & Kjos, D. (2000b). *Cognitive therapy with Dr. John Krumboltz* (reprint): Psychotherapy with the experts video. Boston: Allyn & Bacon.

Carlson, J. & Kjos, D. (2000c). *Cognitive-behavioral feminist therapy with Dr. Lenore Walker* (reprint): Psychotherapy with the experts video. Boston: Allyn & Bacon.

Carlson, J. & Kjos, D. (2000d). *Existential-humanistic therapy with Dr. James Bugental* (reprint): Psychotherapy with the experts video. Boston: Allyn & Bacon.

Carlson, J. & Kjos, D. (2000e). *Narrative therapy with James Madigan* (reprint): Psychotherapy with the experts video. Boston: Allyn & Bacon.

Carlson, J. & Kjos, D. (2000f). *Satir family therapy with Jean McLendon* (reprint): Psychotherapy with the experts video. Boston: Allyn & Bacon.

Carlson, J. & Kjos, D. (2000g). *Solution focused therapy with Insoo Kim Berg* (reprint): Psychotherapy with the experts video. Boston: Allyn & Bacon.

Duncan, B. L., Hubble, M. A., & Miller, S. D. (1997). *Psychotherapy with "impossible" cases.* New York: Norton.

Gould, W. B. (1993). *Frankl: Life with meaning.* Pacific Grove, CA: Brooks/Cole.

Langs, R. (1992). *A clinical workbook for psychotherapists.* London: H. Karnac (Books) Ltd.

Mahoney, M. (1991). *Human change processes.* New York: Basic Books.

Shea, S. C. (1998). *The art of interviewing.* Philadelphia W.B. Saunders.

Welch, I. D. (1998). *The path of psychotherapy: Matters of the heart.* Pacific Grove, CA: Brooks Cole.

TABLE 3.1 Engagement Skills, Descriptions, and Outcomes

SKILL	DESCRIPTION	OUTCOME
Attending and Joining Skills		
Internal attending	Focus on the client and counselor's reaction to the client.	Client feels heard and respected, and gains space to focus on self. Counselor gains information through awareness of own thoughts and feelings.
Physical attending—counselor focus	Body posture, behaviors, and demeanor that communicates interest in and respect for the client.	Client feels attended to and respected.
Physical attending—client focus	Observation of the client's body posture, behaviors, and demeanor.	Counselor gains information that may be useful in diagnosis and treatment.
Verbal attending—counselor focus	Appropriate verbal responses and silence that maintain a client focus, and match and pace client's verbal responses.	Client feels heard and is more able to maintain focus.
Verbal attending—client focus	Attention to client's pace, and use of words and periods of silence.	Counselor gains information that guides interactions and may be useful in diagnosis and treatment.
Active Listening Skills		
Minimal prompts	Sounds and one- or two-word responses that serve to show attentiveness and respect and helps maintain client focus.	Client feels heard and is encouraged and helped to maintain focus.
Reflecting content	Reflection of both stated and implied content that help maintain client focus.	Client feels understood.
Reflecting feeling	Reflection of both stated and implied feelings that help maintain client focus.	Client feels both heard and understood.
Silence	The use of appropriate, comfortable, and empathic silence.	Client feels respected and is given time to consider or process information and ideas.
Empathic Responding Skills		
Empathic responding	Hearing and communicating both overt and covert feelings and related meaning.	Client feels deeply understood and connected to counselor.
Encouragement Skills		
Marking behaviors	Taking notice of client's characteristics, thoughts, and behaviors that contribute to desired change.	Client is encouraged to recognize and use productive behaviors or thoughts.
Eliciting positives	Helping clients identify and acknowledge personal strengths and positive characteristics.	Client gains confidence in self and is encouraged to continue.

PART III ASSESSMENT

CHAPTER 4

DIAGNOSTIC ASSESSMENT

ASSESSMENT: PAST AND PRESENT

In today's accountability-focused world, assessment in the context of psychotherapy is considerably different than it was in the 1970s and 1980s. Then, assessment conducted by a psychotherapist usually included an extensive initial evaluation interview, which might have taken one to three sessions to complete. If diagnostic or treatment issues remained, it might also have included a psychological assessment battery consisting of a Minnesota Multiphasic Personality Inventory (MMPI) or another standardized personality inventory, and one or more projective tests, such as the Rorschach or Thematic Apperception Test (TAT), or a sentence completion test. Sometimes individual intelligence testing was also included. The purpose of this approach to assessment was to develop a wide ranging and comprehensive picture of the client. While some of this assessment information was directly pertinent to the course of treatment often it was not. It was only with the introduction of DSM-III in 1978 that specifying a formal psychiatric diagnosis based on specific diagnostic criteria slowly began to be required by third-party payors. Prior to that time, and probably until the mid 1980s, psychotherapists routinely did not or would not submit a diagnostic formulation to an insurance company in order to be reimbursed for psychotherapy services rendered. It should also be noted that third-party payors often authorized and paid for ongoing, long-term psychotherapy with goals that ranged from return to baseline functioning to self-actualization.

Today, the purpose of assessment is to assess the individual's symptomatic distress, functional capacities and impairment, coping resources, and of singular importance, to monitor progress in treatment. This approach tends to be more limited and narrow in focus, and more pertinent to specified goals of treatment than in years past. Not surprisingly then,

55

formal psychological assessment batteries have become the exception rather than the rule, and a brief diagnostic interview focused-functional assessment.

Whether a therapist meets only once or one hundred times with a client, an effective therapist will be observing and evaluating a client's presenting concerns, symptoms, functioning and resources, and determining what, if anything, needs to be done. Training and experience with the requisite assessment skills is essential to providing effective therapy.

Chapter 4 deals with formal diagnostic assessment, while Chapter 6 describes focused-functional assessment and ongoing assessment. Chapter 5 describes diagnostic, clinical, and treatment formulations. A clinical case exemplifies the various dimensions and skills of formal-diagnostic assessment.

WHAT YOU WILL LEARN IN THIS CHAPTER

1. A description of the assessment process in relationship to the treatment process. Introduction to three different types of assessment utilized in the context of counseling and psychotherapy: formal–diagnostic, focused–functional, and ongoing assessment or treatment monitoring.
2. The six components and the skills of focused–functional assessment.
3. Application of focused–functional assessment in an illustrated psychotherapy case.

THE ASSESSMENT PROCESS: DEFINITIONS AND TYPES

Assessment is defined by Maxmen and Ward (1995) as "a time-limited, formal process that collects critical information from many sources in order to reach a diagnosis, to make a prognosis, to render a biopsychosocial formulation, and to determine treatment" (p. 19). Four components are emphasized in this definition: diagnosis, prognosis, biopsychosocial or clinical formulation, and treatment formulation. In our book, Maxmen and Ward's definition of assessment is what we mean by the term *formal–diagnostic assessment* which is the focus of Chapter 5. Diagnostic assessment differs considerably from focused–functional assessment and ongoing assessment which is the focus of this chapter.

Formal–diagnostic assessment refers to data collected about the client's current problems, current functioning and mental status, relevant social, developmental, and health history and behaviors, and, particularly, the expectations and resources the client brings to therapy.

Focused–functional assessment refers to data collected about an individual's type and level of symptomatic distress, for example, anxiety symptoms, as well as type and level of functional impairment, and, decreased job performance due to clinical depression. Currently, managed behavioral health care organizations (MBHOs) typically utilize what is called medical necessity, also called treatment necessity, as the basis for the authorization of behavioral health care, such as psychotherapy. With regard to psychotherapy, medical necessity refers to the determination that psychotherapeutic treatment is "appropriate (and) necessary to meet a person's health needs, and is consistent with the diagnosis and clinical standards of care" (NCQA, 1998). Accordingly, MBHOs put a premium on focused–functional assessment because, in their view, clinical standards of care means that the goals of psychotherapy are to simply to return the individual to some level of stability. In other words, the goal of treatment is to: (1) reduce symptoms and (2) improve functional status. Other treatment goals that are growth-oriented such as individuation, self-actualization, or spiritual integration, would be inconsistent with the criteria of medical necessity, and would be unlikely to be authorized.

Ongoing assessment, including treatment monitoring, refers to a regular and informal assessment of key dimensions of client functioning at each session. This assessment is undertaken irrespective of whether the presenting problem is depression, violence, an eating disorder, loss of an important relationship, marital discord, or addiction. During each session the therapist would evaluate and assess the following:

- Type and level of symptoms
- Type and level of functioning
- Mental status, especially safety issues
- Health status, particularly medication and substance use
- Treatment progress

OVERVIEW OF THE DIAGNOSTIC ASSESSMENT PROCESS

For the therapist-in-training with no prior clinical experience, the diagnostic assessment may seem daunting, which it is, but it does not have to be overwhelming. By bearing in mind the purpose of the diagnostic assessment, the assessment process can be manageable. The purpose of the diagnostic assessment is two-fold: first, to understand why the client has decided on therapy, what symptoms are present, and how those symptoms create trouble; and, second, to understand what the client is motivated to work on, as well the client's resources, particularly, readiness for change.

The formal–diagnostic assessment is considered to be one of the most important and basic skills of the effective therapist. We use the term formal–diagnostic assessment instead of the more traditional designation, initial clinical evaluation, because changes in health care questioned the value and utility of the traditional initial evaluation.

In a traditional initial evaluation, the therapist or clinician performed a relatively exhaustive inquiry of the patient's story. This evaluation, which might be spread out over the first three sessions, typically included a history of the initial complaint, current and past psychiatric illness and treatment, past family psychiatric history, social and developmental history, medical and substance use history, current job, relational and family functioning, social functioning, intrapsychic dynamics and personality style, and a mental status examination. Managed care advocates questioned both the costliness and the clinical utility of this evaluation method. It was noted that seldom did this information inform treatment decisions and managed care advocates claimed that it was of limited value in monitoring the course of treatment.

The formal–diagnostic assessment, on the other hand, is a much more focused and intentional approach to assessment. A complete formal–diagnostic assessment can usually be accomplished within the first 30 to 40 minutes of the initial session between client and therapist. The focus of the assessment is to gather information about the client that is *clinically relevant* to the treatment process and outcomes. This includes data on the client's current problems, current functioning and mental status, social, developmental, and health history and behaviors, and, particularly, the expectations and resources the client brings to therapy. For instance, the therapist would consider how a medication that is prescribed for a client's medical condition as well as intake of caffeine and other stimulants might exacerbate or even cause the anxiety symptoms experienced by the client. Similarly, the formal–diagnostic assessment emphasizes client resources, such as the client's coping skills and support system, previous success in making changes, and expectations and readiness for treatment. Since these factors have been shown to significantly impact the outcomes of treatment (Lambert, 1992; Miller, Duncan, & Hubble, 1997; Sperry, et al., 1996) it is critical to elicit this information and utilize it in planning treatment goals and interventions. Although there is some similarity between the data collected in both the formal–diagnostic assessment and the traditional initial clinical evaluation, the main difference is that the formal–diagnostic assessment focuses on collecting data that has foreseeable clinical relevance to treatment outcomes.

Table 4.1 provides a bird's eye view of the components of the formal–diagnostic interview process.

Each of these six components is briefly described and illustrated in an example case report. For a more detailed discussion of the diagnostic assessment and interview process see the texts by Othmer and Othmer (1994) and Hersen and Turner (1994).

1. Presenting Problem

This part of the assessment contains a summary of the client's presenting concern as well as how the impact of these symptoms, stressors and circumstances affect their daily functioning. It also indicates the reason this person is seeking therapy at this particular time. This segment of the diagnostic assessment interview encourages the client to tell their story. Accordingly, the therapist should begin the inquiry with an open-ended question such as, "What concern brought you here?" In the interest of collecting a significant amount of information in a short time period, the diagnostic assessment relies on focused questions or closed-ended questions rather than open-ended questions. This first question

TABLE 4.1   Components of the Formal–Diagnostic Assessment

1. Presenting problem and context
2. Mental status assessment
3. Developmental history and dynamics
4. Social history and cultural dynamics
5. Health history and health behaviors
6. Client resources

is the exception, and it provides a goldmine of information about the client. The therapist observes not only what the client answers but how they answer.

Typically the patient will begin describing symptoms and stressful situations and persons in their lives. The therapist may then ask clarifying questions but quickly moves to asking how these concerns affect the client's ability to function in the various spheres of daily life such as work, family, intimacy, health, and social. The therapist asks about circumstances when the concern(s) are not bothering the client. It is also critical to understand why this person has decided to seek therapy at this time. The "Why now?" question begins the inquiry; it is considered *the* central question for therapists to assess (Budman & Gurman, 1988). The answer to this question provides key information about the client's motivation, coping skills, and support system. Finally, the therapist elicits information about previous symptoms and other psychiatric or substance abuse history. If there has been previous therapy or psychiatric or substance abuse treatment this information is noted. However, since past experience in treatment can be an important predictor of present involvement and response to treatment, it is critical to understand what that experience was, including treatment outcomes. What benefits did the client derive from this treatment? What did they learn about themselves as a result of it? What worked and what did not work?

2. Mental Status Assessment

The effective therapist evaluates mental status as part of the overall assessment of a client's functioning and ability to benefit from treatment. Most mental status assessments are geared toward locating factors that signal the need for immediate attention, for referral to another source, or for more detailed evaluation by a specialist. Generally speaking, we evaluate mental status by making skilled observations of the client's presentation and appearance, orientation, mood and affect, cognitive function, thought processes and content, memory, judgment, insight, use of medication and substances, and danger to self and others. Table 4.2 lists six factors that make up the mental status assessment.

The acronym POMP-CS can serve as a memory aid for the therapist.

1. Assessing Presentation. Describe the client's general appearance including the appropriateness of dress, grooming and hygiene. Note whether the client looks his or her stated age, or appears younger or older. Comment on facial expression, for example, pained, frightened, depressed, and so on, as well as unusual mannerisms. Also, indicate any abnormalities of speech such as slurred, rapid, or slowed.

TABLE 4.2 Outline of Mental Status Assessment

1. Presentation
2. Orientation and attitude
3. Mood and emotional status
4. Perceptual status
5. Cognitive status
6. Safety

2. Assessing Orientation and Attitude. Describe the client's level of orientation to time, place, and person. This is assessed by asking the client to describe the day, date, and year; the time and place of the assessment interview; and, their name. Finally, note the degree of the client's attitude toward the assessment process: is it cooperative, guarded, angry, or suspicious.

3. Assessing Mood and Emotional Status. Both the client's report of subjective feeling (mood and affect) are recorded as well as the therapist's observation. Mood refers to an emotional attitude that is sustained over time, for example, neutral, euphoric, depressed, anxious, or irritable. Affect refers to brief emotional responses which are usually triggered by some stimuli. Affect is typically described as being full, blunted, flat, or inappropriate.

4. Assessing Perceptual Status. Abnormalities of perception include illusions, such as perceptual misinterpretations of an actual stimulus; *hallucinations*, such as false sensory experience in the absence of an actual stimulus; and dissociations, such as sudden alterations in consciousness or identity, such as depersonalization, for example, wherein one feels that he or she is suddenly different, or derealization wherein one feels that somehow the environment has changed and reality is no longer familiar. Depersonalization and derealization are commonly reported in individuals experiencing post-traumatic stress disorder.

5. Assessing Cognitive Status. Cognitive status includes both the form and content of thought as well as memory and insight and judgment. Thought form or process refers to the way, including speed of thought, in which an individual puts together ideas and associations. Thought form can be rated in terms such as poverty of ideas, flight of ideas, pressured speech, perseveration, loosened association, or tangentiality. *Thought content* refers to what an individual is actually thinking about such as ideas, beliefs, obsessions, and so on. Delusions, that is, fixed, false beliefs out of keeping with the individual's cultural background, and obsessions, that is, repetitive irrational thoughts, are examples of thought content. *Memory* is usually described in terms of three types of recall: immediate, short-term, and remote or long-term. Difficulty with memory recall should be tested and recorded for example, asking the individual to recall three items immediately after the therapist identifies the items and then again after five minutes. Insight refers to the degree to which the individual can appreciate the nature of their condition and the need for treatment. *Judgment* is the capacity to deal with social situations and adhere to reasonable social conventions. Judgment is rated as intact, limited, or poor.

6. Assessing Safety: Self and Others. Assessing safety issues is an integral part of any diagnostic assessment; it is not optional. Therapists need to use common sense when assessing suicidality as well as the potential for harm to others. The use of a systematic evaluation scheme is recommended to improve the therapist's clinical judgment. A systematic assessment should include the following: (1) known risk factors; (2) client ideation, intentions, and impulsiveness; and, (3) lethality. Some clinics and hospitals require the use of standardized rating forms to assess and record indicators of harm to self and others. The prediction of violence against others is a perplexing matter for most therapists. Although it is currently not possible to accurately predict violent behavior, and it may never be, therapists will continually be asked to offer such determinations. Since therapists often work with situations that could lead to violence, they need to be mindful of the consequences of their assessments.

3. Developmental History and Dynamics

The developmental history and dynamics section of the assessment contains a summary of the client's personal life. It should provide a concise narrative description of the client's life history from birth to the present. It may include developmental milestones such as when the client began to talk and walk. It should note the family constellation, or description of parents, siblings and birth order, as well as the role(s) the client assumed in the family, among peers, and in school. It may include one or two pertinent early memories or recollections (Dinkmeyer & Sperry, 2000). It should briefly note early life adjustment and traumatic experience, such as physical, emotional and sexual abuse, as well as the presence or absence of best friends. It may include mention of early sexual experience but should describe school experiences and level of education. Perhaps most important, the client should be asked to describe themselves as a person now as well as when they were a child to infer their self-view and level of self-esteem.

4. Social History and Cultural Dynamics

This segment of the assessment contains a summary of the client's past and current social history and cultural factors and dynamics. Social history primarily reflects marital status, current job, and work history. It includes the client's current living situation including specifics about family members who live with the client, financial status, and social supports currently available. It should briefly indicate any military service and the nature of the discharge, and note any legal problems, current or in the past.

Cultural factors and dynamics reflect the individual's cultural identity. A complete cultural assessment should include the following: (1) ethnic identity; (2) age; (3) race; (4) gender and sexual orientation; (5) religion; (6) migration and country of origin; (7) socioeconomic status (SES); (8) acculturation in terms of assimilation (strong affiliation with the dominant culture); traditionality (rejection of the dominant culture); and biculturalism (assuming the cultural norms of both cultures without denying either); (9) language; (10) dietary influences; and, (11) education (GAP, 2002, pp. 20–47). Typically, only three of these eleven factors are commonly reported by clinicians: age, gender, and ethnic identity. For example, the first sentence in the "Identifying Information and Chief Complaint" section of a diagnostic assessment report usually begins with a statement of ethnic identity: "This is a 53-year-old Hispanic male who . . . ." Although gender may be specified, sexual orientation is seldom indicated. Three others are either assumed or specified somewhere else in a diagnostic assessment report. These are language, education, and socioeconomic status (SES). This means that five of the eleven dimensions of culture are not addressed at all by most clinicians. Eliciting information regarding these cultural factors can be accomplished in approximately five to seven minutes, and this information can be summarized in a short paragraph of the diagnostic assessment report.

5. Health History and Health Behaviors

The health history and health behavior segment of the diagnostic assessment includes health history, health status, and health behaviors. Some therapists use a short intake form which includes a brief health history section and which the client completes before the interview. Whether this information is elicited in the interview or is provided on such a form, it is imperative for the therapist to briefly review the health conditions, surgeries, and various medical treatments to ascertain *how* these have impacted the client's life. Prescription medication use, over-the-counter medications, vitamins and herbal supplements, and alcohol and substance use can greatly impact treatment outcomes, so these areas are described in detail.

Assessing Prescription Medication Use. Many prescribed medications, such as painkillers such as Demerol and codeine-containing medication, can greatly influence mood and behavior. These medications are also addictive. Several high blood pressure medications as well as many antidepressants, such as Prozac, Paxil, and Zoloft, affect sex drive and sexual functioning. Thus, it is imperative that the therapist inquire about medication use, not just about the ones clients take regularly but also those they take for temporary relief. It is useful for the therapist to have a copy of a reference text such as the *Physicians Desk Reference* readily available to check on the side effect profiles of medications. Finally, it is important to query clients about their pattern of medication compliance: do they consistently take medications as it is prescribed, or whenever they feel like it or get around to taking it. Are they ambivalent about putting chemicals into their bodies, or have they had serious untoward effect taking medication in the past and now are hesitant to use prescribed medication even thought they know it is effective when they take it?

Assessing OTC and Supplement Use. Therapists also should inquire about over-the-counter medications (OTC), vitamin supplements, and herbal remedies. The reason is that a number of cold, allergy, and sinus medications as well as some herbs and most diet aids contain stimulants, which when added to the client's regular intake of coffee and cola can greatly exacerbate or even cause anxiety symptoms. A full review of drug effects is beyond the scope of this book, but therapists need to consider the possibility that these products can have an effect on behavior, emotion, and cognitions.

Assessing Substance Use. When dealing with the use of drugs there are two primary types of evaluation that therapists need to make. First, assess the nature and extent of the usage. This means the therapist should attempt to find out what drugs are used, how often, how much, and under what circumstances. The therapist also might ask, "How old were you when you started drinking (using)?" This is useful in assessing risk for complications and relapse since the younger and the more involved the use, the higher the risk.

6. Client Resources

This part of the diagnostic assessment is perhaps the most important in terms of planning treatment and even in predicting treatment outcomes. It includes a brief description of the client's strengths and past experiences of success or failure in making personal changes. It describes the client's explanatory model for why he or she is experiencing problems, which will serve as the basis for the client and therapist negotiating a clinical and treatment formulation and plan. It also notes the client's expectations for treatment, including the area or focus the client is motivated to change. Finally, it specifies the client's level of readiness for change be it precontemplative, contemplative, preparation, action or maintenance.

CLINICAL ILLUSTRATION: A CASE REPORT OF JUAN R.

Presenting Problem and Context

Juan R. is a 29-year-old single, Hispanic male accountant who presented with a three-week onset of depressed mood. Other symptoms reported were loss of energy, markedly diminished interest, insomnia, difficulty concentrating, and increasing social isolation. He had not showed up for work for four days prompting the psychiatric referral. Cutbacks at his office led to him being transferred out of a close-knit work group where he had been for 12 years to new site across town. Juan appears to have experienced this transfer as a significant loss, which triggered his depressive symptoms and social isolation.

It is noteworthy that Juan showed up late for the initial evaluation explaining that he couldn't find the address although this clinic is six blocks from his home. He indicated that he had come for the evaluation only at the insistence of the vice president of human resources. And, while he admitted that he felt awful, he was not convinced that he really had a problem that needed psychological treatment. His explanation was that he was "just dragging because I went back to work too soon after having the flu," and that was the reason he had taken the five sick days. Clearly, self-disclosure was difficult for him. He did admit that his job transfer was a significant loss and tentatively agreed that it might have triggered his depressive symptoms, diarrhea, and social isolation.

During the course of the interview, Juan's longstanding sensitivity to criticism became increasingly evident. Accordingly, as the formulation of obsessive-compulsive personality style emerged, the therapist was notably gentle and supportive both verbally and nonverbally.

Mental Status Assessment

The client appears his stated age and is appropriately dressed and groomed. He is oriented to person, place, and time and is cooperative with the evaluation. His intelligence, language skills, and ability to abstract were above average, consistent with his college education. His mood is moderately depressed, while his affect is slightly constricted but appropriate to the situation. No obvious perceptual nor cognitive deficits were noted. His immediate, short-term, and long-term memory appeared to be intact. He denied suicidal and homicidal ideation, intentionality or plan currently. While he has had occasional thoughts that he might be better off dead, he dismisses them stating, "I'd never do it because it's against my religious beliefs." His insight into his current situation is fair, and his judgment is adequate to good.

Developmental History and Dynamics

A review of family systems indicated that Juan is the older of two siblings. His brother Jaime is four years younger, married with two children, and works as a computer programmer for a pharmaceutical manufacturer. Both parents are alive and relatively healthy. Juan's father worked as a senior accountant until the firm he had been at for 28 years downsized and forced him into early retirement three years ago. Two years ago the parents relocated to a retirement village in Arizona. Juan's mother never worked outside the home. Family values included hard work, social conformity, and obedience.

Juan thinks he was most like his mother, but has had a somewhat distant relationship with her since he was a child. However, Juan does recall being fussed over by his aunt, his mother's older sister, until she died when Juan was seven. Juan believes his brother was his parent's favorite. He recalls having few friends growing up, and the one and only best friend he had moved away when Juan was 8 years old. He also recalls being ridiculed by others for being somewhat obese and clumsy in junior and senior high school. He did not date in high school. In college he dated two women, both for short periods of time. Only one of these involved sexual relations, and only on a single occasion. He admitted that the prospect of sharing himself intimately was absolutely overwhelming.

His earliest childhood memory, at four years old, involved seeing his infant brother for the first time. He recalls his parents returning from the hospital. Juan had been frightened staying with his aunt and not knowing where his mother had gone. His mother lovingly placed his baby brother in Juan's old crib, while Juan's father said that the birth was the happiest day of his life. Juan was told to stop whining and asking questions about the baby and to go outside to play or he would be punished. He remembers running outside crying and hiding in the tree fort until it got dark. He felt frightened and confused. Juan described intense feelings of humiliation and rejection following the birth of his younger brother.

A second childhood memory is reported when he was about six years old. Juan was supposed to have been watching his brother in his play pen while his mother went inside to make lunch. Unbeknownst to Juan, his brother had taken a small plastic toy apart and stuffed a piece of it up his nose where it got lodged. Juan began screaming. The mother responded to the crying and spanked Juan for being a disobedient and uncaring brother. Juan recalls running to his bedroom crying and feeling hurt for being unjustly punished and unloved because of the attention his mother was giving his brother. In short, he experienced his brother's birth and the subsequent spoiling of him by his parents as the nullification of the sense of specialness and nurturance he had previously enjoyed.

Social History and Cultural Dynamics

Juan lives alone in a condominium near his office. He reports having one close male friend at the office, two social acquaintances whom he seldom sees, and indicates that he has not been involved in an intimate relationship since college. Juan has worked at the same company since graduating from a local, private university where he graduated with honors. He reports never having been in the military or having any legal difficulty.

Culturally, Juan is a third-generation Puerto Rican. His grandparents arrived in the United States 47 years ago looking for greater freedom and economic opportunities. While he is bilingual, Juan attends a Puerto Rican pride festival every summer and is a member of a professional group of Puerto Rican accountants, he is not otherwise as active in the Puerto Rican community as are his parents. While there are two other Hispanic professionals in his corporation, he says that he prefers to socialize with Anglo colleagues and friends. He was baptized a Roman Catholic but does not consider himself to be a practicing Catholic, at least not since he began college. He considers himself heterosexual and describes himself and his parents as bicultural and upper middle class in values and orientation.

Health History and Health Behaviors

He denied having previous psychological or substance-related problems or treatment, and was not aware of any family history of psychiatric, substance-related, or early deaths, suggestive of suicide. Except for occasional flare-ups of irritable bowel syndrome (IBS), he denies any current health problems. When asked if his IBS had been acting up lately, he reluctantly admitted that he had been experiencing diarrhea off and on for the past week.

Health behaviors include daily exercise and a reasonable diet. He denies the use of alcohol saying, "It makes my IBS worse." He had smoked one to two packs of cigarettes a day for eleven years before quitting some three years ago. He stopped at the advice of his physician when his IBS was particularly problematic, and denies any but occasional cravings. He does, however, continue to drink three to five cans of Coke a day which leave him somewhat jittery and appear to fragment and reduce the depth of his sleep. He also reports taking a multiple vitamin daily but denies the use of any prescription or over-the-counter medications or any mineral herbal supplements. His last physical exam was about one year ago, and although he recently refilled a prescription for IBS symptoms, he had not seen a physician in at least six months.

Client Resources

This client brings the following resources to therapy. His level of readiness for treatment, as noted during the initial session, appears to be moving from the contemplative to the preparation stage of change. He is intelligent, well-educated, and has worked at the same job for 12 years which suggests he can sustain commitments. He has also been successful with at least one previous change effort, and he has been a nonsmoker for nearly three years following his participation in a cigarette cessation program. However, his shyness and rather limited social support system are deficits that will need to be addressed in therapy.

Inventories

The client's score on the Beck Depression Inventory (BDI), given after the initial session, was 27 indicating a moderate to severe level of clinical depression. The profile on Juan's MCMI-III suggested the diagnosis of major depression and obsessive-compulsive personality disorder. Not surprisingly, he scored moderately high on the Somatoform scale, probably indicative of a pattern of expressing distress through gastrointestinal (GI) symptoms.

(The remainder of this Report can be found near the end of Chapters 5 and 6.)

PERFORMING A FORMAL DIAGNOSTIC ASSESSMENT

As noted earlier in this chapter, we believe that the formal diagnostic assessment is a basic skill-set of the effective therapist. For most clients, this type of assessment can usually be accomplished in a single meeting, usually the initial session, with a client. If the first session is scheduled for 50 to 60 minutes, this diagnostic assessment should reasonably take approximately 30 to 40 minutes.

There are 20 basic screening questions listed in the Diagnostic Assessment Interview Format (Table 4.3). These questions and a set of detailed inquiry questions are offered to guide your assessment effort. They have been designed to facilitate a natural flow and rhythm to the interview process. All 20 screening questions are structured in a linear questioning format. They can and should be supplemented with circular questioning (as described in Chapter 9).

There are six components of the assessment format and our clinical experience with a number of trainees has indicated that approximately 12 to 15 minutes should be sufficient to adequately cover the presenting problem and mental status assessment; with another 10 minutes or so for the developmental history, social-cultural history, and health history; and 7 to 8 minutes for client resources. That leaves 10 or more minutes to talk about any concerns that the client may have about therapy and for scheduling future sessions, or if a referral will be made, about that referral. Client resources questions, particularly, about expectations for treatment and interview wind down questions naturally lead into this kind of discussion. It is important to keep track of time as the assessment proceeds so that there is sufficient time to delve in client resources, since this component is critically related to treatment process and outcomes.

Skill Learning Exercise 4.1

This skill exercise will give you the experience of doing a formal diagnostic assessment. We suggest you pair up with someone in your class or study group and complete this type of assessment with each other. Conduct a 30- to 40-minute diagnostic assessment interview with one person serving as the therapist and the other taking the client's role; then switch roles. We suggest you follow the diagnostic assessment interview format (Table 4.3). Use the 20 basic screening questions to guide your inquiry. You may wish to take some notes while the client answers. As the client for this skill learning exercise, we suggest that rather than playing a role that you be yourself. This will not only allow you to respond more easily and openly to the therapist's questions but will permit both of you to identify the ways in which your personal history and background has influenced your current circumstances.

TABLE 4.3   The Formal–Diagnostic Assessment Interview Format

FOCUS	BASIC SCREENING QUESTIONS	DETAILED INQUIRY
1. Presenting problem and context (foster engagement and establish context for formal–diagnostic assessment)	1. What concerns brought you here? 2. Why now? 3. Have you (or relatives) ever experienced this or other psychological problems? 4. How has this been affecting your daily functioning?	1. Clarify type of symptoms and stressors 2. Elicit coping skills, social support, and related client resources 3. Elicit previous psychiatric/AODA history and treatment outcomes, family history 4. Life functioning re work, family, social, intimacy, health, self-management
2. Mental status Presentation Orientation and attitude Mood and emotional status Perceptual status Cognitive status Safety issues	5. How do you feel about being here today? 6. How has this affected your spirits/mood? 7. Have you had any unusual experiences? 8. How has your memory been serving you? 9. Have you had thoughts that life isn't worth living?	Note age, dress and grooming, mannerisms, quality/rate of speech, psychomotor activity 5. Orientation re: time, place, and person 6. Probe for anxiety symptoms, etc. 7. Probe for dissociative and psychotic process 8. Probe for form, content, and thought 9. Probe suicidal ideation, intention, and plan; violent impulses and homicidal ideation
3. Developmental history and dynamics	10. How would you describe yourself as a person? 11. You've told me how things are going for you lately. Now, I'd like to shift to how things were when you were growing up.	10. Clarify current self-view, level of self-esteem, personality style 11. Brief developmental history: parents, siblings, developmental milestones, experience in school, best friends, first sexual experience, educational level
4. Social history and cultural dynamics	12. What is your current living situation? 13. What is your ethnic background?	12. Jobs or military, any legal problems, current social support system: family, friends, peers at work/school, financial 13. Ethnic identity, race, age, gender and sexual orientation, religion, migration and country of origin, SES, acculturation, i.e., assimilated; traditional, or bicultural; language, dietary influences, and education
5. Health history and health behaviors	14. Tell me about your health? Health habits?	14. Identify prescription, OTC, and substance usage; health status; health habits

(continued)

TABLE 4.3   Continued

FOCUS	BASIC SCREENING QUESTIONS	DETAILED INQUIRY
6. Client resources	15. How have you tried to make things better (i.e., symptoms)? Results? 16. How would you explain why you're having these symptoms (etc.)? 17. How is it best treated? What do you see as your part in this process? Therapist? 18. When will things begin to change/get better?	15. Probe client's own efforts to change, past efforts and successes in making changes 16. Clarify client explanatory model 17. Identify expectations for treatment and that client is motivated to change 18. Specify readiness for change
Interview wind down and closing	19. Anything I haven't asked you about that would be important for me to know? 20. I've asked you a lot of questions. Do you have any to ask of me?	19. An open-ended query that permits client to add potentially useful information 20. Gives client a sense that the therapeutic relationship is reciprocal and collaborative

Skill Learning Exercise 4.2

Based on the information collected from the formal diagnostic assessment with your client, write up a report of the assessment following the headings in the Assessment Report of the Case of Juan R. (Since no psychological inventories, i.e., the Beck Depression Inventory, are a part of *Skill Learning Exercise 1,* this section of your report can be omitted.) Your course instructor may give you additional instructions for preparing this report.

A CONCLUDING NOTE ABOUT THE FORMAL–DIAGNOSTIC ASSESSMENT

The purpose of the formal–diagnostic assessment is simple and straightforward: To understand the context and determinants of a client's behavior and functioning sufficiently so that an effective treatment plan can be generated which when combined with the client's own resources, the power of the therapeutic relationship, and specific clinical interventions it is likely to result in an optimal treatment process and outcome. This result assumes, of course, that the client has been sufficiently engaged in the therapeutic relationship and therapy process and that the course of treatment is tracked and modified based on ongoing assessment feedback.

REFERENCES

Beitman, B. & Yue, D. (1999). *Learning psychotherapy: A time-efficient, research-based, and outcome-measured psychotherapy training program.* New York: Norton.

Budman, S. & Gurman, A. (1988). *Theory and Practice of Brief Therapy.* New York: Guilford.

Dinkmeyer, D. & Sperry, L (2000). *Counseling and psychotherapy: An integrated, individual psychology approach* (3rd ed.). Upper Saddle River, NJ: Prentice-Hall.

Group for the Advancement of Psychiatry (GAP) (2002). *Cultural assessment in clinical psychiatry.* Washington, DC: American Psychiatric Press.

Hersen, M. & Turner, S. (1994). *Diagnostic interviewing* (2nd ed.). New York: Plenum.

Lambert, M. (1992). Implication of psychotherapy outcome research for eclectic psychotherapy. In Norcross, J. (Ed.). *Handbook of eclectic psychotherapy* (pp. 436–462). New York: Brunner/Mazel.

Miller, S., Duncan, B., & Hubble, M. (1997). *Escape from babel: Toward a unifying language for psychotherapy practice.* New York: Norton.

Maxmen, J. & Ward, N. (1995). *Essential psychopathology and its treatment* (2nd ed.). New York: Norton.

National Committee for Quality Assurance (NCGA) (1998). *MBHO surveyor guidelines for the accreditation of managed behavioral healthcare organizations.* Washington, DC: Author.

Othmer, E. & Othmer, S. (1994). *The clinical interview using DSM-IV: Fundamentals.* Washington, DC: American Psychiatric Press.

Sperry, L. (1995). *Psychopharmacology and psychotherapy: Strategies for maximizing treatment outcomes.* New York: Brunner/Mazel.

Sperry, L., Brill, P., Howard, K. & Grissom, G. (1996). *Treatment outcomes in psychotherapy and psychiatric interventions.* New York: Brunner/Mazel.

CHAPTER 5

FROM DIAGNOSTIC ASSESSMENT TO FORMULATION AND INTERVENTION

After completing a formal diagnostic assessment, the effective therapist begins formulating a treatment plan and interventions. Correct? Actually, not. The effective therapist will first develop an appropriate diagnostic formulation and a clinical formulation as a prelude to developing a treatment formulation. Treatment formulation, as we describe it in this book, is actually a systematic treatment plan based on a diagnostic and clinical formulation. Today, third party payors require that therapists, and other health care providers, submit adequate documentation about proposed treatment in order to receive authorization for a course of psychotherapy or other treatment. Accordingly, therapists are required to submit a formal treatment plan, which is often a standard one- or two-page printed form, that specifies demographic information about the client, the client's presenting problem, a five axes DSM-IV diagnostic formulation, and a treatment formulation which typically consists of targeted treatment goals and interventions and the frequency and number of therapy sessions requested. In deciding whether to authorize treatment, the third party payor's utilization reviewer evaluates the treatment plan for consistency among presenting symptoms and degree of impairment and diagnosis and the proposed treatment goals, methods and number of sessions, and the adequacy of the rationale for this plan. Needless to say, inadequately formulated treatment plans are unlikely to result in authorization for treatment. This chapter addresses the nuts and bolts of the various factors and processes involved in formulating effective treatment.

WHAT YOU WILL LEARN IN THIS CHAPTER

1. The meaning of case formulation and the three different types of formulations: diagnostic, clinical, and treatment formulations; and the importance of the case formulation in achieving effective treatment outcomes.
2. Recognition that clients develop their own case formulations and that effective therapy requires that a negotiated case formulation be achieved.

3. A brief introduction to the diagnostic features of DSM-IV.
4. The skills of formulating diagnostic, clinical, and treatment formulations.
5. Application of three types of formulations in an illustrated psychotherapy case.

THREE TYPES OF FORMULATIONS: DIAGNOSTIC, CLINICAL, AND TREATMENT

A case formulation is a way of summarizing diverse information about a client in a brief, coherent manner for the purpose of better understanding and treating the individual. Basically, case formulations consists of three aspects: diagnostic formulations, clinical formulations, and treatment formulations (Sperry, et al., 1992). Table 5.1 provides brief definitions of these types of formulations.

A *diagnostic formulation* is a descriptive statement about the nature and severity of the individual's psychiatric presentation. The diagnostic formulation aids the therapist in reaching three sets of diagnostic conclusions: whether the client's presentation is primarily psychotic, characterological, or neurotic; whether the client's presentation is primarily organic or psychogenic in etiology; and, whether the client's presentation is so acute and severe that it requires immediate intervention. In short, diagnostic formulations are descriptive, phenomenological, and cross-sectional in nature. They answer the "What happened?" question. For all practical purposes the diagnostic formulation lends itself to being specified with DSM-IV criteria and nosology.

A *clinical formulation,* on the other hand, is more explanatory and longitudinal in nature, and attempts to offer a rationale for the development and maintenance of symptoms and dysfunctional life patterns. Just as various theories of human behavior exist, so do various types of clinical formulations exist: psychoanalytic, Adlerian, cognitive, behavioral, biological, family systems, and biopsychosocial. Clinical formulations answer the "Why did it happen?" question.

A *treatment formulation* follows from a diagnostic and clinical formulation and serves as an explicit blueprint governing treatment interventions. Rather than answering

TABLE 5.1   Three Types of Formulations

TYPE	DESCRIPTION
Diagnostic	A descriptive statement that answers the question, "What happened?" It describes the client's presenting problem, symptomatic distress, and functional impairment in DSM-IV terms.
Clinical	An explanatory statement that answers the question, "Why did it happen?" It provides a rationale for the development and maintenance of the client's pattern of symptoms and impaired functioning.
Treatment	A prescriptive statement that answers the question, "What can be done about it?" It is an action plan governing treatment strategies and interventions.

the "What happened?" or "Why did it happen?" question, the treatment formulation addresses the "What can be done about it, and how?" question.

The most clinically useful formulations are those that are client-centered, or as we refer to it throughout this book, client-focused. Client-focused formulations emphasize the unique context and the needs and resources the client brings to treatment. Client-focused formulations are thus *integrative formulations* in that they integrate and incorporate these factors in all three formulation dimensions: diagnostic, clinical, and treatment. In line with the contemporary movement toward integration, this chapter will emphasize integrative case formulations.

THE CASE FORMULATIONS OF CLIENTS AND THERAPISTS

Effective therapists are skilled at developing, eliciting, and negotiating case formulations. What do we mean by eliciting case formulations? Therapists-in-training are surprised to learn that clients have developed case formulations of their own. While clients may not consciously be aware of their formulations, these formulations are nevertheless powerfully operative in the treatment process. Effective therapists not only recognize the presence of these formulations, but elicit them, and then negotiate a common formulation with their clients.

What are these client formulations like? They closely resemble the *structure* of the three formulations we have been describing. Table 5.2 compares the structure of the client and therapist formulations. First, the client's description of their presenting problem or concern, including their symptomatic distress and their rating of their impairment in the various areas of life functioning, is analogous to the therapist's diagnostic formulation. Similarly, the client's explanatory model of their condition or presenting problem is analogous to the therapist's clinical formulation. Finally, the client's expectations for treatment is analogous to the therapist's treatment formulation.

The client and therapist case formulations usually differ in *content*. Whereas the therapist develops a case formulation based on a critical understanding of the scientific basis, for example, biological, psychological and sociocultural, of human behavior, the client's formulation is more likely to be based on a highly personal, idiosyncratic, and uncritical understanding or theory of human behavior. Social psychologists refer to this phenomenon as naive personality theory.

Why is it important to recognize the client's own case formulation? The greater the client's case formulation differs from the therapist's, the less likely that treatment will be effective and the more likely noncompliance or nonadherence will be present. This can show itself in many ways; for example, clients may come late or no-show for sessions; they may fail to do homework or take medication as prescribed; or, they may prematurely terminate from therapy, or, drop out. Imagine that the client's unelicited explanatory model for panic symptoms and difficulty doing grocery shopping and other outside household responsibilities is because of a chemical imbalance in my brain. Imagine also that this client's unelicited treatment expectation is for Xanax, because it really worked for a neighbor, and no-talk therapy. Then, imagine that the therapist, who is considered a specialist in

TABLE 5.2   Comparison of Client's and Therapist's Formulation

CLIENT'S FORMULATION	THERAPIST'S FORMULATION
Description of symptoms and functioning	Diagnostic formulation
Explanatory model	Clinical formulation
Treatment expectations	Treatment formulation

the behavior therapy of anxiety disorders and is adamantly against the use of tranquilizers like Xanax, comes up with a diagnostic formulation of panic with agoraphobia, a clinical formulation of symptoms being caused by avoidance behavior, and specifies a treatment formulation of exposure therapy. In exposure therapy the client will be trained to gradual exposure to feared stimuli in large stores and other open spaces. What is likely to happen? In all likelihood, the client will directly or indirectly reject the plan for exposure therapy directly by refusing to the exposure protocol or by premature termination, or indirectly by half-heartedly being involved in the early exposure attempts. Now, if this therapist elicited the client's case formulation, the therapist could then provide the client with reasons why Xanax, and other medications in that class, is only a short-term treatment and has high addictive potential, and why exposure is preferable. It may be that after further discussion, both agree that a safer and more effective medication such as Prozac, which has FDA approval for use with panic and agoraphobia, will be utilized along with the behavioral approach.

The effective therapist's task then is to elicit the client's case formulation. Eliciting presenting problem and symptoms/impairment, explanatory model, and treatment expectations have already been addressed in previous chapters, particularly in Chapter 4. Next, the effective therapist will develop a case formulation of the client based on their professional knowledge and skills. Finally, the therapist will attempt to reconcile differences between the client's and the therapist's formulation.

The *negotiation process* begins with the therapist acknowledging the client's formulation and the similarities and differences from the therapist's formulation. The ensuing discussion allows the therapist to educate the client about their illness and clarify misconceptions about it and the treatment process. Discussion of the client's expectations for the treatment process and outcomes facilitates negotiating a mutually agreeable direction for treatment and a therapeutic relationship based on cooperation. Then, the specifics of treatment selection can be discussed.

THE DIAGNOSTIC FORMULATION

DSM-IV TR and Diagnostic Formulation

The standard diagnostic classification adopted by managed care and insurance carriers in the United States is the fourth edition, text revision of the *Diagnostic and Statistical*

Manual of Mental Disorders (2000), usually referred to as DSM-IV TR. Parenthetically, it can be noted that a few third-party payors require that the International Classification of Diseases-Tenth Revision (ICD-10), an international classification system which includes many diagnostic codes similar to DSM codes, be used instead. DSM-IV TR claims to be an atheoretical, phenomenonological system; atheoretical meaning that it has no allegiance to the traditional theoretical perspectives: psychodynamic, cognitive behavioral or biological; and, is phenomenonological which means it is simply a descriptive approach to human behavior rather than an explanatory approach like the traditional theoretical perspectives.

While psychotherapists may be more comfortable with a growth or development model of human behavior than with a pathology or medical model, the reality is that third-party payors require that all requests for psychotherapy services specify a five axes DSM-IV TR diagnosis. DSM-IV TR describes 18 distinct major classifications and diagnostic criteria for more than 200 mental disorders. Each disorder has a unique set of descriptive diagnostic criteria. A DSM-IV TR diagnosis can be made when a match exists between the facts from a particular individual's history and clinical presentation and the diagnostic criteria for a particular mental disorder.

DSM-IV TR allows for a multi-axial classification so that interrelated biopsychosocial or systems facets of a person's life may be considered. Five axes are used:

Axis I: Clinical Disorders (e.g., 309.0; Adjustment Disorder with Anxious Mood)
Axis II: Personality Disorder or Mental Retardation (e.g., 301.6: Dependent Personality
  Disorder)
Axis III: General Medical Conditions (e.g., 244.9: Hypothyroidism)
Axis IV: Psychosocial and Environmental Problems (e.g., death of spouse, and change of
  job)
Axis V: Global Assessment of Functioning (e.g., GAF = 55 (current); GAF = 70 (highest
  level past year))

DEVELOPING A DIAGNOSTIC FORMULATION

Here are five guidelines for establishing a diagnostic formulation and formulation statement (Sperry et al., 1992):

  1. *List all the symptoms and functional impairment.* In order to establish a diagnosis, the therapist begins by identifying a cluster of symptoms that are considered clinically significant (Vace & Juhnke, 1997). A symptom cluster or cluster of symptoms refers to two or more symptoms that are manifestations of a psychological disorder, for example, appetite loss, insomnia, depressed mood and anhedonia (loss of pleasure) are depressive symptoms. According to DSM-IV TR, clinically significant means the disorder causes significant symptomatic distress, disability, or impairment of functioning. Furthermore, such symptoms are not normally expected, nor are they a *culturally-sanctioned response* to an event such as the bereavement over the death of a loved one. The therapist then looks for the diagnostic category that best describes the cluster of symptoms presented by the client. Furthermore,

the therapist notes the degree of overall functional impairment: mild, moderate, severe, or, very severe. Obviously, it is important to develop a familiarity with the symptom clusters.

2. *Compare DSM-IV TR criteria with attention to differential diagnosis and to criteria and specifiers for Axes I and II disorders.* The DSM-IV TR encourages therapists to consider the criteria for differential diagnosis rather than to assign multiple diagnoses whenever possible. Also, be attentive to any diagnosis that requires a *specifier* or data to clarify the current or past course of the disorder. Some Axis I disorders specify subtypes of the disorder, for example, anorexia: restricting type or binge-eating/purging type. When a specifier is required, DSM clarifies exactly what to mention and how to record those specifications criteria for each disorder.

3. *Specify diagnoses on Axis I and Axis II, and on Axis III, if applicable.* Consider the Axis I and II diagnoses that best fit the symptom clusters identified and the specific criteria for given disorders.

4. *Fill in the information for the other axes; in particular, specify an Axis IV designation and determine the GAF score for Axis V.* As noted earlier, the GAF is an important overall measure of symptomatic distress and functional impairment. DSM-IV TR proposes three optional scales: defensive functioning scale, global assessment of relational functioning (GARF), and social and occupational functioning assessment scale (SOFAS). All four of these scales are useful in that they are therapist-rated, unlike the various client self-ratings, such as work, intimacy, and social functioning, that are described in detail in Chapter 4. The defensive functioning scale provides good information on coping strategies that are both adaptive and maladaptive and may be very helpful in work settings, while GARF can be particularly useful in monitoring intimate relationship functioning, and SOFAS with work and social functioning.

5. *Write a diagnostic formulation statement incorporating all five DSM Axes.* Some training programs require a written brief giving the rationale for the diagnostic formulation. Usually, it indicates which criteria for a given Axis I diagnosis(es) were met. However, in everyday clinical practice, specifying a five Axes diagnosis is usually sufficient.

6. *Add a cultural formulation statement.* A cultural formulation is a systematic review of cultural factors and dynamics that have been described in the "Social History and Cultural Factors" and which can impact the process of therapy. Some therapists have found it useful to include an additional statement or paragraph to the diagnostic formulation. This paragraph includes a sentence or two on the following: (1) the cultural identity of the individual; (2) cultural explanation of the individual's condition; (3) cultural factors that impact the individual's level of functioning and support system; and, (4) cultural elements that may impact the relationship between the individual and the therapist (GAP, 2002).

THE CLINICAL FORMULATION

A clinical formulation is a way of arranging data in a case in terms of a specific theoretical orientation such as psychodynamic, cognitive-behavioral, Adlerian, biological, or a biopsychosocial or an integrative perspective (Sperry et al., 1992). In so doing, it provides an explanation of why the client developed the particular symptom cluster(s), degree of impairment, and their characteristic personality style or pattern, and why this pattern is maintained. Accordingly, a clinical formulation can be written from a number of perspectives including the psychodynamic, cognitive-behavioral, Adlerian, biological, biopsychosocial, or an integrative perspective.

The biopsychosocial perspective is a holistic and systems perspective for understanding the person and the relationship of the system outside and inside the person that influences both health and illness. Even though this comprehensive model has a long and venerable history, it has only recently gained widespread acceptance following the publication of George Engel's classic article (1977). The biopsychosocial perspective is a conceptualization which includes all the factors that impinge upon the whole person and contribute to changes in health or mental health status. Since it is holistic and comprehensive, this model differs from reductionistic perspectives such as the systems model, the biomedical model, the psychodynamic model, and the behavioral model, to name a few. Rather, the biopsychosocial perspective integrates several concepts from many of these models (Sperry, 1988; 2001). The biopsychosocial perspective proposes that a person can only be adequately understood if the therapist considers all levels of a client's functioning: biological or physical, psychological, and social.

Consistent with the orientation of this book toward integration, we emphasize the development of an integrative clinical formulation in this chapter. Here is a brief description of six common perspectives on clinical formulations.

Psychodynamic Formulation

In this perspective, psychopathology is understood to result from intrapsychic conflicts, developmental impasses, or distorted object relations. Consequently, symptoms are understood as the manifestation of unconscious processes and neurotic character structures. Treatment then consists of resolving these conflicts, strengthening the ego, and modifying the character structure.

Cognitive-Behavioral Formulation

In this perspective psychopathology is learned as a result of aversive events or disordered thinking and faulty cognitive schemas and is maintained by reinforcing events. Consequently, symptoms are understood as the manifestation of maladaptive behavior patterns or disordered thinking and faulty cognitive schemas. Treatment then focuses on specific symptoms and maladaptive behaviors or thoughts based on their antecedents and consequences.

Biological Formulation

In this perspective psychopathology is understood to result from psychobiological disequilibrium and processes. Consequently, symptoms are understood as the manifestation of this underlying psychobiological disequilibrium. Treatment then consists of normalizing this disequilibrium or compensating for the effects of this disequilibrium, usually with medications, in the most efficient, effective manner with the fewest side effects.

Social Formulation

This is a broad perspective involving a wide range of factors including the interpersonal relations, family system dynamics, socioeconomic status, and cultural values and mores. In this perspective psychopathology is understood to result from maladaptive patterns of marginalization, alienation, poverty, prejudices, boundary violations, power and domination, intimacy conflicts, or social skill deficits. Consequently, symptoms can be a manifestation of one or more of these factors. Treatment can involve several types of interventions ranging from social skills training to establishing more functional system boundaries and fostering equality, to education and the elimination of poverty and prejudice.

Adlerian Formulation

In this perspective psychopathology is understood to result from faulty lifestyle pattern (maladaptive schemas or beliefs of self and others) developed in the context of an individual's family constellation as one strives to achieve a sense of belonging and meaning in life. Consequently, the purpose of symptoms is to safeguard the individual's self-esteem in the face of faulty beliefs and failed strivings. Treatment consists of modifying these faulty beliefs and increasing social interest and belonging. The Adlerian perspective is, perhaps, the most integrative of the single-tradition approaches.

Integrative Formulation

This perspective is also known as the biopsychosocial perspective in that it emphasizes the three sets of dimensions: the biological; the psychological—including selected psychodynamic, cognitive-behavioral, and Adlerian aspects; and, the social. In this perspective psychopathology is understood as a complex, holistic response of the individual to stressors as they impact the individual's biological, psychological, and social-cultural vulnerabilities and resources. Consequently, symptoms are understood as the manifestation of the individual's attempt to cope with stressors given their vulnerabilities and resources. Treatment then is directed to the amelioration of symptoms and increasing the individual's levels of life functioning often through a multimodal approach that is tailored to the individual's needs, expectations, and resources.

The reader is referred to Sperry et al. (1992) for more detailed treatment and case illustrations of four types of clinical formulations: psychodynamic, cognitive-behavioral, biological, and biopsychosocial; see Dinkmeyer and Sperry (2000) for a detailed treatment of the Adlerian clinical formulation.

DEVELOPING A CLINICAL FORMULATION

Some specific guidelines for developing a clinical formulation follow.

1. *Specify relevant psychological factors.* Write a brief psychological formulation state-ment. While being mindful of the client's presenting problem, past psychiatric and/or alcohol and drug abuse (AODA) history, development history, and the results of personality assessment inventories (if applicable) (cf. Chapter 4), consider the client's personality, coping style, and internal and external stressors and hypothesize what and how various psychological factors such as intrapsychic conflicts, distorted object relations, maladaptive behaviors, maladaptive beliefs and schemas, and so on, are impacting the client in terms of symptoms and functional impairment. Then, write a brief statement summarizing this psychological formulation.

2. *Specify relevant social factors including cultural and family dynamics.* Write a brief social formulation statement. While being mindful of the client's social history (cf. Chapter 4), consider the client's social context and external stressors and hypothe-size how various social factors, such as family dynamics, marginalization, alien-ation, poverty, prejudices, boundary violations, power and domination, intimacy conflicts, social skill deficits, and so on, are impacting the client in terms of symp-toms and functional impairment. If applicable, write a brief statement summarizing this social formulation.

3. *Specify relevant biological factors, if applicable.* Write a brief biological formula-tion statement. While being mindful of the client's health history and health behav-iors, presenting problem, that is, the acuity and severity of symptoms, mental status assessment and family psychiatric history (cf. Chapter 4), consider the likelihood that biological factors such as heredity, medical conditions, prescription or OTC medication and vitamins, substance use including alcohol, drugs, caffeine, nicotine, and so on, may be causing or exacerbating the client's symptoms. If applicable, write a brief statement summarizing this biological formulation.

4. *Write an integrative formulation statement that incorporates the above brief formu-lation statements.* Make a list of the various biological, psychological, and social factors and dynamics that are impacting the client's symptoms and functional im-pairment. Prioritize these various factors from most to least. Look for interactions among these factors. Then, write a composite formulation statement integrating these factors and dynamics.

THE TREATMENT FORMULATION

The treatment formulation provides a blueprint for treatment intervention and expected treatment outcomes (Sperry et al., 1992; Sperry, 2001). We are assuming that the therapist has already elicited the client's treatment expectations. These include what outcomes the client is hoping for, as well as the client's expectations about roles and responsibilities and the extent of collaboration between therapist and client. Also, we are assuming that a general treatment formulation has been negotiated, that is, a mutual agreement has been reached about overall treatment goal(s) which should reflect overall treatment outcome(s). For instance, when the client can manage the anxiety of leaving home without a panic attack, it is time to terminate therapy because the mutually agreed treatment outcome has been achieved.

After this overall goal/outcome has been agreed upon, it is then possible to formulate a specific treatment plan with targeted treatment goals and specific intervention tactics and methods. It goes without saying that specific goals should be realistic and achievable for the client. It should also be added that these specific goals should be manageable for the therapist. Targeted goals are manageable when specific and measurable steps can be specified. Some examples of manageable goals are: talk to one individual at work before the next scheduled session; reduce the number of angry outbursts from four to one per week; spend twenty minutes every day alone reading or listening to music. Specified in this manner, these manageable goals/steps become the tasks that the therapist and client work on during therapy, and which are assigned between sessions.

DEVELOPING A TREATMENT FORMULATION

Some guidelines for developing the treatment formulation follow.

1. *Specify targeted psychological treatment goals based on the diagnostic and clinical formulations.* Then specify treatment interventions to achieve these goals. Psychological treatment goals are often specified as the opposite of the targeted symptom or skill deficit, that is, when lack of assertiveness is a targeted symptom, the goal might be specified as: increase assertive communication and the targeted intervention might be assertiveness training.

2. *Specify targeted social treatment goals based on the diagnostic and clinical formulations.* Then specify treatment interventions to achieve these goals. Social treatment goals are often specified as the opposite of the targeted symptom or skill deficit, that is, job stress is a targeted symptom, the goal might be specified as: decrease job stress and the targeted intervention might be workplace job accommodation.

3. *Specify targeted biological treatment goals based on the diagnostic and clinical formulations (if applicable).* Then specify treatment interventions to achieve these goals. Biological treatment goals are often specified as the opposite of the targeted symptom or skill deficit, that is, when depressive symptoms are a targeted problem, the goal might be specified as: decrease depressive symptoms and the targeted intervention might be referral for medication evaluation.

4. *Write an integrative treatment formulation statement incorporating these goals/ interventions.* This statement incorporates the psychological and social treatment goals and interventions, and biological goals and interventions, if applicable.

CLINICAL ILLUSTRATION: CONTINUATION OF THE CASE REPORT OF JUAN R.: CASE FORMULATION SECTION

Diagnostic Formulation

The diagnostic formulation includes the following five axes:

DSM-IV TR diagnosis

I. Major Depressive Disorder, Single Episode, Moderate (296.22)
    Occupational Problem (V62.2)
II. Obsessive-Compulsive Personality Disorder (301.82) with avoidant features
III. Moderate obesity
IV. Limited support system; job stressor
V. GAF 45 (at the time of this evaluation)
    GAF 69 (highest in past 12 months)

Cultural Formulation

Juan identifies himself as a third-generation Hispanic who, while bilingual and bicultural, associates more closely with the dominant culture both socially and professionally. While his parents are more closely aligned with the Puerto Rican community, they are part of Juan's support system. There appears to be little, if any, cultural influence to his explanatory model, nor do cultural factors appear to be impacting his level of functioning. Neither are cultural dynamics anticipated to negatively impact the relationship between the individual and his Caucasian therapist.

Clinical Formulation

The following clinical formulation was specified: Juan came to believe that the opinions of others were all that counted. Yet, he was teased and ridiculed by his peers for his personal appearance, especially his obesity. There were also strong parental injunctions against discussing important matters with outsiders. He typically distances and isolates himself from others when he is in unfamiliar or in close interpersonal relations. Presumably, he anticipates and fears the disapproval and criticism of others. He views others as critical and harsh and is convinced that he is viewed by others as inadequate. Therefore, he is slow to warm up and trust others, and tests others' trustability by being late for, canceling, or missing agreed upon engagements. Lack of social skills in relating to new or less known individuals, and a limited social network—he is a homebody who spends much of his time reading novels, watching TV, or listening to music alone—further contributing to an isolated lifestyle and reinforcing his beliefs about self, the world, and others. With the exception of intimacy and social relations he had functioned above average in the life task of work. He agreed that he was experiencing moderately severe depression and was willing to comply with a combined treatment involving medication and time-limited psychotherapy. Anticipating that he would find it quite difficult to accept a referral for medication evaluation to someone he did not already know, and since he knew no psychiatrists, it was suggested that he see his family physician for a medication evaluation. Juan did not appear to be particularly psychologically minded and was assessed to have moderate skill deficits in assertive communication, trust, and friendship skills. Given his obsessive-compulsive personality structure, it was anticipated that he would have difficulty discussing personal matters with health providers, and that he would procrastinate, avoid feelings, and test and provoke health providers. Nevertheless, in terms of success in changing behavior, he continues to be nicotine abstinent some three and half years after completing a smoking cessation program. His support system includes only minimal contact with an older male cousin and a pet dog.

Treatment Formulation   A focused treatment plan was developed. This plan specified a number of treatment targets including ameliorating symptoms, increasing trustfulness, making workplace accommodation, and returning to work.

Focused Treatment Targets

Biological Targets
- Reduce/eliminate depressive symptoms

Psychological Targets
- Reduce shyness
- Increase trustfulness
- Increase assertive communication

Social/Relational Targets
- Decrease shyness and increase friendship skills
- Decrease job stressors
- Return to work
- Enlarge social support system

These goals were designed to facilitate therapeutic outcomes by maximizing therapeutic leverage while minimizing the influence of previous perpetuants and other forms of resistance to change. An initial treatment agreement was established for eight 45-minute individual sessions combining medication and brief psychotherapy. These sessions focused on symptom reduction and returning to work.

The biological target of depressive symptomatology was first addressed. Elicitation of Juan's explanatory model of his illness and treatment expectations suggested he would be a good candidate for medication. A decision was made to refer Juan to his family physician of whom he was quite fond, rather than to a physician, such as a psychiatrist, whom he did not know or have a reasonable level of trust. For someone like Juan, who is overly cautious, the placebo effect can be easily triggered by a referral to a trusted provider.

The therapist contacted the family physician and clarified the nature of collaboration and suggested the need for a medication which would not have the kind of side effects that would easily dissuade Juan from compliance. A medication trial was begun, apparently without untoward effects. Within ten days, Juan's sleep and energy had returned to baseline.

Since job circumstance stressors had triggered Juan's disordered response, the goal of returning Juan to work might not be achieved without some workplace accommodation. A hallmark of the Americans with Disabilities Act (ADA) is that the employers must reasonably accommodate an employee's disability, including the kind of psychiatric disability manifested in Juan. This would require some measure of collaboration between the therapist and Juan's work supervisor. After getting a signed release from the client, the therapist contacted the work supervisor about issues of work stress, peer support, and possible job accommodation. The supervisor agreed that Juan needed a familiar, trusting social support, and was able to assign one of his coworkers to the same office to which Juan had been moved.

With regard to some of the other social and psychological targets, the therapist and Juan mutually agreed that skill-oriented group therapy was probably the treatment of choice to increase trustfulness and decrease his social isolation. Aware that Juan's pattern of avoidance would make entry into and continuation with the group difficult, the plan was for the individual sessions to serve as a transition into the group, after which shorter individual sessions would focus on medication management, probably on a monthly and, later, bimonthly basis.

Individual sessions continued with gradual transition into a time-limited group therapy focused on interpersonal skill development. It was predictable that Juan would test the prescribing therapist and group therapist's trustability and criticalness. Throughout treatment both therapists continued to be mindful of the therapeutic leverage (success with nicotine abstinence, relations with cousin and pet, close knit typing pool) as well as the perpetuants that would likely hamper treatment. As Juan's depressive symptoms ameliorated and a maintenance medication schedule was established, the prescribing therapist began preparing him for transition into the group. Because of his fear and ambivalence of the group process, the therapist suggested, and Juan agreed, that it might be helpful to first meet with the therapist who leads the interpersonal skills group he was slated to join. During the fifth individual session the group therapist was briefly introduced to Juan and a discussion of a three-way treatment agreement ensued. The three agreed that Juan would continue in individual weekly appointments concurrent with weekly group sessions. Assuming things were proceeding well enough, sessions with the prescribing therapist would be reduced to monthly medication checks.

A subsequent two-way discussion between the group therapist and therapist concluded that there was little likelihood that projective identification and splitting would be issues with Juan. Instead, difficulty maintaining active group participation and follow-up on homework between group sessions were predicted. The therapist agreed to encourage and support the patient's group involvement in his concurrent individual sessions with Juan. Finally, the therapist and psychiatrist conferred after the third group session regarding the transition from weekly to monthly sessions with the prescribing therapist.

Case Commentary

It is noteworthy that the diagnostic formulation contains an Axis I designation of Occupational Problem in addition to Major Depression. The reader will note that there is consistency among the three dimensions of the case formulation. Both the biological factor, depression, and the social factor, job or occupational problem, are reflected in both the clinical and treatment formulations. The clinical formulation provided is an integrative formulation that combined elements from the biological perspective, the Adlerian perspective, the social (family systems) perspective, and the cognitive-behavioral perspective. Finally, the treatment formulation articulates treatment goals targeted at basic symptomatic distress and skill deficits which account for the client's impaired functioning.

DEVELOPING DIAGNOSTIC, CLINICAL, AND TREATMENT FORMULATIONS

While the formulation process may appear to be overwhelming for the therapist-in-training, it is a necessary skill that develops with practice and experience. To help you learn, or further refine, this skill we offer the following guidelines in table form. Table 5.3 indicates the steps in developing a diagnostic formulation. Table 5.4 indicates the steps in developing a clinical formulation. Table 5.5 indicates the steps in developing a treatment formulation.

Skill Learning Exercise 5.1

This exercise will give you the experience of sorting through and making sense of a great deal of information about a client for the purpose of deriving a case formulation. We suggest that you work with the information gathered on your client in **Skill Learning Exercises 4.1 and 4.2.** Using the guidelines in Tables 5.3, 5.4, and 5.5 develop three written statements: a diagnostic formulation, a clinical formulation, and a treatment formulation. The diagnostic formulation should include a five axes DSM-IV diagnoses *and* a brief written statement indicating which of the criteria were met, if you specified an Axis I diagnosis. [If there were insufficient criteria for any Axis I diagnosis, specify the code and

TABLE 5.3   The Development of a Diagnostic Formulation

STEPS IN DEVELOPING A DIAGNOSTIC FORMULATION STATEMENT

1. List the client's symptoms and specify level of functional impairment.
2. Compare these symptoms/impairment to specific DSM-IV criteria for Axis I and II diagnoses.
3. Specify an Axis I and Axis II diagnoses and, if applicable, an Axis III diagnosis.
4. Specify an Axis IV designation and determine GAF score for Axis V.
5. Write a diagnostic formulation statement incorporating all five Axes.

TABLE 5.4   The Development of a Clinical Formulation

STEPS IN DEVELOPING A CLINICAL FORMULATION STATEMENT

1. Specify relevant psychological factors. Write a brief psychological formulation statement.
2. Specify relevant social factors including cultural and family dynamics. Write a brief social formulation statement.
3. Specify relevant biological factors, if applicable. Write a brief biological formulation statement.
4. Write an integrative formulation statement that incorporates the above brief formulation statements.

designation: "V 71.09 No Diagnosis or Conditions on Axis I"]. Then, for the clinical formulation you may choose any of the single-theoretical perspectives, psychodynamic or Adlerian, or you might try your hand at an integrative clinical formulation if there are sufficient requisite dynamics. Finally, draft a treatment formulation statement. You may conclude that there is no indication for suggesting your client undertake a formal course of psychotherapy. Nevertheless, your treatment formulation should list some targeted treatment goals. This skill-learning exercise is undertaken with the understanding that the formulation statements you develop are confidential documents. Your instructor will discuss the matter of confidentiality and how to share this information with your client, which is the focus of **Skill Learning Exercise 5.2.**

Skill Learning Exercise 5.2

In this exercise you get experience in eliciting a client's own case formulation, as well as negotiating a collaborative case formulation. We suggest that you get back together with the same client you worked with in **Skill Learning Exercises 4.1 and 4.2.** This exercise requires approximately 60 minutes: 30 minutes for each of the two interviews: one where you are the therapist, and the other where you are the client. You have already elicited the client's presenting problem and description of their symptoms and functioning. Your task is to elicit their *explanatory model* and their *treatment expectations* [cf. Chapter 4]. This

TABLE 5.5   The Development of a Treatment Formulation

STEPS IN DEVELOPING A TREATMENT FORMULATION STATEMENT

1. Specify psychological treatment goals based on the diagnostic and clinical formulations. Then, specify treatment interventions to achieve these goals.
2. Specify social treatment goals based on the diagnostic and clinical formulations. Then, specify treatment interventions to achieve these goals.
3. Specify biological treatment goals based on the diagnostic and clinical formulations (if applicable). Then, specify treatment interventions to achieve these goals.
4. Write an integrative treatment formulation statement incorporating these goals/interventions.

can be done in five to ten minutes. Use the remaining time first to briefly share the highlights of your clinical formulation and discuss the similarities and differences with the client's explanatory model. Then, do the same with your treatment formulation and discuss the similarities and differences with the client's treatment expectations. Finally, negotiate a case formulation that both you and your client find makes sense and is acceptable.

SOME CONCLUDING THOUGHTS ON FORMULATIONS

This chapter described the components of a case formulation. It pointed out that clients and therapists develop case formulations and that effective therapy requires that a negotiated case formulation be achieved. DSM-IV TR was briefly reviewed as a prelude to discussing diagnostic, clinical, and treatment formulations. Guidelines for developing these three kinds of formulations were described and then illustrated in the psychotherapy case that was introduced in the preceding chapter. The main point of this chapter is that case formulation, especially its treatment planning component, is a critical skill required of therapists today. A stark clinical reality today is that adequately formulated treatment plans usually result in authorization for treatment, while inadequately formulated ones are seldom authorized. Finally, adequate case formulations set the therapeutic stage for achieving effective treatment outcomes.

REFERENCES

American Psychiatric Association (2000). *Diagnostic and statistical manual of mental disorders, fourth edition, text revision.* Washington, DC: American Psychiatric Association.

Engel, G. (1977). The need for a new medical model: A challenge for biomedicine. *Science, 196:* 129–136.

Group for Advancement of Psychotherapy (GAP). (2002). *Cultural assessment in clinical practice.* Washington, DC: American Psychiatric Press.

Dinkmeyer, D. & Sperry, L. (2000). *Counseling and psychotherapy: An integrated, individual psychology approach* (3rd ed.). Upper Saddle River, NJ: Prentice-Hall.

Sperry, L. (1988). Biopsychosocial therapy: An integrative approach to tailoring treatment. *Individual Psychology, 44,* 225–235.

Sperry, L. (2001). Biopsychosocial therapy with individuals and couples: Integrative theory and interventions. In L. Sperry (Ed.). *Integrative and biopsychosocial therapy: Maximizing treatment outcomes with individuals and couples* (pp. 67–99). Alexandria, VA: American Counseling Association Books. Press.

Sperry, L., Gudeman, J., Blackwell, B., & Faulkner, L. (1992). *Psychiatric Case Formulations.* Washington, DC: American Psychiatric Press.

Vace, N. A. & Juhnke, G. A. (1997). The use of structured clinical interviews for assessment in counseling. *Journal of Counseling and Development, 75,* 470–480.

CHAPTER 6

FOCUSED AND ONGOING ASSESSMENT

As we indicated in Chapter 4, three types of assessment will characterize assessment in psychotherapy during the start of the third millennium. Assessment will take place throughout the whole course of psychotherapy: before, during and after. The first of the three types of assessment, diagnostic assessment, was described and illustrated in Chapter 4. The other two types, focused-functional assessment and focused-ongoing assessment, are covered in this chapter.

WHAT YOU WILL LEARN IN THIS CHAPTER

1. A brief discussion of focused and ongoing assessment as it relates to treatment outcomes research; and, definitions of basic terms.
2. An overview of the treatment process from beginning to end, including a description of the natural course of a psychological disorder and the recovery process facilitated by psychotherapy.
3. Three types of symptoms and six areas of life functioning/functional impairment.
4. The skills of focused assessment.
5. The skills of ongoing assessment.
6. Application of focused assessment and ongoing assessment in an illustrated psychotherapy case.

MANAGED CARE, TREATMENT OUTCOMES, AND ASSESSMENT

Today, managed care organizations, insurance companies, and other third-party payors, including the federal government, are demanding accountability for reimbursed services. These organizations are increasingly requiring that psychotherapists and other health care providers demonstrate efficiency and cost-effectiveness in the services they provide. This means that therapists must be able to show that their treatment outcomes are positive and are achieved at a reasonable cost. Accordingly, competence in focused assessment and ongoing assessment has become essential for therapists.

As noted in Chapter 4, *focused assessment* refers to assessment of an individual's type and level of symptomatic or clinical distress *and* type and level of functional impairment. Perhaps, a more complete and accurate designation for *focused assessment* would be 'focused clinical and functional assessment,' but for ease of discussion we will utilize the shorter designation, *focused assessment.* Currently, managed behavioral health care organizations (MBHOs) typically use what is called *medical necessity,* also called *treatment necessity,* as the basis for the authorization of behavioral health care, such as psychotherapy. With regard to psychotherapy, medical necessity refers to the determination that psychotherapeutic treatment is "appropriate (and) necessary to meet a person's health needs, and consistent with the diagnosis and clinical standards of care" (NCQA, 1998). MBHOs put a premium on focused functional assessment because, in their view, clinical standards of care and adequate care are defined in terms of restoring clients to the previous level of stability and functioning. Accordingly, behavioral health care is restricted to the *restoration of functionality.* This effectively means that the goals of psychotherapy are limited to: (1) reducing symptoms and (2) decreasing functional impairment. Not surprisingly, more *growth-oriented goals* such as wellness, individuation, personal growth, self-actualization and spiritual integration would be considered inconsistent with the criteria of medical necessity, and are unlikely to be authorized for payment.

Also noted in Chapter 4 was *ongoing assessment,* which refers to the regular and continuous assessment of key dimensions of client functioning across sessions. It is undertaken irrespective of the presenting problem or diagnosis, and its purpose is to monitor both positive and negative developments in the course of treatment. We should add that *ongoing assessment* is synonymous with the designations 'concurrent treatment outcome measurement' and 'treatment outcomes measurement.'

It may be useful to briefly define some common terms related to treatment outcomes and their assessment. In the following section we situate focused and ongoing assessment in the context of the treatment process.

Clinical outcomes: Outcomes that describe the type and degree of *symptoms* or *symptomatic distress.*

Functional outcomes: Outcomes that describe the type and degree of client *functioning* in the dimensions of self-management, intimacy, family, work, health, and social functioning.

Treatment outcomes measurement: The quantification of clinical *and* functional outcomes during a specific time frame, that is, anxiety symptoms and work, intimacy and social functioning. Also referred to as *focused assessment.*

Treatment outcomes monitoring: The periodic monitoring of treatment outcomes over time to assess overall impact of psychotherapy or other behavioral health treatments for the purpose of optimizing treatment decisions about the course of treatment. Can be continuous—every session—or episodic—every third session. Also referred to as concurrent treatment outcome measurement and *ongoing assessment.*

Treatment outcomes management: The use of outcomes monitoring information to increase the overall effectiveness and efficiency of a clinic's or practice's therapeutic services, that is, for therapist or client profiling, or case mix adjustment.

THE TREATMENT PROCESS: FROM BEGINNING TO END

Psychological disorders tend to have a natural and predictable course in terms of duration and severity. For example, a case of untreated moderate depression could be expected to last between four and nine months. However, the use of appropriate clinical interventions such as medication and/or psychotherapy will often limit the course of depression to about two months. Knowing about the natural course of psychological disorder and the expected course of its treatment is not only useful in understanding the treatment process but is also helpful in understanding the role and value of the three types of assessment.

The Natural Course of a Psychological Disorder

For relatively uncomplicated behavioral health cases, the natural course of a psychological disorder follows a predictable trajectory. First, life functioning in one or more areas begins to decline. As this occurs mild symptoms and distress are noted. All the while the individual attempts to cope as best they can. Demoralization and a decreased sense of well-being begins to set in, but they keep trying. However, as their coping resources become strained further declines in functioning occur while acute symptoms become more distressing. Eventually, as they continually experience their failure to cope, they move into the sick role which usually follows a call for help (Frank & Frank, 1993). By seeking professional help their sick role status is confirmed and legitimized. During this time individuals are relieved of personal responsibilities to varying degrees. In western culture, social convention allows individuals to remain in the sick role for a limited period of time after which they are expected to recover and increasingly return to their previous responsibilities.

Figure 6.1 illustrates the usual course of a psychological disorder and its natural recovery process without psychotherapy or other behavioral health treatments.

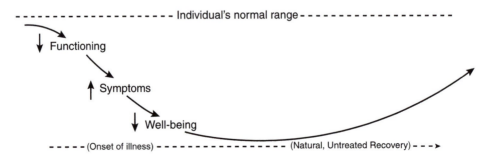

FIGURE 6.1 Trajectory of the course of a psychological disorder.

The Course of Clinical Treatment and the Recovery Process

The application of psychotherapy or other clinical interventions tends to increase the rate of recovery, i.e., recovery is typically shorter in duration than if the condition is left untreated. Recall that the sick role is legitimized when professional treatment is sought. Recovery typically follows the pattern of increased hopefulness, followed by decreased symptomatology, followed by return of functional capacity. Kenneth Howard has operationalized this healing sequence as *remoralization*, *remediation*, and *rehabilitation*. He calls this predictable sequential process of treatment recovery the *Phase Theory model* (Howard et al., 1993).

For many depressive and anxiety disorders this is approximately four to nine or even twelve months. Remaining in the sick role for longer periods of time usually suggests a complicated case which may be interpreted by caretakers and health care providers as representing disability-proneness. Not surprisingly, indices of *well-being*, or remoralization, tend not rise much, if at all, even when treatment is provided. Similarly, *life functioning* remains low while *symptoms* may or may not remain at high levels.

Figure 6.2 represents an uncomplicated course of illness and a course of treatment. In this instance treatment was successful.

While effective clinical interventions often result in positive treatment outcomes, most notably, recovery, other outcomes do occur. In Figure 6.3, three different trajectories following clinical treatment interventions are illustrated. The upward curved trajectory on the right indicates a predictably successful course of treatment which can be referred to as an *A-Tracking*. This means that improvement would be noted in ongoing assessments or trackings. The flat, horizontal curve indicates that there has been little or no appreciable clinical change noted because progress in symptom reduction or return of functional capacity has stalled. This can be referred to as a *B-Tracking*. The downwardly deflected trajectory on the right suggests that the client has actually worsened. This means that indicators of well-being and/or life functioning scores have reportedly declined or symptoms have reportedly increased. This can be referred to as a *C-Tracking* (Sperry, Brill, Howard, & Grissom, 1996).

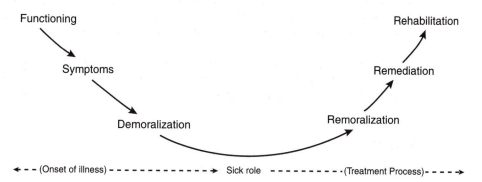

FIGURE 6.2   Trajectory of the course of a psychological disorder as impacted by the treatment and recovery process.

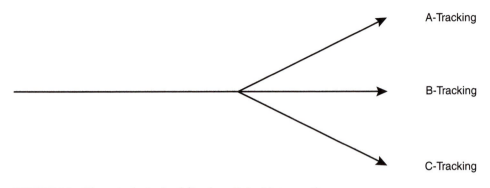

FIGURE 6.3 **Three trajectories following clinical interventions.**

FOCUSED ASSESSMENT

Focused assessment, as we have noted, refers to assessment of an individual's type and level of *symptomatic distress* and type and level of *functional impairment*. This section provides an extended description of symptom manifestations and types as well as areas or spheres of life functioning.

Symptomatic Manifestations

Symptoms are a relatively complex phenomenon. It is common knowledge that the same symptom, such as depression, can be experienced quite differently by two individuals. Symptoms have differing manifestations, can be characterized by type, have several triggers, and have various purposes.

Many clients with chronic, long-standing behavioral health disorders experience troubling dysphoria, anxiety, and other symptomatic expression. At the very least, it is essential to differentiate symptoms by manifestation and type. Manifestation refers to the channels through which symptoms are expressed. Type refers to the intensity, quality, and timing of the symptom. For example, there are three different channels or manifestations of symptomatic expression: biological, cognitive, and behavioral.

- *Biological manifestations:* heart palpitations, hyperventilation, shaking
- *Cognitive manifestations:* flashbacks, self-doubt, rumination, self-criticism
- *Behavioral manifestations:* avoidance, aggressiveness, nonassertiveness

Symptom Types

Similarly, there are three types of symptoms: acute, persistent, and warning (Sperry, 1995).

Acute symptoms refer to the full-blown incapacitating symptoms that signal acute decompensation. They are so intense as to interfere with normal functioning. Acute symptoms are usually experienced as intolerable, meaning they are moderately to severely painful. Efforts to distract oneself from the pain is difficult if not impossible. In terms of severity rating, acute symptoms tend to be reported in the moderately severe to markedly severe range of pain. For instance, an individual may be able to continue to tolerate the pain and function adequately with a mild tension headache, but not be able to tolerate the pain or function at all with a severe migraine or cluster headache.

Persistent symptoms refer to the chronic low grade symptoms that are reasonably tolerable, minimally impair function, and are usually not ameliorated by medication. Persistent symptoms are like the mild tension headache in the above example. However, because this symptom is experienced constantly, or nearly constant, individuals become discouraged. They may erroneously conclude that they always will have these symptoms and never feel better. It should not be surprising that many chronically mentally ill, such as those who are symptomatic for two or more years, are disability-prone. Individuals suffering from persistent symptoms tend to have a past history of exhaustive trials of several medications without lasting relief. Because medication has little or no effect on this type of symptom, other treatment intervention should be explored. Chronic pain is a persistent symptom. Fortunately, there has been notable success in the treatment of chronic pain. Not surprisingly, treatment for chronic pain is extremely useful in greatly reducing the discouragement and increasing both well-being and functioning. In short, persistent symptoms are treatable.

Warning symptoms refer to symptoms which gradually increase in intensity and precede an acute episode. Table 6.1 compares these types.

TABLE 6.1   Description of Symptom Types

SYMPTOM TYPE	SYMPTOM EXPRESSION	TIMING	INTENSITY	INTERVENTION
Acute symptoms	Full blown clinical manifestations are moderate or severely painful.	Abrupt onset; usually follows warning symptoms.	Very intense; functioning is markedly impaired.	Medication, hospitalization, and/or behavioral techniques
Persistent symptoms	Same as acute symptom but presents in subclinical manifestations.	Ongoing, more or less constant	Mild intensity, may minimally impair daily life functioning; often present in disability-prone	Distraction techniques or other behavioral techniques
Warning symptoms	Negative changes in mood, appetite, sleep, thoughts, behavior	Appear a few days or weeks before a relapse of acute symptom	Intensity is low and increases; if not treated leads to acute symptoms	Increase medication dose or initiate medication; crisis techniques

Source: Adapted from Sperry, 1995.

TYPES AND LEVELS OF LIFE FUNCTIONING

It is clinically useful to distinguish symptoms from functioning. Unfortunately, DSM-IV does a disservice to clinicians by mixing symptoms and functioning in its Axis I, II, IV criteria as well as in Axis V, the so-called Global Assessment of Functioning (GAF) Scale. There is considerable clinical advantage and merit to separating and differentiating symptoms from functioning. This differentiation facilitates the establishment of a *primary treatment focus.*

It also is clinically useful to differentiate functional status, or functional level, from functional capacity. *Functional status* refers to an individual's current or actual level of life functioning. It is assessed by client self-report or a rating scale. *Functional capacity* refers to the extent and limits of the individual's *maximal* or potential level of functioning in one or more areas. For instance, it is not surprising, at the outset of treatment, for a client with major depression and an avoidant personality disorder to have both a lower functional status and functional capacity for intimate relationships, as noted on the Intimacy life functioning dimension than a client with major depression, but no personality disorder, who has a high functional capacity for intimacy but whose functional status is currently low, that is, low levels of intimacy just after beginning treatment.

There are six areas or dimensions of life functioning that clinicians have found useful and which the Social Security Administration uses in Social Security Disability (SSD) evaluations. They are self-management, intimacy, family, social, health, and work. Table 6.2 provides a brief description of each of these dimensions (Sperry et al., 1996).

In terms of the *biopsychosocial model,* one of these dimensions reflects *biological functioning:* health; two reflect *psychological functioning:* self-management and intimacy. The remaining three reflect larger *social functioning:* work, family, and social. Health and work are particularly germane to behavioral health today since they are most directly related to disability-proneness, disability and return to work issues. In Western culture, work, particularly career and occupational status, has become a principal component of self-identity and a primary source of self-esteem for many individuals. Perceived health status influences an individual's sense of well-being as well as capacity for responsibility, and as such reflects on one's attitudes toward disability. For instance, two middle-aged male sales representatives are hospitalized for depression for ten days. Both are equally symptomatic and do not function as sales reps during their hospitalization. After discharge, one goes back to work and quickly returns to baseline work or job functioning while the other's work or job functioning remains relatively low for a protracted period of time. After a long enough period of time without returning to work, the second individual is likely to ask for or be asked to apply for permanent disability compensation. An obvious difference between these two individuals is degree of *disability-proneness,* which is a psychological vulnerability often reflecting a view of self as deficient and/or entitled which is reinforced by family, social support system, and others.

ONGOING ASSESSMENT

The measurement of treatment outcomes is essential to an accountability-oriented approach of psychotherapy. Effective treatment outcomes require that clinicians continu-

TABLE 6.2   Dimensions of Life Functioning

DIMENSION	DESCRIPTION
Self-management	Addresses the client's level of functioning with regard to the client's control over, conception of, and satisfaction with himself or herself.
Intimacy	Addresses the client's level of functioning with regard to the intimate relationship with a significant other, being supportive and feeling supported by the significant other, carrying out expected responsibilities, and sexual functioning.
Family	Addresses the client's level of functioning with family members, including handling of family stress and conflict, carrying out expected responsibilities, and the support of and by other family members.
Health	Addresses the client's level of functioning with regard to health habits, personal hygiene and grooming, and overall sense of physical well-being.
Work	Addresses the client's level of functioning at work (or school), including interactions with fellow workers and supervisors (or students and teachers), ability to complete job (school) assignments, and the like.
Social	Addresses the client's level of functioning in social and community settings, including interactions with others, feeling supported by others, and carrying out expected responsibilities.

Source: Based on Sperry, et al., 1996.

ously monitor progress over the course of treatment. Ongoing assessment or monitoring of treatment involves comparing focused-clinical and focused-functional assessment for the most recent therapy session with similar data collected at the outset of treatment. Self-report or rating scales are used to accomplish this type of assessment.

During each session the therapist must be prepared to evaluate and assess the following:

■ Mental status, especially safety issues
■ Health status, use of medication, supplements, and substances
■ Client resources, especially readiness for change
■ Functional status; especially symptoms and functioning
■ Treatment progress, as noted by *ongoing assessment*

The first three of these assessment dimensions were addressed in Chapter 4. This chapter addressed the last two. Skill Learning Exercise 5.1 provides specific instructions on performing functional assessments and ongoing assessments. Now, we return to the case report of Jon R., which began in Chapter 4 to illustrate both functional and ongoing assessment.

CLINICAL ILLUSTRATION: CONTINUATION OF THE CASE REPORT OF JUAN R.: PROGRESS NOTE

Focused Assessment

In terms of focused-clinical assessment, Juan estimated his depressive symptoms to be 3/10 on the mood scale (1 = worst, 10 = best, 5 = average mood) in the past two weeks. This is the lowest he can recall his mood ever being. He estimates his usual mood is 6–7/10.

In terms of focused-functional assessment, Juan rates himself at about 3/10 now, as compared to 6/10 prior to the job change. His ratings on the six areas of life functioning at the present are (on a 1–10 scale where 1 = lowest and 10 = highest): self-management 4; work 2; family 4; intimacy 2; health 3; and social 3. He rates his sense of well-being at 1/10.

Ongoing Assessment

After the second session, the therapist's progress note for Juan R. read:

Observation and Assessment   It has been two weeks since the initial diagnostic assessment session with Juan. He did accept the referral to his family physician, L. Winslow, M.D., for a medical evaluation of his depressed moods. Dr. Winslow sent a report indicating that he concurred with my diagnostic impression of major depression and prescribed Celexa 20 mg for 7 days and then 40 mg thereafter. Juan immediately began taking the medication, today being his tenth day. No side effects were reported. He reports that he has been sleeping through the night for the past eight days and awakens refreshed. His energy level also has increased greatly since he has been on the medication and he has been taking daily walks. He is feeling less depressed and reports his mood to be 5/10 on the mood scale for the past two days. His functional ratings are: self-management 6; work 4; family 4; intimacy 3; health 6; and social 4. He rates his sense of well-being at 8/10. Discussed the status of job accommodation. . . .

Assessment   Some resolution of acute symptoms noted; reasonable response to medication and therapy.

Plan   Continue with medication; I will call Juan's work supervisor re job accommodation. Scheduled appointment in one week.

After the third session, the therapist's *Progress Note* for Juan R. read:

Observation   The client reports considerable improvement since our last session, which was one week ago, which he attributes to medication, daily exercise, and feeling hopeful about his work situation after hearing that accommodation will begin next Monday. No medication side effects were reported. mood scale: 6/10. Functional ratings are: self-management 6; work 8; family 5; intimacy 3; health 8; and social 5. He rates his sense of well-being at 8–9/10. Discussed idea of group therapy. . . .

Assessment   Mood appears to have returned to baseline in response to medication, exercise, therapy, and job accommodation. A significant improvement in work functioning rating since the initial diagnostic assessment is noted.

Plan   Continue with medication and exercise. Will continue discussion of group therapy referral. Scheduled appointment in one week.

Case Commentary

The therapist indicates an awareness of the type and level of symptoms and functional impairment. The symptoms are of the acute type, and the therapist is sensitive to the clinical significance of the client's rating of work functioning. Also noted is that the client is showing improvement in both symptoms and functioning over the three sessions. This would represent an A-tracking and suggests that the treatment formulation is effective. However, if little or no progress was noted by the third session the effective therapist would do well to reconsider the treatment formulation.

PERFORMING FOCUSED AND ONGOING ASSESSMENTS

There are several ways of performing focused assessments and ongoing assessments. This chapter described a rather simple and straightforward approach that is easily learned and adopted by therapists-in-training. This approach involves client self-rating of their overall level of symptoms or symptomatic distress and level of functioning or functional impairment. This assessment approach can be accomplished by writing or verbal self-report. We have found that therapists-in-training quickly learn to perform these kinds of assessments, and we recommend that the therapist verbally elicit these client self-ratings, at least initially. Table 6.3 provides a format for verbally eliciting these self-ratings.

Skill Learning Exercise 6.1

This skill exercise will give you the experience of doing a focused assessment. We suggest you pair up with the person with whom you completed the formal diagnostic assessment exercise in Chapter 4 (Skill Exercise 4.1). Use the focused assessment format for symptoms and functioning (Table 6.3). Take turns in the role of client and thera-pist. As therapist ask the client to rate themselves on the symptomatic distress and the six life functioning areas. Record these findings in the case report you began in Skill Exercise 4.1.

CONCLUDING COMMENTS ON FOCUSED AND ONGOING ASSESSMENT

1. While you may have found the description of the treatment process from the onset of the psychological disorder through the therapeutic and recovery process both in-

TABLE 6.3 Focused Assessment Format

SYMPTOMS AND SYMPTOMATIC DISTRESS

Mood Scale

Rate your *overall* mood this past week on a 1 to 10 scale: where 1 = the worst you can ever imagine feeling, where 10 = the best you can ever imagine feeling, and 5 = an average mood for you:

| 1 | 2 | 3 | 4 | 5 | 6 | 7 | 8 | 9 | 10 |

Anxiety Scale

Rate your overall feeling of nervousness and anxiousness this past week on a 1 to 10 scale: where 1 = feeling you were going to die or have a heart attack or go crazy, and where 10 = being perfectly calm and anxiety-free:

| 1 | 2 | 3 | 4 | 5 | 6 | 7 | 8 | 9 | 10 |

FUNCTIONING AND FUNCTIONAL IMPAIRMENT

Rate your level of functioning in the past week in each of these areas on 1 to 10 scale where 1 = lowest and 10 = highest

1. Family functioning	1	2	3	4	5	6	7	8	9	10
2. Health functioning	1	2	3	4	5	6	7	8	9	10
3. Work functioning	1	2	3	4	5	6	7	8	9	10
4. Social functioning	1	2	3	4	5	6	7	8	9	10
5. Intimate functioning	1	2	3	4	5	6	7	8	9	10
6. Self-management functioning	1	2	3	4	5	6	7	8	9	10

WELL-BEING SCALE

Rate your overall feeling of psychological well-being this past week on a 1 to 10 scale: where 1 = the worst it could possibly be, and 10 = the best it could be:

| 1 | 2 | 3 | 4 | 5 | 6 | 7 | 8 | 9 | 10 |

teresting and informative, we hope that this description also increased your understanding of the relationship between symptom-formation, functional impairment, and well-being, also referred to as demoralization-remoralization.

2. In the discussion of the therapeutic-recovery process, we also described three types of tracking, A, B, and C, and trust that you will make the connection that the course of treatment, for example, the therapeutic and recovery process, is a function of several factors including previous psychiatric history and response to prior treatment(s), type of symptoms and level of functional impairment, as well as client resources, the degree to which the client is able to engage in the treatment process, for example, the *engagement* phase of psychotherapy. In the past, therapists might describe a client who was not making progress in treatment as resistant, which essentially attributed the lack of movement in therapy to an unconscious process which was a label that was

not particularly helpful to either client or therapist. Currently, the emerging view of the dynamics of change in the therapy process is more differentiated and enlightened, and hopefully allows the effective therapist more therapeutic options. For example, clients who are predicted to follow a downward course, a C-tracking, do much better with intensive case management than they do with weekly traditional therapy sessions. Similarly, clients with B-trackings invariably do better with novel multimodal focused treatments than continuing with the same sort of single modality treatment.

3. *Focused assessment* and *ongoing assessment* are becoming requisites of documenting treatment efficacy and cost-effectiveness. Effective therapists will most likely use some form of these two types of assessment in their therapeutic work. While this chapter has described and illustrated a rather simple self-rating approach to accomplish these kinds of assessment, there are some standardized outcome measures that are commercially available such as the *Compass PC* (Sperry, Brill, Howard & Grissom, 1996) and the *Outcomes Questionnaire 45* (OQ-45) (Lambert & Finch, 1999). Both of these assessment systems elicit clinical/functional and ongoing assessment from *both* the client and the therapist. Beitman and Yue (1999) offer a less formal approach for assessing psychotherapy outcomes. One advantage of the Beitman and Yue approach is that it has been used extensively in psychotherapy training programs.

REFERENCES

Beitman, B. & Yue, D. (1999). *Learning psychotherapy: A time-efficient, research-based, and outcome-measured psychotherapy training program.* New York: Norton.

Frank, J. & Frank, J. (1993). *Persuasion and healing: A comparative study of psychotherapy (3rd ed.).* Baltimore: Johns Hopkins Press.

Howard, K., Lueger, R., Maling, M., & Matinovich, Z. (1993). A phase model of psychotherapy: Causal mediation of outcome. *Journal of Consulting and Clinical Psychology, 61,* 678–685.

Lambert, M. & Finch, A. (1999). The outcomes questionnaire. In M. Maruish (Ed.). *The use of psychological testing for treatment planning and outcomes assessment* (2nd ed., pp. 831–870). Mahweh, NJ: Lawrence Erlbaum.

National Committee for Quality Assurance (NCQA) (1998). *MBHO surveyor guidelines for the accreditation of managed behavioral healthcare organizations.* Washington, DC: Author.

Sperry, L., Brill, P., Howard, K. & Grissom, G. (1996). *Treatment outcomes in psychotherapy and psychiatric interventions.* New York: Brunner/Mazel.

Sperry, L. (1995). *Psychopharmacology and psychotherapy: Strategies for maximizing treatment outcomes.* New York: Brunner/Mazel.

PART **IV** INTERVENTIONS

■ ■ ■ ■ ■ ▬▬▬▬▬▬▬▬▬▬▬▬▬▬▬▬▬▬▬▬▬

CHAPTER 7

COGNITIVE AND BEHAVIORAL INTERVENTIONS

WHAT YOU WILL LEARN IN THIS CHAPTER

1. The role of cognitive and behavioral interventions in counseling.
2. What cognitive restructuring is and how and when to use it.
3. Some of the important behavioral interventions including:

   a. desensitization, exposure, and relaxation skills
   b. social skills training
   c. modeling and behavioral rehearsal

COGNITIVE AND BEHAVIORAL INTERVENTIONS: OVERVIEW

Many counseling theorists separate interventions along the lines of changes in thinking, feeling, and doing. This chapter looks at how to change both thinking (thoughts) and doing (behavior). Most cognitive restructuring methods trace their roots to Aaron Beck (Beck, Rush, & Emery, 1979). The general goal of these therapies is to identify thought patterns that are based in irrational or faulty logic and to change them by challenging them directly. Dysfunctional thinking styles are viewed as the source of unhappiness rather than the event itself. Before the client can learn more adaptive thoughts and coping strategies to rehearse and practice, the ineffective patterns must be identified. These thought patterns, often called schemas, are thought to be quite general and play a role in how a person responds in many different situations. By changing the general pattern, work on specific problems becomes much easier.

Most behavioral methods are rooted in conditioning and learning theory and the works of Pavlov, Skinner and Hull. The basic principle is that unhealthy behavior (neurosis) is a product of learning and can be eliminated through unlearning or new learning. There are literally hundreds of techniques currently available to change behavior.

COGNITIVE RESTRUCTURING

A cognition is the same thing as a thought. The main goal of cognitive restructuring is to help clients recognize their faulty thinking and change it. When people feel anxious or depressed they are thinking about life in a negative and self-critical way. Cognitive therapists believe that these negative thinking patterns are at the source of depression and anxiety. For example, when you think of losses that you have experienced, you are often sad or depressed; when you believe you are in danger because you think something bad is going to happen, you feel worry or anxiety. In contrast, when people are taught to think about their problems in a more positive and realistic way, they experience increased self-esteem.

Cognitive restructuring is often considered the first step when using cognitive behavioral strategies. These strategies are used to help clients:

1. Become aware of automatic thinking patterns and how they influence others as well as themselves.
2. Change the way that they process information and behavior.
3. Learn to change their beliefs about self, others, and the world.

Through this process clients learn to identify useless or ineffective thinking patterns. David Burns (1999) in his important book *Feeling Good* developed a checklist of the major forms of twisted or distorted thoughts.

1. All-or-nothing thinking: You look at things in absolute, black-and-white categories.
2. Overgeneralization: You view a negative event as a never-ending pattern of defeat.
3. Mental filter: You dwell on the negatives and ignore the positives.
4. Discounting the positives: You insist that your accomplishments or positive qualities "don't count."
5. Jumping to conclusions: (A) Mind reading—you assume that people are reacting negatively to you when there is no definite evidence for this; (B) Fortune-telling—you arbitrarily predict that things will turn out badly.
6. Magnification or minimization: You blow things way out of proportion or you shrink their importance inappropriately.
7. Emotional reasoning: You reason from how you feel: "I feel like an idiot, so I really must be one." Or "I don't feel like doing this, so I'll put it off."
8. *Should* statements: You criticize yourself or other people with *shoulds* or *shouldn'ts. Musts, oughts,* and *have tos* are similar offenders.
9. Labeling: You identify with your shortcomings. Instead of saying "I made a mistake," you tell yourself, "I'm a jerk," or "a fool," or "a loser."

10. Personalization and blame: You blame yourself for something you were not entirely responsible for, or you blame other people and overlook ways that your own attitudes and behavior might contribute to a problem.

Once these thoughts are identified, the client needs to clarify how and when they are being used. The responses often occur automatically as in a habit.

AUTOMATIC THINKING PATTERNS

When people feel bad it is because they are thinking about things in a negative way. It is the thoughts and not the actual events that create upset feelings. These thoughts often occur involuntarily or automatically. This process occurs with both healthy and unhealthy people. Most of the time we are barely aware of these (automatic) thoughts, however, with a little training it is possible to become conscious of these thoughts and actually change them.

It is helpful to teach clients the *A-B-C* of emotion. (Ellis, 1962) This allows the client to understand the role thoughts play. *A* stands for the actual event; *B* stands for your beliefs about the event; and *C* stands for the consequences of the beliefs including the feelings and behavior. For example,

A = Lost job
B = I can't do anything right
C = Depression

If your thought *B*—"My boss is really a jerk" then *C* might have been feeling angry. If you thought *B*—"Now I can go to school and do what I really want" the *C* might be feelings of joy.

The first challenge for the therapist is to help the client become aware of their automatic thinking patterns. Don Meichenbaum (1994) has identified five ways to accomplish this.

1. Ask Directly

This procedure involves directly asking the client about thoughts or beliefs that trouble them. It is perhaps the most common procedure used in talk-oriented therapies. Questions can pertain to events that have occurred prior to the interview, during the session, or anticipated in a future encounter. You ask directly for a description of thoughts in problem situations.

"What thoughts did you have as you were talking to her?"
"What is happening to you at this moment? Get in touch with your thoughts and feelings as we discuss this event."
"As you anticipate talking to her tomorrow, what thoughts and feelings pop into your head?"

Many clients will have trouble with these questions since you are asking them about things that they might not have looked at prior to your question. Automatic thoughts are often not conscious thoughts but rather patterns of behavior and thinking that are passed on from generation to generation. They often go unquestioned or unchallenged and are not brought into awareness. The challenge is to bring these patterns into awareness and make them conscious so that the client can rewrite or rescript their responses, and, therefore, their life.

Some clients find it easier to study their feelings, while others prefer to examine their thoughts, and some, their actions. At this stage it is important to create a safe holding environment where the client can create awareness. The therapist must be careful to not question or challenge these patterns until later in the session. Questions that focus on feelings might be helpful in creating conscious awareness. Ask directly,

"You look (state feeling i.e., angry, glad, sad, mad . . .) right now. What is going on?"
"What makes you feel this way?"
"When you feel this way, what do you think? What images or pictures are going on?"
"When you say that, how do you feel?"

Again, it is important to present these questions in an unthreatening and safe fashion.

2. Imagery Reconstruction

This process involves asking clients to relive or remember an event. The process usually involves using relaxation procedures prior to asking the client to carefully review what occurred during an event. The events may be positive or negative. This process is often used in Adlerian psychology to help the client see the pattern of their behavior. That is, since all behavior is goal-directed, any two sequenced behaviors show a movement toward a goal. This process helps the client to gain awareness and understanding of the seemingly meaningless or insignificant events. Once clients learn this process they can replicate it as needed to create more awareness and insight into their thoughts and behavior patterns. They learn that behaviors do not simply occur but actually have a pattern. Ask directly,

"What exactly did she say to you?"
"How did you respond?"
"Can you use the exact words and say it in the same way?"
"How did you feel as you responded?"
"What did she do and say next?"
"What was your reaction. . . ."

3. Advice Giving

This process is used to help someone who cannot provide their own direct imagery. The therapist asks the client to give advice to someone who has a similar problem situation. In order to do this they have to guess about another person's thoughts and feelings. The therapist has the client talk about the kinds of thoughts and feelings someone might need to have to keep this problem or situation. After exploring how not to handle the situation, the therapist explores how they came up with their answer and what thoughts, feelings, and behaviors the person might need to change to create a different outcome.

4. Self-monitoring

Clients can be taught to record their thoughts, feelings, and behaviors to problem situations. This process not only provides useful information but also helps the client to take some control over their situations and life by creating a record. Some clients are more than willing to do record keeping while others need to be motivated. Clients can easily be shown that record keeping is similar to the process of analysis that occurs in therapy. By doing the process on their own they can learn to be more self-sufficient. Just list the (1) situation; (2) thoughts; (3) emotions; and, (4) behavior/action.

5. Processing Thoughts and Behavior

Clients need to begin by becoming aware of how they process information. This involves looking at the ways in which they selectively look at information—past, present, and future. It is accomplished by asking the client to generalize thoughts and feelings to other situations. "What are some other situations in which you have had the same thoughts?"

The first challenge this process poses for therapists is that they must educate the client in how one's beliefs affect the way that they process information and construct the world in which they live. This can be accomplished through word pictures such as the metaphor of prejudice suggested by Padesky (1990). This process helps the client see the belief and understand the nature of the cognitive restructuring process. Padesky asks the client if they know anyone who is prejudiced (e.g., racial or gender prejudice). The therapist then explores with the client the characteristics of someone who is prejudiced. They discuss how a person who is prejudiced tends to selectively attend to data, overgeneralize, ignore, distort, discount, use stereotypes, and does not accept data that is incompatible with their prior beliefs. The client and therapist discuss ways that a prejudiced person's beliefs might be changed. The therapist then indicates that our core beliefs tend to operate or act as if we are prejudiced, distorted, or discounted. Together the therapist and client explore the impact, cost, and personal price of being prejudiced about oneself.

A similar metaphor is that of mental contamination. This procedure helps the client recognize how their thinking processes often are influenced by factors beyond their awareness. The therapist draws the comparison to physical contamination such as radiation, radon, or pollution. Just as our bodies might become contaminated by poisonous gases, our minds become contaminated by bias, stereotypes, and prejudices. Our parents, the news media, and church, for example, are all means by which we are contaminated. The client is then taught how to be sensitive to contamination and to create a filter to screen them out. When using either of these metaphors the therapist always translates the learning into very concrete behavioral strategies.

The second challenge for the therapist is to help the client actually stop the automatic beliefs and change the content of the self-message. Many clients are all too aware of their self-defeating thoughts but are unsure about how to create self-enhancing ones. There are several strategies that are used to modify core beliefs and automatic thoughts. Some beliefs are easy to change while others are more resistant and take hard work over an extended period of time. Some experts recommend using a scaling technique in order to determine the strength of a belief (Beck, 1995). Therapists can ask clients to rate the strength of their old belief and then their new belief. For example, *new belief:* Money is only one way to measure success (75 percent). *Old belief:* Because I didn't get the biggest raise, I'm not successful (55 percent).

There are no hard and fast rules about what the percentages mean. A belief can seldom be reduced completely but scores below 30 percent are usually sufficient. At this point in the process the emphasis changes to creating self-enhancing thoughts that challenge or are incompatible with the self-defeating ones. These may involve situational coping statements or positive self-statements.

FOUR STEPS TO HAPPINESS

A process that pulls together the identification process is four steps to happiness (Burns, 1999). This process can be applied to all kinds of problems. The steps are:

1. *Identify the upsetting situation.* Help the client describe the event or problem that is upsetting them. Find out who or what they are feeling unhappy about.
2. *Help them to identify their negative feelings.* Help them with words like sad, angry, frustrated, anxious, guilty, and hopeless. Then help them rate the negative emotion on a scale from 1 (least) to 100 (most).
3. *Use the triple column technique.* Become aware of the negative thoughts that are associated with the feelings. Have the client identify what they are saying to themselves about the problem. Write these thoughts in the automatic thoughts column and record how much they believe each one between 0 (not at all) and 100 (completely). Identify the distortions in these thoughts and substitute rational responses in the far right hand column and record how much they believe between 0 (not at all) and 100 (completely). Make sure the rational responses are convincing. That is, they are valid statements that question the automatic thoughts.
4. *Have the client identify how much they believe in each of the automatic thoughts between 0 and 100.* It is very likely that their beliefs in these thoughts will be greatly reduced.

The daily mood log can be used to help identify the problem and its impact.

THE DAILY MOOD LOG

Step One: Describe the upsetting event_____

Step Two: Record your negative feelings—and rate each one from 0 (the least) to 100 (the most). Use words like sad, anxious, angry, guilty, lonely, hopeless, frustrated, etc.

EMOTION	RATING	EMOTION	RATING	EMOTION	RATING
1.		3.		5.	
2.		4.		6.	

Step Three: The Triple Column Technique

AUTOMATIC THOUGHTS	DISTORTIONS	RATIONAL RESPONSES
Write your negative thoughts and estimate your belief in each one. (0–100)	Identify the distortions in each Automatic Thought.	Substitute more realistic thoughts and estimate your belief in each one. (0–100)

Although this process seems simple, it will require that the client practice identifying and stopping self-defeating thoughts and replacing them with coping thoughts. The client is urged to practice using the four-step sheet. Once cognitive restructuring is learned, it can help the client to construct a more positive mental picture of troubling situations. By changing the picture, the situation as well as the corresponding issues change.

DESENSITIZATION, EXPOSURE, AND RELAXATION SKILLS

This section focuses on how to help clients learn to deal with stress and anxiety. Desensitization and exposure skills are important to all therapists.

Systematic desensitization is a procedure that is used to help individuals deal with anxiety-provoking situations. This is the same process that is used to help people deal with allergies. In behavioral terms the individual becomes allergic to a specific situation and becomes anxious and tries to avoid the situation. The desensitization process inoculates the individual by having them recall the anxiety-provoking situation while in a relaxed state. This process builds a tolerance or immunity to the anxiety provoking situation. Desensitization or exposure skills fall under the technique of surrendering to your symptoms. In this process, the individual essentially exposes themselves to their fears and anxieties that allows them to become flooded with uncomfortable symptoms. After a time, the symptoms reach their crest and fade away. As these symptoms disappear, the client often experiences exhilaration instead of the shame and humiliation that they felt when they let the fear get the better of them. This approach believes that an individual learns an anxiety response to a specific situation. For example, when a person has been in a bad car accident and is often nervous or anxious to be in a car, they are helped back into a car by sitting in it while it is not running, then going for short distances, having a friend along, and having their favorite music playing, and so forth. If someone is afraid of riding in a boat, you put them in a boat and have them ride in the boat until their anxiety subsides.

The first step in the process is learning to relax. *Relaxation* is based on the observation that by relaxing one's muscles it is possible to reduce anxiety. It is often useful as a general intervention to teach clients relaxation procedures. The most common procedure is that of deep muscle relaxation. In this process, the therapist begins by showing the client how to get comfortable and to close their eyes. The therapist then systematically goes through each muscle group and teaches the client how to tense and relax the muscles in order to allow feelings of tension to leave the body. The therapist uses a calming voice to create a safe context.

Once clients recognize the difference between tensed and relaxed muscles they can learn to create a relaxed state very quickly. The client can then learn to use their breathing and imagination to unwind. For example, by breathing in a slow deep fashion the client can close their eyes and imagine that they are at a special imaginary or real place where they are relaxed, such as a beach, meadow, or mountain top, for example.

The process of desensitization begins by helping the client develop a hierarchy—a list of a series of increasingly stressful situations. For example, for a client with fear of flying, a situation low on the list might be learning they have to take a trip. A situation in the middle of the list might involve driving to the airport. High on the list might be waiting at the gate for the flight to board. Once the list is developed, the counselor has the client relax using whatever procedure works for them. They then ask the client to visualize the scene that is lowest on their hierarchy. Once the client has visualized the situation completely they are asked to continue to focus on being relaxed. This process continues by pairing relaxation with situations at increasing levels of the hierarchy. The pace of the desensitization process is determined by the client's ability to relax completely while imagining the anxiety-provoking situation. The final step of the process is helping the client to relax in the actual anxiety-provoking situation.

Clients often protest this approach claiming that their phobias are really dangerous. Dogs and snakes will bite and cars and boats can really hurt you. It is important to realize that the fears that get in the way of productive living are irrational. The fear of rattlesnakes about to strike is no phobia; however, people with snake, dog, car, or boat phobias are afraid of all boats, all cars, all dogs, and all snakes even the ones that are not dangerous. For example, people with a fear of insects might have a daddy-long-legs walk across their arm, for those afraid of dogs, you might have a friendly dog come and play with them.

Sometimes clients cannot face their fears as dramatically and they need to expose themselves to anxiety-provoking situations more gradually. This allows them to stop and back off whenever their anxiety becomes too intense. The most important thing to do is to continuously challenge their fears until they disappear.

A new therapy known as *eye movement desensitization and reprocessing* (EMDR) is becoming very popular. This approach claims to have the advantage of removing phobias in three sessions or less. Francine Shapiro (1995) designed this approach to help clients deal with traumatic memories. The approach integrates a variety of therapeutic interventions to reduce the suffering caused by traumatic experience. This approach requires special training. More information can be obtained from the EMDR Institute, P.O. Box 51010, Pacific Grove, CA 93950. An excellent video entitled *EMDR Working with Grief* that shows Dr. Shapiro demonstrating this approach is available from Zeig Tucker & Thiesen Publishers, 3614 N. 24th Street, Phoenix, AZ 85016.

In summary, desensitization and exposure skills are some of the oldest behavioral strategies developed to alleviate anxiety. Formal desensitization is time-consuming to implement. Most therapists use a less formal method to help clients alleviate anxiety and treat phobias. Just like the old saying, you need to get back on the horse after it throws you, desensitization helps clients to get back into the saddle of their life.

SOCIAL SKILLS TRAINING

Traditional mental health services follow a defect model. This type of model explains personal problems by finding a defect or a conflict inside an individual to account for his or her dysfunctional behavior. Modern approaches seem to be shifting focus to help clients develop their strengths and solutions. They emphasize the power of personal responsibility and the ability to learn the skills needed to live a different lifestyle. Frequently, clients need direct help in developing or learning the skills required to solve their most pressing problems. Skills such as assertiveness, problem solving, and communication are not present and need to be learned.

Training is based on several assumptions. The first is that interpersonal behavior is based on a set of skills that are primarily learned behaviors. Therefore, how one behaves is directly connected to their repertoire of social skills. A second assumption is that social skills are situation-specific. It is important to know that cultural and situational factors determine social norms or what is expected of an individual in a specific situation. The final assumption is that the effective use of social skills requires reinforcement. In other words, they need to work effectively within the social context.

Several structured programs are available (Lewis, Carlson & Collins, 2002) that can be used in group and individual therapy settings as well as in bibliotherapy. The process involves direct instruction teaching the skills needed to survive in social situations.

Assertiveness Training

Training in assertiveness should help clients to clarify their intentions. If an individual does not know what they want, it is less likely they will get it. Goal clarity is an important component of assertion training and an essential prerequisite of assertive behavior. To clarify or understand intentions, clients can take daily notes on the thoughts, feelings, and behaviors that they find hard to express. Once their intentions are clear, the client needs to learn how to ask for feedback, how to give feedback, and to express acceptance of other people's points of view (Lewis, Carlson & Alberti, 2002).

Alberti and Emmons (2000) offers clear guidelines for assertiveness training. Clients are taught to stand up for their own rights without infringing on the rights of others. The first step is to assess the client's actual behavior. The therapist and client then need to identify the hoped for response or goal. The therapist then creates a simulation where they can model the new behavior for the client. This is followed by having the client practice the new behavior with the therapist before taking their new learning into real life.

Problem-Solving Training

This training involves three necessary skills: (1) receiving skills, which include attending to and accurately perceiving cues and contextual elements of interpersonal situations; (2)

processing skills, which include generating response alternatives, weighing the consequences of each alternative, and selecting optimal options; and, (3) sending skills, or using the chosen option for an effective social response that integrates both verbal and nonverbal behaviors.

The therapist usually helps the client to identify the problem area and to develop a preferred way to respond. The new response is often practiced in the therapy session and potential problems or roadblocks are identified and discussed. The client is urged to practice and report what happens at the next meeting.

Communication Skill Training

Effective communication can be broken down into three basic parts (Myers & Smith, 1995): (1) giving an understanding statement, (2) taking partial responsibility, and (3) offering to help. An understanding statement introduces feelings into discussion, particularly empathy. A partial responsibility statement indicates that the client is willing to accept a role in creating or solving a specific problem. A final way to enhance communication is through an offer to help. Taken together these components deliver a message of wanting a change, but with a willingness on the part of the requester to be actively supportive in the process. The outcome is a decrease in defensiveness and more open lines of communication.

The therapist listens carefully to the client's communication in the therapy session to assess if they are able to effectively send and receive messages.

MODELING AND BEHAVIORAL REHEARSAL

Behavioral rehearsal is also known as role-playing and is used to help clients learn new ways to respond. Rather than just talking about a problem or challenge in the abstract, the therapist teaches new behaviors by acting out situations and developing alternative responses. The therapist models the behavior that the client needs to learn. Clients can observe successful behavior and then imitate the behavior. It is important to note that imitation and modeling work much more effectively for learning behavior or specific actions than feelings or thoughts.

In *behavioral rehearsal* a client is allowed to try out a set of behaviors that they would like to carry out in their real life. The therapy setting provides a safe atmosphere for the practice of new behaviors. Through practice or simulation, the client can develop the courage to achieve the behaviors in the called for situation. For example, a common problem that clients bring to therapy is the desire to make new friends. In the therapy session they can practice making eye contact, initiating a conversation or greeting, making small talk, and inviting the person to do something. The therapist provides encouragement, support, and feedback that allows the client to learn social skills that will make the real life debut successful. Some therapists use video programs to help learn social skills (Lewis, Carlson, & Collins, 2002). Programs describe the necessary social skill, demonstrate with a real person, and then allow the viewer to turn off the video and practice before returning to a discussion with others who have just practiced this same new skill.

The goal-specific and active, solution-oriented nature of these approaches helps reduce the fears and powerlessness felt by people who experience depression and anxiety. These techniques are helpful for treating a wide variety of behavioral problems. Cognitive problems such as test anxiety or phobias and interpersonal difficulties respond especially well to behavioral rehearsal and modeling. The emphasis on learning, rather than psychopathology, allows for a wide variety of applications (families, schools, medical, community, or other areas of work).

SUMMARY

This chapter has provided an overview of cognitive and behavioral interventions. These procedures are utilized by most therapists at some time in the treatment process. Cognitive restructuring has become the treatment of choice for many psychological problems. The strategies of desensitization, social skill training, modeling, and behavioral rehearsal are helpful in creating behavioral change. Therapists need to be able to use these skills as the client's problem(s) dictates.

REFERENCES

Alberti, R. & Emmons, M. (2000). *Your perfect right.* San Luis Obispo, CA: Impact Publishers.

Beck, A. T., Rush, A. J. & Emery, G. (1979). *Cognitive therapy for depression.* New York: Guilford Press.

Beck, J. (1995). *Cognitive therapy: Basics and beyond.* New York: Guilford Press.

Burns, D. D. (1999). *Feeling good: The new mood therapy.* New York: Avon.

Ellis, A. (1962). *Reason and emotion in psychotherapy.* New York: Lyle Stuart.

Lewis, J., Carlson, J. & Alberti, R. (2002). *Seven skills for addiction-free living: Assertiveness.* Boston: Allyn & Bacon.

Lewis, J., Carlson, J. & Collins, L. (2002). *Seven skills for addiction-free living: Social skills.* Boston: Allyn & Bacon.

Meichenbaum, D. (1994). *A clinical handbook/practical therapist manual for assessing and treating adults with post-traumatic stress disorder* (PTSD). Waterloo, Ontario: Institute Press.

Myers, R. J. & Smith, J. E. (1995). *Clinical guide to alcohol treatment.* New York: Guilford Press.

Padesky, C. (1990). Schema as self-prejudice. *International Cognitive Therapy Newsletter, 6,* 16–17.

Shapiro, F. (1995). *Eye movement desensitization and reprocessing: Basic principles, protocols and procedures.* New York: Guilford Press.

CHAPTER 8

PSYCHODYNAMIC INTERVENTIONS

WHAT YOU WILL LEARN IN THIS CHAPTER

1. The role of psychodynamic interventions in counseling
2. The definition of insight and the role insight plays in counseling
3. Interpretation in counseling and how counselors gain interpretation skills
4. Intervention skills that contribute to clarification and insight including:

    a. summarizing
    b. clarifying meaning
    c. establishing connections
    d. challenging discrepancies, incongruencies, and destructive behavior
    e. exploring transference and countertransference

PSYCHODYNAMIC INTERVENTIONS: OVERVIEW

All therapy involves examining some part of one's life. As we look at our lives, we begin to make sense of what we are doing and how what we do helps or hinders our life purpose: Psychodynamic interventions are based on the concept that we have fears, intentions, and defenses that we are not consciously aware of, but which influence our thoughts, feelings, attitudes, and behaviors. Counselors use psychodynamic intervention skills to address clients' underlying anxieties and fears, positive and negative motives, and adaptive and maladaptive defense mechanisms. We examine interventions that help clients gain insight so that they are better able to understand their emotions and responses and thus learn to make conscious choices about their lives. The interventions we explore in this chapter come from a number of perspectives but are all variations of interventions that counselors use to help clients learn more about themselves.

Suggested practice activities let you try out some of these skills for yourself and examples from actual counseling sessions and video clips of these sessions give you an opportunity to observe some of these skills in action. We also consider the issues of transference and countertransference in therapy and how counselors can successfully and therapeutically manage transference in a session.

You will learn how and when to use these skills with your clients and view video-taped examples of these skills demonstrated by expert therapists in actual counseling sessions. As you learn to identify these skills, observe them in action, and purposefully practice them, you will begin to develop the ability to use them intentionally and strategically in therapeutic settings.

PSYCHODYNAMIC INTERVIEWING SKILLS—
UTILITY AND VALUE

Clients often come to counseling with statements such as "If I only knew why I get so mad, maybe I could control my temper better." Or, "Why does my son act like this anyway? We've tried to be good parents, to give him what he needs, but he's just impossible. If we could only figure out what's wrong with him or what's wrong with us."

How easy it might be if we had wonderful insight and the ability to say to our clients, after a brief assessment, a statement that went something like this: "You have this problem because you behave, think, believe, or feel thus and so and so you need to do, think, believe, or feel this way and everything will get better." Then the client would follow our directive and all would be better. Unfortunately, even though at times we feel that is what clients expect, it just does not work that way. Insight cannot be given, it must be found. We can share our ideas with our clients about their problems but they need an experiential *knowing* to be able to actually change. Therefore, much of the dialog that promotes insight focuses on *how* something occurs rather than *why* it occurs.

Indeed, simply telling clients that they need to do more of this or less of that often elicits responses such as "I already tried that, and it didn't work." The process of change, particularly change in patterns of behavior, beliefs, and personal rules does not come easy. Psychodynamic interventions help clients look at life-long patterns and the messages, rules, and traditions that govern their lives. By seeing a pattern of behavior, clients have the option to change by developing new ways of responding to and dealing with life problems. However, it is important to remember that insight does not necessarily mean change nor does change always depend on insight.

Some psychodynamic interventions are seen by clients as challenging or confrontational as they may suggest a new way of viewing a situation or challenge long-held beliefs. These interventions help clients see the patterns of their behaviors and explore how these patterns contribute to their problems as well as helping them identify and explore the beliefs and rules that underlie their behaviors. Through this exploration, clients can gain insight that, in turn, provides clues for developing new and more effective responses, behavior patterns, beliefs, and rules. However, this challenge may put pressure on clients, so that they experience a heightened anxiety and become defensive. Therefore, it is probably more helpful to "gently point out defensive behaviors, but at the same time, provide a holding environment to help the patient manage whatever anxiety or unpleasant feelings emerge" (McCullough, 1997, p. 13). She suggests that both confrontations and interpretations be presented in a tentative manner to allow the client to confirm or deny the interpretation.

SUMMARIZING

Clients may get so lost in their own story they lose sight of the meaning or intent and how various factors link together. Thus, it might be helpful to summarize the key points for the client, paying attention to how one piece links to another. In summarizing, the counselor pulls together key pieces of the client's story in a way that helps the client stay on track. Effective summarizing is based on careful listening on the part of the counselor as well as careful attention to the focus of the treatment plan. Brief summarizations are also helpful when making a transition and may be useful in helping both the client and the counselor see an issue or event more clearly. Novice counselors may get caught in long retelling of what the client has reported. This is counterproductive and may encourage the client to again retell portions of the story to make sure the counselor understands. Experienced counselors listen for the key points of the story that relate to the therapeutic purpose and craft their summarization around these points.

Summarizations also allow for counselors to plant seeds and ideas. For example, if the summarization is about how someone or something made the client's angry, the counselor might summarize using slightly different words such as "You got angry" or "You found yourself getting angry." Such responses subtly change the meaning of the client's statement to suggest anger as a choice rather than an inevitable response.

In the following interchange (Carlson & Kjos, 2000b), O'Hanlon uses summarizing statements early in the session not only to let the family know he hears them, but also to suggest a slightly different way of viewing the daughter's behavior.[1]

> **M 4:**   We live together, and that was our main project. Giving her more self esteem and . . .
>
> **F 1:**   For her to communicate to us.
>
> **M 5:**   To us.
>
> **F 2:**   Not us to her but from her to us. When we ask her a question or something, she just shuts up and walks away and mumbles.
>
> **TH 4:**   Okay, so you two are pretty good about in your view coming to her and telling her what's going on or asking her what's going on. Sometimes she . . .
>
> **F 3:**   Most, all the time. I should say 99 percent of the time.
>
> **TH 5:**   99 percent of the time?
>
> **F 4:**   And that's going high.

[1]M is mother, F is father, D is daughter, TH is O'Hanlon.

TH 6: All right she would, when you ask her something, walk away, and you hear her mumbling something so you know she's got something going on but you're not sure what it is or it seems like she's mad or something?

F 5: Yeah, she gets very upset when we try talking to her or asking her a question. To us, we're her parents. You should be able to talk to your parents about anything, you know, and she won't talk to us about nothing. Because she feels that it's her personal life.

TH 7: Right. So sometimes she has this sense, you know, lookit, you guys lay off, it's my life. Don't bug me about this stuff. I have my own private stuff.

F 6: That's the attitude I get.

TH 8: All right. And you two say we're not trying to bug you. We want to find out what's going on with you, have a little more communication going back and forth?

F 7: Yes, but it's been this way for many, many, many, many years.

M 6: She's afraid to tell us things. I think that's the whole thing. She thinks that we are going to get angry with her or say no to her, but she has done this since she's been a little girl, afraid to tell me things, or she'll tell us at the very last minute if she's going some place it will be, I'm going out, and I'm leaving right now. Well, you didn't plan on her going out, or you didn't . . .

TH 9: You were expecting something different. It happened occasionally when she was younger, but it's gotten more in the years since she's grown up, and you've told them that, that you don't want to hear disapproval or you're afraid they'll get upset or whatever so you just learned to keep quiet, spring it on them at the last minute, and then you're out of there. And that you two would prefer a little more notice so you could plan ahead and all that kind of stuff.

M 7: Right.

TH 10: And a little more back and forth communication.

M 8: Right.

F 8: Just about anything.

ACTIVITY I: **PRACTICE SUMMARIZING**

With a classmate or in a small group, take turns being the client with the others being the counselors.

1. The client begins by briefly telling about some memorable event they recently experienced.
2. After the client tells about the event, each member of the group summarizes what he or she heard.
3. The client then gives individual group members feedback on the summarization. Was it accurate? Was there a somewhat different perspective? If so, how did the client experience that?

ENCOURAGING CLIENTS TO ELABORATE

Earlier you learned about reflecting feelings, thoughts, and behaviors and that one's feelings, thoughts, and actions are linked. Our emotions both influence and are influenced by our thoughts and behaviors. Our thoughts both influence and are influenced by our feelings and behaviors. Our behaviors both influence and are influenced by our feelings and thoughts. And, underlying these thoughts, feelings, and behaviors are motivations, fears, and defenses. One of the ways that clients begin to identify their patterns is to identify what they do or think or feel in specific problem situations. We can use open-ended verbalizations and gentle commands to encourage clients to elaborate on their emotions, thoughts, or behaviors.

Shea (1988) defines open-ended verbalizations as those that call for more than a brief answer. These are questions that begin with words such as "How" or "What." Thus when a client reports on an argument with a neighbor, the counselor might ask a question such as, "What kind of thoughts were going on in your mind when this was going on?" or "How do you feel now as you think back on that argument?" Open-ended verbalizations are more productive when they focus on the client's perspective. Thus the focus is on what the client is doing, thinking, and experiencing or feeling. Counselors-in-training often get caught up in the story and may shift the focus away from the client. Remember the goal is to help the client elaborate or clarify his or her perceptions, thoughts, and feelings.

Gentle commands are simply statements that give some direction but do not limit the client (Table 8.1). Thus, statements such as "Tell me how a typical day goes at your house. Just start at the very beginning and work all the way through to the end for me" (Carlson & Kjos, 2000a) directs the family to tell Bitter about how they work or do not work as a family. Gentle commands can be direct or implied. As with "how" or "what" questions, they serve to give direction to the client and help the client discover links between behavior, feelings, and thoughts.

In the following excerpt Jon Carlson (Carlson & Kjos, 2000b) uses several open-ended verbalizations to help Gina gain some insight into her thinking and behavior concerning her ex-husband.

TABLE 8.1   Gentle Commands

LEAD	EXAMPLE
Share with me . . .	Share with me what you are feeling as you tell me about this.
Help me understand . . .	Help me understand what you are telling yourself about this relationship.
I'm not sure I understand . . .	I'm not sure I understand just how you would know when you had settled this for yourself.
I'm wondering about . . .	I'm wondering about what you think you could have done differently in this situation.

CL 111:   I probably would have, if I could do it again. I would step back from responsibilities of the home and devote more time, maybe, to him, because he was a needy person. He needed things, attention, and I thought I was giving it to him, but he says I wasn't, and now looking back at how . . .

TH 112:   What do you think he wanted that he wasn't getting? What do you think was missing?

CL 112:   Happiness.

TH 113:   How would you give him happiness?

CL 113:   Well, I couldn't. But allow him to find it himself.

TH 114:   How would you do that?

CL 114:   By letting him mess up. Allow him his mistakes [mhm] and to go forward from there.

TH 115:   Mhm. You didn't do that?

CL 115:   Mm-mm. I tried to fix things.

TH 116:   So you weren't like your mom?

CL 116:   No, I was my dad.

TH 117:   Your dad.

CL 117:   My dad took care of everything.

TH 118:   Right.

CL 118:   Still does in a way, so I jumped up and started doing it.

TH 119:   Mhm. How can you let go of that? That sounds like it's a pretty tall order. It sounds like it really requires that you have to put yourself in somebody else's shoes for a while.

CL 119:   I'm tired of doing it all the time. Why, and then looking back I think why do I have to do this all the time. Wait a minute, this is not my problem. So I think self-preservation is making me step back [mhm] and not do so much. It's hard. [sure] I have to fix things. It's something I'm working on.

Gina notes a pattern in her behavior. She has to be like her dad and take care of or fix everything, even if it is not something she can take care of or fix. And, Gina notes that self-preservation is motivating her to step back. What emotions, thoughts, and behaviors are linked in Ginas' case? Do they make sense? Do you think Gina's insight into her need to take on others' problems and her realization that she needs to take care of herself will effect a change in her life?

Open-ended verbalizations and gentle commands encourage clients to evaluate their actions, and link emotions to thoughts and behaviors. This, in turn, leads them to articulate behavior patterns and thus be able to decide whether to change these patterns or not. Thus, Gina might say about herself, "When I see that someone I care about is having a problem, I feel responsible and think I have to take care of the problem for them." Gina has decided that she would like to change that pattern and is working on doing that.

CLARIFYING

Several years ago, Richard Bandler and John Grinder (1975) proposed a meta-model for therapy based on transformational linguistics. They identified areas where therapists would want to challenge a client in order to help the client reach a deeper understanding. Counselors who pay attention not just to what the client says, but to what the client does not say will notice deletions, distortions, and generalizations.

Deletions

A deletion is when important information is left out. For example, the client presents for counseling saying, "I need counseling because I'm always so angry." The counselor might wonder, "Does this person just go around being angry at anything and everything or is this person angry about or at something or someone specific?" The counselor's response might be "Angry at what or who?" Indeed, the focus of more than one session may be sorting out just who the client is angry at or what the client is angry about.

In the following excerpt Insoo Kim Berg helps Robin identify just what calm looks like. She helps her add information that has been deleted.

CL 7:   I'd be much more calm.

TH 8:   Calm about [CL Right] your reaction to whatever.

CL 8:   Right, right.

TH 9:   Okay. That makes sense. Okay, okay. So suppose you are, so suppose you are calm. [CL Mhm] You say, oh well. You know one of those things in life [CL Mhm] and be able to go on. [CL Mhm] I guess that's what you're talking about.

CL 9:   Right, right.

TH 10: Instead of being frantic, you just say, okay, well, you know, [CL Right] take it with a grain of salt and just go on with your life.

CL 10: Right.

TH 11: What, what would that be like for you?

CL 11: It would be control. I'd have a lot of self-control.

TH 12: Self-control (Carlson & Kjos, 2000i).

For someone else, calm might mean something entirely different such as serene or docile. But for Robin, calm means self control, and once Robin is able to express this, both she and Berg have a focus that they might not have had if each held a different view of calm.

Distortions

Distortions, in this model, are the representation of processes as fixed or closed events. It is marking *closed* on something that is still going on as if one has no control over it. "I really regret my relationship with my mother" might be a distortion of "My mother and I don't get along very well." Distortions are often indicators of the client being stuck in a situation and, while not happy with it, believing that getting out of the situation will be worse if possible. How might you help a client reword the following distortion? "I really hate myself for not quitting smoking."

In the following exchange (Carlson & Kjos, 2000h), Robert Wubbolding challenges Juan concerning his writing and picks up on his distortion concerning finishing a play.

TH 111:   Have you written anything on that one play that's inside you?

CL 111:   Yeah, I did, I did, and, um, that came out pretty well too. My roommate took a monologue from that, took it to this Irene Ryan competition downstate, and people said, "Where did that monologue come from," and he said "Oh, it's my roommate" and, uh, uh, so, but I never finished that thing, so . . .

TH 112:   You never did finish it.

CL 112:   I never finished it, but it took him . . .

TH 113:   Up 'til today.

CL 113:   Yeah, up 'til today. But it's very personal I think, I think I'm just waiting for the actual story to finish before I go back to it. So, oh, I don't know. But it's good to be talking like this. I mean, I just, you know, who wants to hear it, I mean. So . . .

When we pay attention to and challenge the client's distortions, we challenge the beliefs that keep change from happening. We open the way for future possibilities. Rather than a play that he never finished, Juan has a play that he is still finishing.

Generalizations

Generalizations are words or phrases we use to shift from a specific to a universal perspective. The adolescent girl says "Nobody understands me." You wonder, "Who, in particular fails to understand her? Is she afraid that I won't understand her either?" We challenge the client's generalizations to help make sense of what is going on. Often generalizations serve to make the problem look insurmountable. Consider words such as nobody, everybody, always, or never. How can we help our client be more specific? One approach to generalizations is to accent or highlight the generalization by repeating it back to the client, possibly as a question. "Nobody?"

Can you identify the generalization in the following exchange between Lazarus and Juan? (Carlson & Kjos, 2000f) Notice how Lazarus responds.

CL 45:   I'm getting hungry I think. You know, I always thought it would be insurance. I thought it would be insurance.

TH 46:   Insurance?

CL 46:   People say, oh you got your Master's. Big deal, you know. But if you say that, that is a cultural currency, and you think, I'll take it.

TH 47:   People say, we get into this people say.

In paying attention to, and challenging, our clients' deletions, distortions, and generalizations, we can help them begin to get a fuller view of what they are feeling and thinking and how this impinges on the way they experience their lives. As we focus our clients' attention to their language, they become more aware of how language influences their thoughts, feelings, and behavior.

MAKING CONNECTIONS

Earlier we talked about paying attention to *how* something occurs in order to find out *why* it occurs. What is going on just before an argument? What leads up to an anxiety attack? How does the couple manage to get into an argument? As we listen to clients tell about how events occur and what kinds of thoughts, feelings, and actions go with these events, we can help clients make connections that will lead to insights.

Much of our everyday behavior is governed by rules we have learned or made for ourselves through experience. However, not all of these rules are useful and we often make our own problems because of negative expectations, failure to act, or other behaviors based on these rules.

Pete, who was in the process of a divorce, complained time and again about his mother and her need to continually criticize him. In many ways, he blamed her for his marital difficulties in that she did not approve of his wife and was critical and nonaccepting toward her. As part of the divorce, Pete and his wife sold their house and Pete needed to find a new place to live. At his next counseling session, his counselor observed that Pete seemed somewhat agitated. He reported that the house was sold and he was moving in with his mother. Knowing the problems Pete had with his mother, the counselor's first reaction was to ask Pete why he was doing that. Instead, she simply encouraged Pete to talk about what he was doing. In the process, Pete reported that his sister had moved in with their mother after her divorce. "Ah, a family tradition," the counselor responded. Pete stopped for a minute, and then said, "You know, I really don't have to move in with my mother, do I?"

When we are able to make the connections between behaviors, thoughts, or emotions and outcomes, we can choose whether to change. Counselors can help clients discover connections between what they are doing, thinking, feeling, and self-talk so that they can begin to see patterns and triggers and be aware of how they change unproductive patterns. Gentle commands and questions help enrich the client's perceptions and develop the components of a pattern (Table 8.2).

ACTIVITY II: MAKING CONNECTIONS

Complete the following statements using thoughts, feelings, behaviors, and/or self-talk.

When I'm nervous, I _____.

When I'm running late, I _____.

When I'm anxious, I _____.

After I've had an argument with someone, I _____.

When I'm worrying about something, I tend to _____.

TABLE 8.2   **Examples of Statements for Making Connections**

LINKS	STATEMENT TEMPLATE
Emotions ← Thoughts	*Example:* When I begin to feel anxious I think about how many things can go wrong.
Emotions ← Self-talk	*Example:* When I tell myself "I can handle this." I start to calm down.
Emotions ← Behaviors	*Example:* When I act like I'm confident, I begin to feel less anxious.
Behaviors ← Thoughts	*Example:* When I start arguing with someone, I think "I just failed again."
Behaviors ← Self-talk	*Example:* When I procrastinate and have trouble getting started on a project, I ask myself what it is I'm afraid of that keeps me from tackling the project.
Thoughts ← Self-talk	*Example:* When I start thinking that I'm never going to amount to anything, I remind myself of some of my real accomplishments.

Can you think of other "When I _____, then I _____" statements about your-self? Choose one and, in consultation with a classmate, friend, or small group, brainstorm some things you might do instead of your normal response.

By encouraging a client to talk through a decision or fully describe an event, the counselor can help the client begin to understand the event and other events in their lives. However, it is important to maintain a client focus. Often, clients want to tell about what someone else is doing without connecting that behavior to themselves. The counselor listens to the reporting and then reflects from the client's perspective. In the following interaction Guerin begins with an observation about the family and checks it out. He encourages the family to talk about a pattern in their lives and how it works for them—no fighting if you do not talk.

TH 239:   Everybody holds up unto themselves. Do you do that too? Everybody goes off into their box, right? Pam does. She says, "Leave me alone." Mother says does and you do too. How come?

M 86:   It's easier that way.

TH 240:   It's easier. What makes it easier, Judy?

M 87:   Well, there is no fighting, no arguing, or . . .

TH 241:   So, if you start talking about what's upsetting you then the fight would ensue?

M 88:   Well, it might if it was something said that . . .

TH 242:   You mean if it was critical or . . .

M 89:   Yeah, if it was something, yeah . . .

TH 243:   But suppose it was just sadness or upset . . .

M 90:   Oh, I think we can talk about that. I think we talk about that if it was something sad or something . . .

TH 244:   So, if the tears are coming from frustration and anger and it's frustration and anger with somebody else and you try to talk about it, then it's not safe. But if it's 'cause there has been a loss, or your feelings have been hurt, or you are frustrated because things are not going well at work, then you can talk about that.

M 91:   Probably, yeah.

TH 245:   Now, what Adrian tells me is that you have upset feelings. I'm not sure they are hurt, that you and Pam somehow can't have the kind of connection you would like to have with your daughter. Is that accurate?

THERAPEUTIC CONFRONTATION SKILLS

Confrontation is bringing to the attention of the client the discrepancies between what they are saying and what they are doing both in and out of the session. Such interventions put pressure on clients to think about what is going on with them and may give them more information about themselves. The ability to note discrepancies and use them effectively in therapy is an important skill for counselors who want to be truly effective. The manner in which we present confrontations affects the way they are heard and accepted or rejected by the client. As with other types of interventions, counselors gauge when and how they will confront and how subtle or how direct they will be.

Confronting Body Language

You are no doubt aware of the classic discrepancies in body language and what an individual says—individuals who say one thing while their facial expressions and movements indicate another, such as the "I'm so glad to see you," accompanied by a slight frown and a turning away. However, there are many, more complex, nonverbal communications that therapists get from clients and the challenge is to know when to notice them, whether they indicate a discrepancy and, if they do, decide whether or not to confront them.

One of the difficulties with identifying discrepant body language is that gestures, expressions, and other nonverbal communications may be culturally derived. In some countries, for example, a negative is accompanied by an upward bob of the head which, in other countries, might be interpreted as an affirmative. Looking one straight in the eye may be a sign of respect in one culture and a sign of disrespect in another. Maintaining eye contact can be seen either as an important part of good communication or as intrusive and rude. With each client, therefore, counselors need to be observant and willing to check out their impressions before making definitive assumptions about whether or not there is a discrepancy between a client's nonverbal and verbal message.

A second issue in confronting nonverbal communication is determining how much weight should be given to a particular gesture, movement, or facial expression. Therefore, early in the relationship, it is important not to make assumptions or assign a meaning to a nonverbal response. For one person, a frown may mean disagreement, for another, concentration.

Finally, as a counselor-in-training, it is important to be observed and to observe yourself to see what you might be communicating by your nonverbal response. Does your empathic look tend to look more like a frown of disapproval? Do you appear to be attentive or *off in space?* As you view yourself on video, pay particular attention to what you are communicating through your nonverbal responses.

Confronting Immediate Behavior

Counselors pay attention to the behaviors of their clients in session and the context of these behaviors. They may then choose to confront a behavior in the session when such behavior might lead to client insight. The client frequently might change the subject when a particular issue is under discussion, shift to talking in the second person, laugh inappropriately, or simply stop talking and maintain a long silence. Often, these behaviors alert the counselor to the fact that the issue at hand is uncomfortable or even off limits. Not all immediate behavior should be confronted, nor should a particular behavior always be confronted each time it occurs.

In confronting immediate behaviors in session, the counselor may give the client important information that leads to insight. In supervision, Jim talked about a female client he was working with who apologized consistently. "She apologizes if she's early and she apologizes if she's late. If she's on time she worries that she's late—or early." Jim was encouraged to point this out to the client, possibly in the same wry manner he had presented it to his supervisor. This led to further discussion of her need to continually apologize and what that was all about in her life. As a result of the discussion, they made an agreement that when she began to apologize to Jim, he would say, "There you go again." As time went on, when the client began an apology, she would stop herself with, "There I go again." She also began to look at the times when she felt she needed to apologize and what it signified in her life. This led to her talking about the guilt she felt related to the abuse she experienced as a child and adolescent.

In-session behaviors can provide cues to issues that need to be explored as well as to the client's progress. Margaret was working with a man who consistently used profanity. Uncomfortable with the profanity, Margaret chose not to confront it until she felt she had a better relationship with the client. After a time, she brought up the profanity and suggested that a lot of anger seemed to be linked with it. This led to several sessions in which the client was able to talk about the death of his father, the loss of a partner, and his ongoing battle with his mother. As they continued to work, Margaret noted that her client was using less and less profanity and, at the same time, reporting that he was having fewer conflicts, both at home and on the job.

In the following clip Bugental (Carlson & Kjos, 2000d) challenges Gina's immediate behavior by pointing out both nonverbal and verbal behavior.

> **CL 78:** So, that in one way I do believe that you should be critical of yourself. But it shouldn't be distractive. [TH Mhm] It shouldn't get you into depression and

you shouldn't lose your self-esteem over it. You shouldn't stop functioning because of it.

TH 79:   Now, I'm going to play mean [CL Okay] and point out you suddenly switched to the second person. You're saying "you" shouldn't.

CL 79:   Okay, meaning that . . .

TH 80:   What about Gina, first person.

CL 80:   First person. I . . .

TH 81:   Ahh, the faces come back. [CL laughter] Did you see it?

CL 81:   Yeah. I thought, uh oh, making faces again. Um, I could say with me, yeah, that I shouldn't be so critical of myself.

Confronting Destructive Behaviors

Counselors also need to confront a client's destructive behavior—whether it be self-destructive or behavior that is potentially destructive to another. The most obvious areas of destructive behaviors concern harm to self or others. In the following excerpt, McCullough (Carlson & Kjos, 1999) confronts a young woman who is in a physically abusive relationship.

LM 70:   You said he was hitting you so much in the head that you didn't know if you were going to wake up.

CL 70:   Yeah. It happens a lot. I mean . . .

LM 71:   That happens a lot. Where you don't know if . . .

CL 71:   He's a black belt in karate. I mean, there is no way I can protect myself from him. Not at all.

LM 72:   Ah, that's, this is hard for me to hear. That's, you know, and I'm in the business of listening to painful stories. Ah, what is it like for you hearing that from me?

CL 72:   It's scary.

CL 73:   Yeah. Uhuh.

LM 74:   What's scary about it?

CL 74:   I don't know. Maybe, I know I should like leave him, I know everybody is saying leave him, but nobody's in my shoes to say just get up and go, you know. It's impossible just to get up and go. I mean nobody thinks I don't like my son to see what happens, what goes on. I just have to deal with it until I can make my own money.

LM 75:   You said . . . Let me go back. You said it was scary, my reaction.

CL 75:   Yes.

LM 76:   It is so painful for me to hear it's scary. It tells you something.

CL 76:   That I have a problem. Yeah.

LM 77:   Yeah, that really bad things are going on, and that you're in a lot of danger.

Note that McCullough does not tell the client to get out. The client knows she should get out, but somehow keeps talking herself out of it. Here, McCullough reflects her own response to hearing this story and reminds the client that she is in a lot of danger. Later in the session, McCullough uses a more direct confrontation.

LM 98:   Well, words are one thing. When people get mad they say things to try to hurt, but, but he's using physical violence, and there's no excuse for that. And you keep saying that there's some excuse for what he's done to you. Some part of you knows that's not true.

The following sequence of interventions are helpful in confronting behavior related to moral responsibility or a moral dilemma (Doherty, 1995, pp. 42–45).

1. Validate the language of moral concern when clients use it spontaneously.
2. Introduce language to make more explicit the oral horizon of the client's concern.
3. Ask questions about clients' perceptions of the consequences of their actions on others, and explore the personal, familial, and cultural sources of these moral sensibilities.
4. Articulate the moral dilemma without giving your own position.
5. Bring research findings and clinical insight to bear on the consequences of certain actions, particularly for vulnerable individuals.
6. Describe how you generally see the issue and how you tend to weigh the moral options, emphasizing that every situation is unique and that the client will, of course, make their own decision.
7. Say directly how concerned you are about the moral consequences of the client's actions.
8. Clearly state when you cannot support a client's decision or behavior, explaining your decision on moral grounds and, if necessary, withdrawing from the case.

INTERPRETATION SKILLS IN COUNSELING

In earlier chapters, we discussed the importance of observing the client, and paying attention to your own internal responses to the client as well as listening to what the client says and how it is said. All of this information is important in formulating interpretive responses that are based on both the content of what the client says and our own intuition. The intuition one has as a beginning therapist is based on life experiences. Your cultural background, whether you grew up in an urban or rural setting, the breadth of knowledge you have accumulated about people and how they live, and your unique life experiences all contribute to your intuitive sense. Counselor preparation also is designed to enhance your ability to be intuitive in that you study such areas as human development, personality theory, mental disorders, family systems, and group process.

However, as you learn counseling skills, you also can learn to expand your ability to hear and understand what is being said as well as what is not being said. You might build mind pictures of what an event looks like. You may consider both what the client is doing and what the client is not doing. You can listen for any rules, guidelines, or traditions that the client uses to guide behavior. You can pay attention to what it might feel like to be in a client's situation. As the client talks, you may note feelings in yourself such as confusion, anxiety, frustration, sadness, boredom, or impatience. What might these feelings tell you about the client? About yourself? In all of this you should begin to see patterns in the client's life that are made up of beliefs, emotions, thoughts, behaviors, and consequences. This information will serve as a guide in tailoring your responses to your client to help the client gain insight.

Many interventions can lead to client insight, and, indeed, many clients come to their own insight simply by telling their story. There are, however, some ways of working with clients that are more effective than others in promoting insight. The following interventions often are useful in helping clients gain new perspectives and, thus, insight.

Guidelines for Interpretation

The following guidelines, strategies, and techniques are helpful in promoting client insight in that they help clients hear and be clear about what they are saying, explore connections, and challenge their perceptions about their problems.

1. Develop an effective working relationship before attempting interpretive interventions. While we might have wonderful insights about our client, it is premature to begin using interpretation until the client trusts us and is committed to change.
2. Allow the clients to discover their own insight whenever possible. As you have probably surmised, it does not really help to have someone tell you why you do something. However, it is helpful to discover how you came to do what you do in specific situations, how you learned to think or believe specific concepts, or how you developed the beliefs that you hold. Interpretations are most effective if clients are guided to figure them out on their own. You may believe that Mary is having difficulty with her boss because her boss reminds Mary of her mother with whom she continues to have conflicts, but Mary may not be ready to agree with you. However, simply by saying, "I wonder if your boss reminds you of anyone else in your life," might lead Mary to find the link and thus her own insight. Interpretations should generally be given tentatively rather than as pronouncements. Leads such as "I wonder if . . ." or "Perhaps you . . ." allow the client to choose to accept, edit, or reject your interpretation (Table 8.3).
3. Note how the client reacts to your attempts toward insight and how your interpretations are received. If your attempts are well received, your rapport with the client will grow. However, premature attempts may lessen the rapport between you and the client (McLoughlin, 1995).

Levels of Interpretation

There are varying levels of interpretation and, as with other types of therapeutic interventions, how we approach interpretation depends on the client's readiness or level of open-

TABLE 8.3   Examples of Leads That Might Lead to Insight

Can you think of another situation like this?

How do you see this in terms of . . .?

What do you think this is all about?

How is this like . . .? or Is this anything like . . .?

I am reminded of the incident you told me about . . .

ness or defensiveness. Sometimes insight comes simply through the opportunity to talk through problems or issues with an empathic listener. In other cases, only a few hints or suggestions, or possibly just a nonverbal communication on the part of the counselor will cause the client to stop and think. In other instances, the counselor might put together a scenario of how something occurs in the client's life, linking behavior, feelings, responses, and outcomes. There are times when the counselor needs to prompt a bit, using leads and questions that help the client look at issues in a different way. And, at times, the counselor will need to be more directive, focusing the client's attention on possible patterns, motivations, and rationales.

Probably the most common form of interpretation is in helping clients make links between situations or events and their personal responses. Responses to stress, anticipation of a problem, or the perceived need to adapt or defend, as well as states of mind that might influence responses, are areas that might be subjects of these kinds of interpretations (Horowitz, 1989). Some questions or ideas the counselor might consider in crafting these kinds of interpretations to help clients gain insight are those that build a "When you, then you" scenario.

DEALING WITH TRANSFERENCE AND COUNTERTRANSFERENCE

There are varying perspectives concerning transference and countertransferences in therapy and the interested scholar can find years worth of readings on the subject. While we only touch on this extensive subject, it is important to understand some of the basic ideas about transference and countertransference. Both transference and countertransference are based on the relationship and, in turn, influence the relationship between the client and the counselor.

Transference involves the feelings and ideas the client has concerning the counselor which are reenactments of previous relationships. These feelings and ideas, whether accurate or inaccurate, can serve as positive and negative influences on the progress of therapy. Some of the simplest forms of transference are seen in how clients change opinions of themselves or what they do based on how the counselor reacts. A client treated with respect might think "I must be worth something, this counselor seems to respect me." That is one of the reasons counselors are very careful about or avoid altogether giving advice or telling a client what to do.

Clients who experience a negative transference are more likely to stop coming for counseling, so counselors need to pay attention to how the client is experiencing therapy. What do they expect from the therapist? How are they feeling about the therapy? Is it helpful? Are they comfortable in the relationship? If the relationship between the client and counselor is under stress, it is important to address the relationship in session.

> . . . the therapist's sensitivity to the ups and downs of the relationship and her or his ability to attend to relational stresses could directly influence clients' willingness to confront their own dysfunctional relational patterns, as well as increasing their confidence in asserting their psychological needs within a relational context (Bachelor & Horvath, 1999, p. 151).

In the following interchange, note how Jill Scharff (Carlson & Kjos, 2000g) addresses the client's discomfort with her questions.

TH 25:   Mhm. Well, although you are terribly out of time, I take it you must actually be doing alright grade-wise [Oh, yeah] to then get an award. A sort of scholarship you said?

CL 25:   Yeah. I got two scholarships, and I got a list of awards. National scholar, I don't know what they were. I was on the Dean's list the past two semesters.

TH 26:   What do you mean you don't know that they were?

CL 26:   It sounds, okay, I was on the Dean's list twice. I was, two scholarships . . .

TH 27:   For what?

CL 27:   Money scholarships that I applied for.

TH 28:   Mhm, for current courses or for future?

CL 28:   For current. [O.K.] That was just, you know, I applied, and I had, I filled the requirements of . . .

TH 29:   The qualifications?

CL 29:   Yeah, the qualifications. Grade point average, [Yeah] financial need, and I applied. So, I got two of those, and I had, there is some other stuff that I don't know, I got a little plaque, and it says all the school stuff on it that I got.

TH 30:   What does it say?

CL 30:   I just told you. I don't remember.

TH 31:   Well, I'm very interested in that. You don't remember.

CL 31:   National Merit Scholar Award. I don't know. There were like four or five things on there, and two of them were Dean's list, two of them were scholarships, and there might be two other ones, one or two other ones. National All American Scholar, not National Merit Scholar, I don't know.

TH 32:   It's very interesting that you don't know what it is.

CL 32:   It wasn't like . . .

TH 33:   Maybe, you don't know how big a deal it is, or you don't want to know how big a deal it is.

CL 33:   No, it was a big deal. It was pretty cool.

TH 34:   It sounds like a pretty big deal to me.

CL 34:   Yeah, well.

TH 35:   But I have a feeling like you're kind of blowing it off like don't get too interested in this. [It's ah] Do you think I'm sounding too much like a mother?

CL 35:   No.

TH 36:   Wanting to know about your successes?

This transaction leads to further exchanges concerning the client's relationship with his mother and how that has affected and continues to affect his life.

Countertransference broadly relates to the feelings the client brings up in the therapy. Countertransference can provide important clues to the counselor concerning the client's issues. Intuitive leaps in counseling are often based on countertransference. Such a leap occurs when the counselor notes that certain feelings, memories, or moods come to mind as the client talks and shares this in some way with the therapist. This resource is probably most available to counselors who are able to be fully present with the client.

Countertransference also provides the counselor information about themselves. Because of this, countertransference issues are often the subject of supervision. Does this client sound whiney and unlovable because he or she is whiney and unlovable, feels whiney and unlovable or because the client reminds the counselor of someone else?

One of the ways that counselors respond to transference and countertransference is through *immediacy.* Immediacy is the counselor's responding to something as it occurs in the session. As the term implies, the focus on immediacy is on the here and now. Cormier and Cormier (1998) define three categories of immediacy:

> In using immediacy in counseling the therapist reflects on a current aspect of (1) some thoughts, feelings or behavior of the *counselor*, (2) some thoughts, feelings or behavior of the *client*, or (3) some aspect of the *relationship*. (p. 47)

In addition to contributing to client insight, immediacy, when used appropriately, serves to enhance the client counselor relationship. Note how Ivey uses immediacy as he concludes his session with Robin (Carlson & Kjos, 2000e).

TH 97:   So, now we are indeed running out of time, and I was wondering, Robin, if you could give me a little feedback about our talk together and what sense you make of it.

CL 97:   I guess primarily that I do need to look at some of those pictures and that would be something good. I could take different people in my family, what strength did they give me, what weakness did they give me. And sort of know what my limits are, what my abilities are, and draw from those rather than, or learn from my weaknesses.

TH 98:   I just totally love the idea of the papers all over the place and getting a chuckle out of that. I love the smile. That's wow, what a source, and what a resource for making an impact, but impacts don't come along . . .

CL 98: Well, sometimes I wonder when my son spills the milk on the floor for the third time, you know, okay.

TH 99: I'm making no impact here. I better let it go. There is a challenge there all the time. So the idea that hanging in, making an impact, drawing on those strengths, and being aware that I guess maybe even taking joy in some of your imperfections.

CL 99: Yeah. In other words, don't beat myself up because of the way I am.

TH 100: My Baptist images are very different from yours, and I say hey I like that idea of the chuckle. My church . . .

ACTIVITY III: PRACTICE IMMEDIACY

Select two members of your small group to ask each other the following questions in turn, while the rest of the group observes:

1. What client behavior do you find (or think you would find) most annoying?
2. What counselor behavior do you find (or think you would find) most annoying?
3. What behaviors do you observe in me that help you know what I am feeling or thinking?
4. Observers give the two feedback on what they observed during the interaction.
5. Repeat with other group members.

SUMMARY

Counselors use psychodynamic interventions to help clients gain insight that then can lead to change. Psychodynamic interventions focus primarily on the here and now of counseling and both are based on the relationship between the client and the counselor and play an important part in furthering that relationship. These interventions are based not only on what the client is saying, but also on how the client is saying it and what the counselor is observing, both externally and internally.

TABLE 8.4   Psychodynamic Skills, Description, and Outcome

SKILL	DESCRIPTION	OUTCOME
Summarizing	Focus on significant issues, share meaning.	Client feels heard, may gain new perspective.
Open-ended verbalizations and gentle commands	Direct client towards deeper thinking and communications.	Client moves to deeper self-exploration.
Clarifying deletions, distortions, and generalizations	Focus on incomplete, distorted, or unclear communications.	Client develops clarity of thought and deeper self-understanding.
Establishing connections	Help client develop between feelings, inner conflicts, thoughts, and behaviors (When you—then you).	Client becomes aware of how behaviors influence outcomes.
Confronting discrepancies, incongruencies, and destructive behaviors	Help client recognize discrepancies, incongruencies, and destructive behaviors.	Client encouraged exploration of internal conflicts.
Exploring transference and counter transference	Encourage understanding of interpersonal behaviors and motivations.	Client/counselor relationship enhanced. Client gains insight into how relationships influence behavior.
Immediacy	Focus on here and now or the session.	Client gains increased self-awareness.

REFERENCES

Bachelor, A. & Horvath, A. (1999). The therapeutic relationship. In M. A. Hubble, B. L. Duncan, & S. D. Miller, (Eds.). *The heart and soul of change: What works in therapy* (pp. 133–178). Washington, DC: American Psychological Association.

Bandler, R. & Grinder, J. (1975). *The structure of magic, I. A book about language and therapy.* Palo Alto, CA: Science and Behavior Books.

Carlson, J. & Kjos, D. (1999). *A case of domestic abuse: Brief character change demonstrated by Leigh McCullough, Ph.D.* Brief Therapy Inside-Out Video. Phoenix: Zeig, Tucker & Co.

Carlson, J. & Kjos, D. (2000a). *Adlerian therapy with Dr. James Bitter* (Reprint): Family Therapy with the Experts Video. Boston: Allyn & Bacon.

Carlson, J. & Kjos, D. (2000b). *Adlerian therapy with Dr. Jon Carlson* (Reprint): Psychotherapy with the Experts Video. Boston: Allyn & Bacon.

Carlson, J. & Kjos, D. (2000c). *Bowenian therapy with Dr. Phil Guerin* (Reprint): Family Therapy with the Experts Video. Boston: Allyn & Bacon.

Carlson, J. & Kjos, D. (2000d). *Integrative therapy with Dr. Allen E. Ivey (Reprint): Psychotherapy with the Experts Video.* Boston: Allyn & Bacon.

Carlson, J. & Kjos, D. (2000e). *Existential-humanistic therapy with Dr. James Bugental* (Reprint): Psychotherapy with the Experts Video. Boston: Allyn & Bacon.

Carlson, J. & Kjos, D. (2000f). *Multimodal therapy with Dr. Arnold Lazarus* (Reprint): Psychotherapy with the Experts Video. Boston: Allyn & Bacon.

Carlson, J. & Kjos, D. (2000g). *Object relations therapy with Dr. Jill Savege Scharff* (Reprint): Psychotherapy with the Experts Video. Boston: Allyn & Bacon.

Carlson, J. & Kjos, D. (2000h). *Reality therapy with Dr. Robert Wubbolding* (reprint): Psychotherapy with the experts video. Boston: Allyn & Bacon.

Carlson, J. & Kjos, D. (2000i). *Solution-focused therapy with Insoo Kim Berg* (reprint): Psychotherapy with the experts video. Boston: Allyn & Bacon.

Carlson, J. & Kjos, D. (2000j). *Solution-oriented therapy with Bill O'Hanlon* (Reprint): Family Therapy with the Experts Video. Boston: Allyn & Bacon.

Cormier, S. & Cormier, B. (1998). *Interviewing strategies for helpers: Fundamental skills and cognitive behavioral interventions.* Pacific Grove, CA: Brooks/Cole.

Doherty, W. J. (1995). *Soul searching.* New York: Basic Books.

Horowitz, M. J. (1989). *Nuances of technique in dynamic psychotherapy.* Northvale, NJ: Jason Aronson Inc.

McLaughlin, B. (1995). *Developing psychodynamic counselling.* London: Sage Publications.

Truax, C. B. & Carkhuff, R. R. (1967). *Toward effective counseling and therapy.* Chicago: Aldine.

Wubbolding, R. (1998). *Psychotherapy with the experts.* Boston: Allyn & Bacon.

CHAPTER 9

INTERVENTIVE AND SOLUTION-FOCUSED INTERVENTIONS

THERAPEUTIC AND INTERVENTIVE INTERVIEWING: AN OVERVIEW

Traditionally, the clinical interview was thought of as having two phases: a diagnostic interviewing phase and a therapeutic interviewing phase. The purpose of the diagnostic phase was to elicit data primarily through who-what-when-where-how questions, while the purpose of the therapeutic phase was to facilitate insight and change in beliefs and behaviors. Usually, the first few sessions with a client were devoted to diagnostic interviewing. Based on the diagnostic information collected, the clinician would develop a case formulation and a treatment plan. Only after this was completed could formal counseling or psychotherapy proceed, of which therapeutic interviewing was the primary intervention. In short, diagnostic interviewing preceded and was separate from therapeutic interviewing.

Today, the distinction between diagnostic interviewing and therapeutic interviewing is blurring (Sperry, 1997). This blurring reflects current concerns with cost containment, wherein brief therapy—even single session treatment—is becoming normative (Hoyt, 1995; Johnson, 1995). Therapeutic interviewing includes a wide range of interventions including therapeutic confrontation, interpretation, cognitive-behavioral interventions as well as a variety of systemic and strategic interventions including interventive interviewing. Chapter 7 focused on cognitive-behavioral interventions, while Chapter 8 describes the skills of interpretation and therapeutic confrontation. This chapter focuses on interventive interviewing while Chapter 10 describes other systemic and strategic interventions.

WHAT YOU WILL LEARN IN THIS CHAPTER

1. What interventive interviewing is and how it originated.
2. The significant impact that interventive interviewing can have on the therapy process.
3. A description of ten key interventive interviewing questions—including scaling questions that are probably the most often used intervention of this type.

4. How and when to use these interventions.
5. How interventive interviewing links individual and couples/family therapy.

ORIGINS OF INTERVENTIVE INTERVIEWING

In 1987, a Canadian psychiatrist and family therapist, Karl Tomm, M.D., proposed the concept *interventive interviewing* to describe questioning that seeks not only to elicit data or information from the patient, but also to impact how a client processed information. Tomm suggested that clinical interviewing is a powerful intervention. He believes that its purpose is much broader than asking questions in order to establish a diagnostic formulation. He defines interventive interviewing as "an orientation in which everything an interviewer does and says, and does not do and does not say, is thought of as an intervention that could be therapeutic, nontherapeutic, or countertherapeutic" (Tomm, 1987a, p. 4).

In short, Tomm contends that the intent of a clinician's questioning should be twofold: to impact the patient's cognitive processing of the questions themselves, as well as to elicit specific content answers (Tomm, 1987a). In other words, therapeutic change and diagnostic information can and should be gathered simultaneously.

White and Epston (1990) have similarly described interventive interviewing within a narrative therapy perspective. Human experience, within the narrative metaphor, is seen as influenced by dominant stories or narratives that structure an individual's or family's life experiences. From this perspective, psychotherapy focuses on the elicitation of the patient's dominant narrative, and replacement by a more useful alternative narrative, which resolves the clinical concern.

Almost at the same time that Tomm and White and Epston were describing their approaches, another variant of interventive interviewing was being articulated at the Brief Therapy Center in Milwaukee. Steve de Shazer (1985, 1988, 1991) and Insoo Berg and Scott Miller (Berg & Miller, 1992) have described several forms of solution-focused questioning which are clearly interventive interviewing strategies. The questioning strategies they describe can powerfully reframe a client's problems and concerns. These include exception questions, outcome questions, coping questions, and positive description questions. But perhaps the most important of their contributions have been scaling questions.

Interventive interviewing, a unique method of interviewing, was described, without naming it as such, more than 50 years ago by Alfred Adler, MD, the founder of Alderian psychology, also called individual psychology (Adler, 1956; 1964). In his classic 1932 paper, "Techniques of Treatment," Adler described an interview protocol including both diagnostic and therapeutic questions that appears remarkably similar to the strategy of what is today called interventive interviewing (Adler, 1956, pp. 408–409). However, while Adler may have first proposed this interviewing approach, clinician-theorists like Tomm, White, Berg, de Shazer, and Miller have considerably refined and specified this effective and unique intervention strategy and skill set (Sperry, 1997).

The remainder of this chapter describes the clinical use and value of this type of intervention, and then provides an in-depth look at ten common interventive questions. Illustrative examples of various questions focusing on a single theme—depression—are used to provide the reader a context for comparison.

INTERVENTIVE INTERVIEWING/QUESTIONING SKILLS: THEIR CLINICAL USE AND VALUE

Basically, therapy is a process that facilitates change. Interventive interviewing facilitates this change process by framing questions that not only elicit useful information, such as linear-diagnostic questions, but that provokes change in the mental and emotional landscape in the client as they process and respond to interventive questions (Tomm, 1987a). In the process of answering the clinician's question, various changes begin occurring within the client, such as expansion or change of one's frame of reference with circular questions, getting in touch with one's sense of self-efficacy as with empowering questions, or mobilizing one's problem solving skills as with reflextive questions.

The value of interventive questioning is multifaceted. Rather than spending the entire first one or two sessions asking a large set of predictable diagnostic, information-seeking questions as a basis for establishing a formulation and a treatment plan, and then following up with therapeutic questions and interventions in subsequent sessions, the interview process is short-circuited. One or two diagnostic questions set the stage for immediately following up with interventive, change-provoking questions that provoke change. Thus, within the very first session or encounter between clinician and client, therapeutic change and movement can occur. In fact, it should be expected. It also means that clients do not have to spend a session or more telling their entire story all over again as they have already done so with an intake clinician or a previous therapist.

Furthermore, some types of interventive questions, such as outcomes questions and scaling questions, are particularly useful in making the therapy process more focused, less vague, and airy-fairy as some clients would say. Scaling questions may be the most commonly used intervention to clarify clinician–client interactions. Asking a scaling question or two can reduce the sense of vagueness and indefiniteness that both clients and clinicians experience when they appear to be talking about the same reality, but neither are sure. And, neither feels particularly hopeful or empowered about changing the situation. For example, back-to-back scaling questions such as "Where has your mood been for the last week or so on a 1 to 10 scale where 1 is the worst and 10 is the best?" (Client: 4); "What could you do to raise it to a 5 or 6?" This kind of questioning can lead to a very specific and different kind of discussion than if the clinician predictably asks "How have your moods been lately?" (Client: "Pretty bad."); "Why do you suppose that is?" (Client: "I'm not sure.").

Furthermore, interventive questioning is of great importance in a variety of approaches for working with individuals, couples, and families within a systemic perspective. Clearly, interventive interviewing has been articulated and nurtured within the systemic perspectives of family therapy, strategic therapy, narrative therapy, and solution-focused therapy. Not only is interventive questioning the coin of the realm for many of these approaches, it also serves as a convenient bridge between individual therapy and couples and family therapy. Until recently, the specialities of couples and family therapy has developed largely independent of individual psychotherapy. Family therapists traditionally have been trained in specialized programs apart from those being trained in individual psychotherapy. Interestingly, graduates of such training programs tend to be quite versatile, not only capable of working with couples and families but also with individual clients. As a result, many of those who were traditionally trained in individual therapy had little, if any, formal training in couples and family therapy, and usually work only with individual clients. Until recently they have not been expected to work with couples and families. Of course, the revolution in health care, and particularly in managed behavioral health care, has greatly changed the way most clinicians practice today. Irrespective of one's initial training, managed care expects clinicians to deal with an individual client's needs whether they include work, relational, or family issues. In fact, many managed care organizations have a preference for adding clinicians to their providers networks who are skilled in brief therapies, particularly in systemic and solution-focused approaches. As traditionally trained individual therapists upgrade their skills to be able to work with a broader clientele, they typically become acquainted with interventive interviewing methods such as scaling questions which have significant value in both individual and family treatment contexts.

Diagnostic-Linear Questions

Before describing these ten interventions it will be useful to contrast them with *diagnostic-linear* questions. While diagnostic-linear questions characterize diagnostic interviewing, they are intended to be information-seeking rather than change-provoking questions (Tomm, 1987a). Interventive questions, however, are by definition primarily change-provoking questions.

Description. Diagnostic-linear questions are basically data-gathering or information-seeking questions that typically follow a Who?—What?—When?—Where? format and sequence. They are based on linear assumptions about nature; for example, A causes or effects B. Most clinical interviews begin with at least some diagnostic-linear questions, as they are extraordinarily effective and useful in establishing the chronology of events. It should come as no surprise that many clinicians exclusively use this question-type in most, if not all, of their clinical interviewing.

Purpose. The purpose is to orient the clinician to the clinical situation, collect data, and establish a chronology of events. Some examples of linear questions are: "What brings you to counseling? When did your symptoms begin? How long have you been depressed? What do you think triggered it? What conditions make it better? What makes it worse?

Clinician Intention. In utilizing this type of questioning, the clinician functions much like a detective attempting to follow up a lead in a criminal investigation by asking specific focused questions. The clinician's intention in asking linear questions is to seek information and, ultimately, to be able to generate a formulation as to the cause and effect of the individual's symptomatic distress or impairment. For example, a clinician interviewing someone with depressive features might ask a series of criterion-based questions (DSM-IV criteria for Major Depression). Upon eliciting six or nine criteria they conclude that the individual suffers from this disorder with sufficient severity to reasonably formulate that the causative factor is, in large part, biologic.

Examples. Here are some examples of linear questions:

Individual therapy context:
- *General data gathering questions:* What brings you to therapy? When did your symptoms begin? How long have you been depressed? What do you think triggered it? What conditions make it better? What makes it worse?
- *Linear sequencing to establish a diagnosis:* You say your moods have been sad lately. How long? How has your sleep been? Are you having difficulty falling asleep or awakening during the night or early in the morning? What about your appetite? Your concentration?

Couples therapy context:
- How would you describe your wife's moods lately? How does it affect you? What do you do about it?

How a Clinician's Intentionality Determines Question Types

It is important to clarify that the impact of the question-type does not depend soley on semantic content or syntax. Rather, it depends primarily on the clinician's intentions and assumptions in asking the questions. Interestingly, Tomm (1988) illustrates how the exact same sequence of words can constitute a diagnostic-linear, strategic, circular, or reflexive question. For instance, if a clinician is working with a family and asks the adolescent son "What does your mom do when your dad comes home and misses dinner?", If this was framed as a single question, it would be considered a *diagnostic-linear question.* If it were asked as part of a planned sequence of questions to explore the circular interaction between the parents, it would then be a *circular question.* If the original question was asked to prompt the parents to become observers of their own behavior and mobilize their awareness to modify their actions, then it would be a *reflexive question.* If the question were asked because the clinician anticipated what the adolescent would probably say, and wanted this information released in order to confront either parent of their intolerant behavior, it would be a *strategic question.*

TEN TYPES OF INTERVENTIVE INTERVIEWING QUESTIONS

While there are numerous types of interventive-focused question types, this chapter focuses on ten question-types that are easily learned by clinicians-in-training and are commonly utilized by effective clinicians. Table 9.1 provides an overview of these ten interventive questions.

1. Circular Questions

Description. Circular questions can be quite useful in understanding and mapping the individual's relational world. This type of question is based on a circular rather than linear view of reality or causality. For instance, in linear causality it can be said that event A *effects* event B, but not vice versa. However, in a circular view of causality, event A can be said to *effect* event B but at the same time event B also *effects* event A.

Purpose. Circular questions are most helpful in eliciting the type and extent of relational patterns that connect individuals (Tomm, 1987a). They are questions about comparisons or differences, and form the basis for reframing specific life circumstances and affects. Presumably, while processing the clinician's circular question, the client expands his or her perspective on a situation that previously was framed negatively.

Clinician Intention. The clinician's role in using circular questions is analogous to an explorer who sets out to discover new territory or a medical researcher who discovers the genetic basis of a troubling chronic disease. Similarly, the clinician's intention is to prompt the client to reframe a troubling relationship or symptom in a new way. The simple but skilled use of circular questioning can facilitate such an expanded perspective.

Examples. Here are several examples of how a clinican can phrase circular questions. Notice how these clients are asked to step outside their own perspectives and make comparisons or differences that introduce new distinctions.

- *Individual therapy context:* "Besides you, who else worries about your daughter's depression? Who worries more, you or your husband? When your daughter is depressed, how do you respond? How do you respond to her response? How does your husband react to this?"
- *Couples therapy context:* "When you start talking in that tone, how does your partner respond? How do you respond to her response?" [To partner] "Is that the way you experience it? When you become quiet, does your partner draw closer to you or move further away? Do you see this in a similar or different way?"

2. Reflexive Questions

Description. Like circular questions, reflexive questions are based on circular assumptions of reality. They ask the listener to shift to a different point of reference in terms of person, place, or time. As a result, reflexive questions help individuals generate new perspectives and contexts.

Purpose. Reflexive questions are intended to influence a client, couple, or family in an indirect or general manner (Tomm, 1987b; 1988). Their intent is to mobilize the listener's

TABLE 9.1   Ten Interventive Interviewing Question Types

QUESTION-TYPE	PURPOSE OF THE QUESTION	CLINICIAN'S ROLE/INTENTION	EXAMPLE OF THE QUESTION
Circular	Expands one's perspective on the situation	Explorer out to make a new discovery	What would your wife believe is the basic cause of your depressed moods?
Reflexive	Mobilizes one's own problem solving processes	Guide or coach to mobilize one's own resources	Suppose you were to imagine yourself free of depression. What would that be like?
Strategic	Confronts or leads the individual to action	Judge suggesting how one should act	When are you going to stop talking so pessimistically about your future?
Externalizing	Separates one's sense of self from the problem, symptom, etc.	Emergency technician freeing one from entrapment	What are you like as a person when your life is not dominated by depressed moods?
Empowering	Elicit's one's sense of self-efficacy	Facilitator drawing out one's strengths	On those occasions when you were not depressed, what were you thinking and doing then?
Scaling	Measures strength of the problem or its solution	Scientist making exact measurements	Suppose your mood is 4 on a 1 to 10 scale tomorrow. What could you do to raise it to 5 or 6?
Exceptions	Spotlights successful efforts that have gone unnoticed	Detective doing a thorough investigation	What's different about times when your mood is better? What accounts for that difference?
Positive description	Replaces negative goals with positive goals	Motivational speaker	What will you be doing instead of feeling depressed and dejected?
Outcomes	Elicits one's goal or endpoint for change	Strategic planner clarifying outcomes	How will you know when you've finally overcome your depression?
Coping	Explores coping strategies (past successes)	Facilitator finding hope when things are bleak	What are you doing to keep your depression from becoming worse?

own problem solving processes. They prompt the listener to reconstruct meaning or shift contexts. This type of question encourages listeners to think about the implications of their current perceptions or behaviors and consider alternatives.

Clinician Intention. The clinician's role in utilizing reflexive questioning is analogous to a coach who prompts and guides a player to a higher level of performance. In the therapeutic context, the clinician, through the skilled use of reflexive questioning, guides the client to mobilize their own intellectual or emotional resources to solve previously unsolvable problems.

Examples. Here are some examples of how a clinician can phrase reflexive questions. Notice how the listeners, the clients, are prompted to mobilize healing resources that they might not previously have believed they could, for example, be successful at therapy or overcome their depression.

Individual therapy context

- Suppose this therapy is successful and someday in the future you reflect on it, what will you consider to have been the turning point?
- Suppose you were to imagine yourself free of depression. What would that be like?

Couples therapy context

- Suppose you were to share with him how worried you are about him and his depression, what do you suppose he might think and do?
- Just suppose he was resentful about your family, but feared bringing it to your attention, how could you convince him it was safe to talk about it?

3. Strategic Questions

Description. While strategic questions are the mainstay of strategic therapy approaches (Haley, 1963), they are also an essential component of interventive interviewing. Strategic questions are directive in nature and are intended to provide a corrective influence on a client, couple, or family. The directiveness of the clinician is usually masked since the corrective statement is packaged in the form of a question (Tomm, 1988). While some clients may bristle at being asked this question-type, others find it quite compatible with their typical pattern of interaction. Unlike the other nine question types described in Table 9.1, strategic questions are essentially linear questions.

Purpose. Their purpose is to alter the individual's behavior in a therapeutic direction. While based on linear assumptions of causality, this type of question assumes that when the clinician discovers dysfunctionality, they can proceed to correct or change it. Strategic questions are a powerful mode of influencing individuals, couples, or families either overtly or covertly.

Clinician Intention. The clinician's role in utilizing strategic questioning is analogous to a judge suggesting how a defendant should act, or the type of questioning a trial attorney would use in cross-examining a witness. In a therapeutic context, the clinician attempts, through the use of strategic questioning, to confront, in an indirect fashion, the client's resistance to change.

Examples. Here are some examples of how a clinician can phrase strategic questions with individuals and couples.

Individual therapy context
- When are you going to stop talking so pessimistically about your future?
- When are your going to take control of your life and start looking for a job?
- Is this habit of making excuses something new for you?

Couples therapy context
- Why don't you talk to your wife about your worries instead of your talking to your daughter about them?
- What would happen if for the next week you would suggest she make breakfast every morning instead of staying in bed until noon?
- How come you're not willing to try harder to get her up and around?
- Would you prefer making sure she gets up every morning or confronting her with your fears that she might overdose?

4. Externalizing Questions

Description. Externalizing questions are questions that facilitate the client's experiencing a problem, or the context that supports the problem, as external to themselves. Problem externalization is an effective way of reducing a client's perceived sense of feeling helpless or trapped (White & Epston, 1990). Externalization questions help a client in framing their symptoms or conditions as separate from their selfhood.

Purpose. The main purpose of externalizing questions is to separate one's sense of self from the presenting problem, symptom, or impairment so that one does not feel so hopeless, helpless, defeated, dominated, or guilt-ridden and, thus, unable to plan, act on, or cooperate with a change effort.

Clinician Intention. The clinical use of externalizing questions is analogous to an emergency technician freeing an accident victim from a car wreck with jaws of life technology. Through the use of externalizing questions the clinician can loosen the stranglehold that helplessness, guilt, or hopelessness has previously bound the client, allowing them to begin to believe that change may, indeed, be possible.

Examples. Here are some examples of how a clinician can phrase externalizing questions with individuals and couples.

Individual therapy context
- What are you like as a person when your life is not dominated by depression?

- What percent of your day does it seem that depression controls you? What percent of your day does it seem that you can control the depression?
- In what ways are you able to organize your life the way you want it to be, despite the depression?

Couples therapy context
- What are the earliest signs that let you know that your father's way of treating your mother is starting to infiltrate your relationship with your spouse?
- How does criticalness of your partner manage to seduce you when you've been so determined to escape its influence?

5. Empowering Questions

Description. Empowering questions are particularly useful in drawing out a client's strengths and building on whatever past successes they have had inside or outside of psychotherapy. Talmon (1990) and White and Epston (1990) have illustrated several question-types that are framed to empower and reconstruct selfhood, once a client or family has framed their problems and concerns as somehow separate from themselves. In this regard, empowering questions are similar to externalizing questions.

Purpose. The main purpose of empowering questions is to elicit the patient's sense of self-efficacy by drawing on their previous knowledge, experience, and previous successes in other areas of life and bringing them to bear on the therapeutic task at hand.

Clinician Intention. The clinician's use of empowering questions is analogous to an organizational consultant facilitating the process of team building by drawing out each team member's personal and professional strengths and loyalties to the team. Through the use of empowering questions the clinician draws out the client's strengths and sense of self-efficacy so that they come to believe, perhaps against great odds, that life can be different.

Examples. Here are some examples of how a clinician can phrase empowering questions with individuals and couples.

Individual therapy context
- In those occasional instances when you were not depressed, what were you thinking then?
- When you see yourself refusing to accept a lifestyle of depression, what does that then say about you as a person?
- Imagine you are looking into a crystal ball and can see you yourself as no longer depressed, what will you be doing differently with your life? How will you manage to make that a reality?

Couples therapy context
- Can you both imagine, for a moment, having total control over the situation with your son's acting out behavior. What would you do differently?

- If you were to think of a very small but significant step in the right direction that would give you just one ray of hope that your marriage would get back on track, what would it be?

6. Scaling Questions

Description. Questions that ask for metaphoric descriptions to be quantified. Clinical experience suggests that individuals benefit from looking at their problems as continuous rather than dichotomies.

Purpose. Scaling questions help the individual and the clinician map the strength of various aspects of the problems or the solutions (de Shazer, 1991). The general form of the question is, "On a 1 to 10 scale, with 10 equal to the worst problem you could have and 1 equal to the least, what would you rate the current problem?"

Clinician Intention. The clinician's use of scaling questions is analogous to a meteorologist carefully tracking hurricane force winds over a period of days to predict the hurricane's potential destructive impact. The clinician utilizing scaling questions is able to more accurately assess the client's perception of symptomatic distress, impairment, and progress to change than he would get by asking less focused questions.

Examples. Here are some examples of how a clinician can phrase scaling questions with individuals and couples.

Individual therapy context
- On a 1 to 10 scale, with 10 meaning "I'll do whatever it takes" and 1 meaning "There's nothing I can do about it," how would you rate your readiness today to solve this problem?
- What could make your readiness go up one point? Go down one point?

Couples therapy context
- If I (clinician) were to ask your wife how she would rate your readiness for change, what would she have guessed your rating would be? How do you account for the difference?
- On a scale of 1 to 10, with 10 meaning you have totally achieved the goals you came to couples therapy for, and 1 meaning that you haven't started yet, where would you rate yourself today? (The couple says: 4). What do you need to do to move from 4 to 5?

Addenda: Fostering Client-Centeredness Through the Use of Scaling Questions. Finally, another important value for utilizing scaling questions should be mentioned. Scaling questions truly can faciliate the therapy process in approaching the time-honored ideal of being truly "client-centered" or "client-driven" (Berg, Sperry & Carlson, 1999). That is because scaling questions assess the client's ideal—not the clinician's ideal—of what constitutes an adequate resolution to their presenting problem or concern. Because the client rates on his own scale, not on the clinician's expert scale, the clinician can say "Are you content to live with your mood at a 5 level?" If the client says "Yes, it's as good as things can be for now," the clinician does not have to be disappointed because the client did not set his endpoint at a 7 or 8, which may have been the clinician's ideal for this client.

Besides being a very effective method of intervention, this kind of questioning is very respectful of the client. It says to the client: "I know you know what you want for yourself. I know you know what's good for you. So you just tell me." As a result, clinicians do not have to take all the responsibility for coming up with the right solutions or answers for the client, since much of the responsibility is given back to the client. It is very different than saying "I know what's good for you; to get your mood up to 7 or 8."

7. Exception Questions

Description. This type of question assumes that there are times and circumstances when the client's problem or symptoms does not occur, and attempt to learn whether those times and circumstances can be a foundation for further change. This question type emphasizes any unrecognized, successful client action(s) that could serve to leverage therapeutic progress in some way or another.

Purpose. The purpose of exception questions is to spotlight successful efforts on the client's part that have been unrecognized (Berg & Miller, 1992). Exception questions assume that clients can and do change on their own, but that the client may ignore those changes, unless they are attended to by the clinician. It also assumes that important changes can occur, even prior to the first session.

Clinician Intention. The clinician's use of exception questions is analogous to a detective conducting a careful investigation and finding a significant piece of evidence that others have overlooked, and this evidence is critical in a successful prosecuting of the case. The clinician utilizing exception questions highlights successful effort, no matter how small, that the client has overlooked, and that are critical in encouraging the client to continue the difficult and painful process of therapy.

Examples. Here are some examples of how a clinician can phrase exception questions with individuals and couples.

Individual therapy context
- What is different about those occasions when your symptoms are not so strong or noticeable? What might be causing those exceptions? How do they occur?
- When are you already doing some of what's needed to accomplish your goal?
- During the past week, were there any occasions when the problem did not occur?
- Have there been times when the problem almost occurred but you were successful at neutralizing it?

Couples therapy context

- Sometimes a couple will notice a change between the time they call for an appointment and their first session. What kinds of changes might you have noticed?
- You say there's been no change in arguing and fighting since we met last. Well, what might you have done to keep things from getting any worse?

8. Positive Description Questions

Description. Clients, particularly early in therapy, tend to utilize negative language in describing their goals and aspirations (Tomm, 1987b). For instance, they describe what will likely be *missing* when they have achieved what they hope for: they will not feel depressed anymore, they will stop smoking, or their spouse will be less irritable and critical. The assumption is that negatively framed goals and actions indicate that the client is not really free to experience their unique sense of self, but rather merely is free from constraints or restraints. Thus, reframing in positively described language is an important therapeutic undertaking. With the use of positive description questions the clinician addresses the possibility of positive, achievable goals and actions as a replacement for the client's negatively stated goals, plans, and behaviors.

Purpose. The purpose of positive description questions is to prompt the client to replace negative goals and plans with positive goals and plans (Berg & Miller, 1992).

Clinician Intention. The clinician's use of positive description questions is analogous to a motivational speaker at a corporate sales meeting who so enlives and activates the previously beat down and reactive sales force so that they shift their forecast from maintaining present market share to increasing it by 10 percent in the next quarter. The clinician utilizing positive description questions prompts the client to shift language in a more proactive and positive direction. As a result, negatively focused goal language is replaced with more positive language regarding treatment goals and outcomes that are realistically achievable.

Examples. Here are some examples of how a clinician can phrase positive description questions with individuals and couples.

Individual therapy context
- "What else can you be doing tonight instead of using drugs?"
- "What kinds of feelings will you notice instead of those hopeless and depressed feelings?"

Couples therapy context
- "What will your financee say when she simply disagrees with you instead of insulting you?"
- "What will you do when you start feeling more positive about your relationship?"

9. Outcome Questions

Description. One of the reasons why clients terminate from therapy prematurely is that they are dissatisfied with their treatment. Often, this means that the clinician and client had different goals for the therapy. When treatment goals are not discussed and specified, and there is little or no goal-alignment between clinician and client, therapy cannot be successful and satisfying.

Purpose. The purpose of outcome questions is to elicit and specify the client's goal or endpoint for change (Berg & Miller, 1992).

Clinician Intention. The clinician's use of outcome questions is analogous to an organizational consultant leading a strategic planning session and helping a group of sales managers clarify their one-, three- and five-year sales goals and expected market share. Similarly, the clinician utilizing outcome questions assists the client to clarify and specify their specific expectations for the outcomes of psychotherapy.

Examples. Here are some examples of how a clinician can phrase outcome questions with individuals and couples.

Individual therapy context
- Who will notice, without being told by you, that you made progress in therapy? What will they notice?
- Suppose in the middle of the night tonight, a miracle happens, and the problem that brought you into therapy is solved. But, because it happens while you are asleep, you don't realize it. Tomorrow when you wake up, what will tell you the problem has been solved? What will be the first sign that this is happening? This is the so-called miracle question (de Shazer, 1988).

Couples therapy context
- How will you know when you are both getting what you want from couples therapy?
- If we had video camera that would tape you whenever your relationship was going well, what would we see you both doing on that tape?

10. Coping Questions

Description. During the course of some therapies, it becomes evident that there are few, if any, useful exceptions, or that the client feels so hopeless that she cannot even imagine a positive outcome from therapy and so is unable to respond to outcome questions. Instead, the client may report suicidal thoughts or plans. When circumstances seem ominous or the client becomes increasing hopeless about change, that is the time to explore the client's coping strategies. In the process of exploring coping strategies, the client's life is indirectly reframed in terms of the capacity to heroically cope with difficult external influences (Berg & Miller, 1992).

Purpose. The purpose of coping questions is to explore the client's coping strategies as well as their past successes in making personal changes.

Clinician Intention. The clinician's use of coping questions is analogous to an optimistic labor mediator finding hope for a settlement in a negotiation when both sides are far apart and things seem bleak or hopeless. Similarly, the clinician utilizing coping questions assists the client to explore times in which they have been successful in making and sticking with changes, and the self-management, problem-solving and relationship skills that the client brought to bear in those circumstances.

Examples. Here are some examples of how a clinician can phrase coping questions with individuals and couples.

Individual therapy context
- What are you doing to keep your depression from really getting you down?
- It seems like you're pushed to your limit. How do you manage to keep yourself going?
- What kind of things have you been doing to fight the urge to hurt yourself?
- How have you managed to keep things from getting worse?

Couples therapy context
- Given how worried you are about your daughter's cancer, how do you both manage to keep going every day?
- With all these financial burdens and problems with your kids, how have you been able to keep your marriage together?

HOW AND WHEN TO USE INTERVENTIVE QUESTIONING: A MAP FOR THERAPY

How does a clinician use these interventive interviewing questions in the practice of counseling and psychotherapy? This depends on a number of factors, such as the client's need, disposition, and timing, for example, when in the course of treatment—the first session or the middle of therapy. We suggest the following strategy.

In the Initial Interview

1. Begin the first interview with an open-ended question or two, such as, "What brings you to counseling?"
2. Follow-up with a few data gathering questions, or linear questions, in order to specify the type of symptoms and/or impairment as well as the sequence of events regarding the narrative of precipitants, consequences, relationships, etc., for example, "When did you first notice these depressed feelings?"
3. Specify the level of distress and impairment with scaling questions, for example, "On a scale of 1 to 10 with 1 being the worst you can imagine feeling and 10

the best, what is your mood now? At its worst in the past two months? At its best?"

4. Then, follow that with outcome questions, for example, "When do you expect to be feeling much better? How will you know when you've finally overcome your depression?"

5. From then on, depending on the client's responses to the outcome questions you might move into positive description questions, circular questions, exception questions, etc. with the purpose of aiding the client in moving toward their outcome goals.

In Subsequent Sessions

Using an interventive interviewing approach in subsequent sessions means you tailor the questioning strategy or protocol in such a way as to assist—which may range from encouraging or supporting to prodding or to confronting—your client in moving in the direction of achieving their outcomes. It may involve interspersing some linear or data-gathering questions along with any of the various interventive questions, as are appropriate to the situation. We suggest you become totally familiar with the purpose and clinician role/intention of each of the ten question-types in Table 9.1. Your choice of a question type follows from situational demand. For example:

1. When the client is feeling quite discouraged and helpless, coping, empowering, and positive description questions are particularly useful.
2. When the client appears to be frightened or ambivalent about making changes, externalizing and exception questions may be essential.
3. When the client appears stuck and resistant to moving toward their outcome goals, strategic questions may be essential, particularly when therapeutic confrontation and/or clinical interpretations have not been particularly effective (see Chapter 8).
4. When gaining insight or another frame of reference is needed, circular and reflexive questions are indicated.
5. Finally, recall that scaling questions can be utilized anywhere in the course of treatment to assess the client's perceptions of distress, impairment, and motivations, and readiness for change, as well as progress toward their outcome goals.

SUMMARY

Recent demands on clinicians to function more efficiently and cost-effectively, as well as several exciting and significant developments in the fields of counseling and psychotherapy, have markedly changed the way in which counseling and psychotherapy is conducted today. Among these changes are the utilization of therapeutic interviewing strategies even from the outset of treatment. This chapter has described the emergence and development of interventive interviewing over the past 60 years. Interventive interviewing is a broad strategy for impacting change in a client while at the same time eliciting information. It is distinctly different from traditional diagnostic interviewing which emphasizes data gathering through diagnostic-linear questioning. While providing the clinician with considerable therapeutic leverage in assisting the client to achieve mutually agreed upon treatment goals and outcomes, interventive interviewing also bridges or links individual psychotherapy with couples and family therapy. Ten interventive question-types have been described and illustrated in this chapter, and specific guidelines have been provided for utilizing this interviewing strategy in the course of treatment, whether in the first session or the tenth.

REFERENCES

Adler, A. (1956). *The individual psychology of Alfred Adler.* H. L. Ansbacher & R. R. Ansbacher (Eds.). New York: Harper & Row.

Adler, A. (1964). *Superiority and social interest.* H. L. Ansbacher & R. R. Ansbacher (Eds.). Evanston, IL: Northwestern University Press.

Berg, I. & Miller, S. (1992). *Working with the problem drinker.* New York: Norton.

Berg, I., Sperry, L., & Carlson, J. (1998). Intimacy and culture: A solution-focused perspective—Interview. In J. Carlson & L. Sperry (Eds.) *The intimate couple* (pp. 33–40). New York: Brunner/Mazel.

de Shazer, S. (1985). *Keys to solutions in brief therapy.* New York: Norton.

de Shazer, S. (1988). *Clues: Investigating solutions in brief therapy.* New York: Norton.

de Shazer, S. (1991). *Putting differences to work.* New York: Norton.

Haley, J. (1963). *Strategies of psychotherapy.* New York: Grune & Stratton.

Hoyt, M. (1995). *Brief therapy and managed care.* San Francisco: Jossey-Bass.

Johnson, L. (1995). *Psychotherapy in the age of accountability.* New York: Norton.

Sperry, L. (1997). The rediscovery of interventive interviewing. In J. Carlson & S. Slavik (Eds). *Techniques in Adlerian Psychology* (pp. 107–110). Washington, DC: Accelerated Development/ Taylor & Francis.

Talmon, M. (1990). *Single-Session Therapy.* San Francisco: Jossey-Bass.

Tomm, K. (1987a). Interventive interviewing: Part I. Strategizing as a fourth guideline for the therapist. *Family Process, 26:* 3–13.

Tomm, K. (1987b). Interventive interviewing: Part II. Reflexive questioning as a means to enable self-healing. *Family Process, 26:* 167–183.

Tomm, K. (1988). Interventive interviewing: Part III. Intending to ask lineal, circular, strategic, or reflective questions? *Family Process, 27:* 1–16.

White, M. & Epston, D. (1990). *Narrative means to therapeutic ends.* New York: Norton.

CHAPTER 10

SYSTEMIC AND PSYCHOEDUCATIONAL INTERVENTIONS

WHAT YOU WILL LEARN IN THIS CHAPTER

1. Understand how structural techniques can change systems.
2. How to use systemic and structural techniques to create disequilibrium.
3. How to create different perceptions of reality as a precursor to change.
4. How to create different behavior through psycho-education and pattern interruption.

OVERVIEW

Interventions can be made by changing the ongoing transaction patterns and/or social context. This involves changing a family's hierarchical structure, its boundaries, alignments, and coalitions. The therapist intentionally creates situations that challenge and unbalance the social environment. The intervention increases the stress on the system and opens the path for structural change.

The structures that we live in influence us for better or worse. For example, in some families, structure is well organized in a clear hierarchical pattern allowing the members to relate effortlessly. In other families, there is little structure and minimal opportunity for meaningful interaction. According to Minuchin (1974) in both situations, developmental or situational events increase family stress, rigidity, chaos, and dysfunction throwing the family into crisis. The birth of child, loss of a job, move to a new town, or having children leave the home for college are examples of such events.

It is believed that a person's symptoms are best understood as rooted in the context of family transaction patterns. The family, or system, is treated as the client. The hope is that through structuring or restructuring the system, all members of the family and the family itself will become stronger (Minuchin, 1974). Therefore, in order to create lasting change, the therapist must modify the balance and alliances so that new ways of interacting become realities.

Structural strategies can be used to create organizational or structural changes. Relative position, power, role, loyalty, and boundaries among the subsystems are the focus of these changes. Alfred Adler promoted what Sherman and Dinkmeyer (1987) have called *place psychology*. Place psychology concentrates on how clients subjectively perceive their place in both the system and the world and how they functionally behave toward others in relation to that perception. According to Sherman and Fredman (1986), it is important to examine the sense of place and its significance. Place affects and is affected by many interacting influences.

1. Cultural, ethnic, racial, geographic, and other socioeconomic factors
2. The individual's birth order position within the family
3. The sense of loyalty to the family and the degree of individuation and differentiation among the members
4. The distribution of power and how decisions are made
5. The roles within the system (peacemaker, protector, initiator, humorist, helpless one, etc.)
6. The alliances and collusions among the members and the triangulation that interferes with dyadic relationships
7. The degree of physical or emotional closeness and distance among members (Hoffman, 1981)

When there is a change in any one of these factors the entire system will be influenced and changed. This is the major assumption for the use of structural strategies. Another important assumption is that every behavior is done for a purpose and, therefore, the place and role assumed by each person serves a useful function for the system. The nature of this usefulness needs to be understood by the therapist in selecting the appropriate strategy or technique for change.

The organizational patterns as well as each individual's place are assessed by the therapist verbally and nonverbally as they work with the family. For example, who sits next to whom, how far from whom, looking at whom, leaning toward or away from whom? Who wanders about, when, and how do the others react to it? Who withdraws attention from whom and when? The therapist can intervene and change the patterns that appear to maintain the symptom.

Structural techniques are very important in the beginning stages of therapy. A major move on the part of every therapist is to somehow *join* with the clients without being absorbed into their system. Whether it is called rapport, joining, accommodating, or transference, the therapist has to find a place with the clients. Essentially this creates a new system—the therapeutic one. It includes structuring the therapy (the rules of this new game), empathy, and agreement about what the work of this new group, including the therapist, will be. The therapist lets the client know that they are heard, understood, and valued in their own context.

The objective of structural techniques designed to bring about change is to reorganize the system by getting members to move from one place to another, from one role to another, and to establish and reinforce appropriate boundaries between places in the system, thus causing the system to reorganize itself.

Structural strategies can be used for many purposes:

1. *Create movement.* Clients typically feel stuck in their present positions and do not know how to get out of them. A structural move immediately triggers a shift.
2. *Change perspectives.* Having clients assume a new place or position with its attendant new roles and rules stimulates clients to observe things differently and apply different meanings to the same facts.
3. *Shift distribution of power.* By allying with various subsystems, the therapist can increase the weight of one relative to the others in order to overcome inequities or break oppositional deadlocks.
4. *Disrupt coalitions.* Sometimes two or more people combine in opposition to a third.
5. *Form new alliances.* People can be helped to combine their efforts by cooperating and working together.
6. *Clarify boundaries between and among the subsystems.* Who is included, how, when, and in what functions; who is responsible for what; recognition of the differences among generations; and, reducing too rigid boundaries to allow more sharing and cooperation are the kinds of issues attended to.
7. *Discover new aspects of selves.* By changing places, people have the opportunity to try out new behaviors and to discover new dimensions of their own being.
8. *Normalize the experience of being in a particular place.* People will sometimes view themselves as bad, unworthy, or powerless because they occupy a certain place in the system. The therapist can say something such as, "If I were in your shoes I would be depressed too" or "People in a position like yours generally will do or feel similar things" or "What are the advantages of this position?"
9. *Reframe the meaning of being in a particular place.* One client complained about the burdens of being the oldest child. The therapist replied, "Yes, that's true. That's what happens to most oldest children. But it also trains them for leadership in the world and others look up to them."
10. *Change the family system while working with one individual.* If the assumption is correct that when one person changes position the system has to reorganize, then the therapist can encourage and support one client to assume a new role in the organization, forcing the others to adapt.

TECHNIQUES FOR DISEQUILIBRIUM

Creating a Different Sequence of Events

Enactment allows the therapist to observe how family members actually behave toward one another. The therapist can determine the place that the problem behavior has within the sequence of transactions. Enactment is also the vehicle through which the therapist introduces disruption into the transaction patterns forcing the family to adapt and to develop different rules and more functional roles. Change occurs through dealing with the problems rather than talking about them.

Enactment is always intended to give the family members a different experience of reality. The family members' explanations for their own and each other's behaviors, their notions about their respective positions and functions within the family, their ideas about what their problems are and how they can contribute to a solution, and their mutual attitudes are typically brought into question by these transactional experiences choreographed by the therapist. Enactments may be dramatic or very subtle. The real power does not reside in the emotionality of the situation but rather in the very fact that family members are being directed to behave differently in relation to each other. By prescribing and monitoring transactions, the therapist assumes control of a crucial area—the rules that regulate who should interact with whom, about what, when, and for how long (Minuchin, 1974).

Boundary marking is a special case of enactment. The therapist defines areas of interaction deemed open to certain members but closed to others. This way of marking boundaries also has been called *blocking*. It is a restructuring maneuver because it changes the rules of the game. It may be accomplished verbally by preventing someone from helping someone else or physically by changing the seating arrangement in the therapy session. It is often surprising to see how shifts in boundaries can change patterns that do not respond to verbal interventions. The therapist can mark boundaries in the following ways:

1. Rearrange the seating. For example, the therapist can change seating patterns to prevent disruption of an interrupting child.
2. Reframe the problem. This can be accomplished by getting the family to view the problem differently. For example, seeing a child acting out as trying to get their parents together.
3. Block interaction patterns. This can be accomplished by moving closer to the family member, raising a hand to stop the interaction, or giving a directive.

CREATING DIFFERENT PERCEPTIONS OF REALITY

Reframing is a strategy that puts the presenting problem in a different perspective. The facts of an event do not change but the meaning of the situation is viewed from a fresh perspective. The original meaning of an event or situation is placed in this new context in which an equally plausible explanation is possible. Families often perceive problems in ways that appear to have no workable solution. The new perspective allows the family to work effectively with a problem when they use a different formula or to see it from a new viewpoint. This often involves giving a positive connotation to a negative behavior. Reframing is an important interpersonal skill since there are advantages and disadvantages to every behavior. It is thought that by accepting the behavior, the person will often decrease it.

Reframing does not change a situation, but "the alteration of the meaning invites the possibility of change" (Piercy & Sprenkle, 1986, p. 35). For example, when a partner appears to be tuned out it may actually be that they are being thoughtful about what was just said. The mother who is accused of nagging is reframed by the therapist as one who is intensely interested and caring. The therapist feeds back the pattern of behavior in a different, positive frame of reference so that the clients will see it differently. By viewing the present situation from another perspective allows them to think and feel differently about it. This may create the motivation necessary to approach the problem differently.

Relabeling involves substituting a positive adjective for the negative ones used in the blaming stances of many dysfunctional families. For example, the wife says the husband is *controlling* and the therapist relabels saying that the husband is *overburdened*. This relabels the husband's behavior as a part of the family structure. The therapist can then help the family to divide up the responsibilities of the family in a more equitable fashion. This strategy is very similar to reframing.

Punctuation is a term created by systems theorists to describe patterns of behavior where each individual attributes the problem to the other. The concept is at the heart of circular causality as opposed to linear cause and effect thinking. Circular communication occurs because each participant imposes their own punctuation; each believes that what they do is caused by what the other person says or does. For example, the husband explains that he withdraws because his wife nags and his wife explains that she nags because he withdraws. As long as interactions are punctuated in this fashion there is very little chance of change. These redundant patterns of communication must be identified and repunctuated in order to develop healthier ways of living.

Unbalancing is a term that could be used to describe most of what a therapist does. The basic strategy is to create disequilibrium. In therapeutic terms, it is when the therapist uses their authority/power to break a stalemate by supporting one of the people in a conflict. It is not done randomly and is used only with precision to challenge some of the rights and wrongs, good and bad that keep families stuck. The challenge of unbalancing is with the system and not the individuals.

The goal of this strategy is to change the relationship of members within a subsystem. Many therapists have a difficult time with this concept as it is actually taking sides and, therefore, goes counter to the neutrality mandated of a good therapist. It is important to note that the therapist is not judging who is right or wrong but rather unbalancing the unhealthy stalemate.

The therapist can unbalance the family system in the following ways:

1. Align with a family member who has less power. The therapist aligns with a family member not because he or necessarily agrees with that member's position but because they want to lend power to a family member to modify the structure. The therapist might say, "I can see why you would feel that way" or "She needs to be convinced of your position."
2. Refuse to recognize a family member. This technique is extremely powerful because it challenges the excluded family member's need to belong. A disengaged, oppositional, or controlling member of the family may begin to fight the therapist for a way back into the family. Because the therapist controls this interaction, they can influence how a family member comes back in; that is, the price of admission may be participation or tolerance or whatever facilitates an improved system (Hanna & Brown, 1999, p. 211).

Boundary restructuring is used to realign boundaries by either increasing closeness or distance. Dysfunctional families are characterized by overly rigid or diffuse boundaries.

In very close or highly enmeshed families, the therapist strengthens the boundaries be-tween subsystems and attempts to increase the independence of the family members. For example, family members are urged to speak for themselves, anyone who tries to interrupt will be blocked. This occurs when therapists have to help parents to stop children from in-terrupting their dialogue.

Families that are detached or disengaged avoid conflict to minimize interaction with one another. The therapist must prevent escape or avoidance and help the family members to learn to face one another. This involves learning first to express feelings directly and then to resolve with positive interaction.

Paradoxes are cognitive constructions that frustrate or confuse family members into searching for alternatives to their present situation. The technique is paradoxical because occasionally people must do things in apparent opposition to their goals in order to reach those goals. It gives families and their members permission to do something they are al-ready doing and is intended to eliminate or lower resistance.

Haley (1976), one of the leading proponents of this technique, believes that paradox takes many forms, including the use of restraining, prescribing, and redefining.

1. In *restraining,* the therapist tells the family that they are incapable of doing anything other than what they are doing. For example, a therapist might say, "In considering change, I am not sure you can do anything other than what you are presently doing."
2. In *prescribing,* family members are instructed to enact a troublesome dysfunctional behavior in front of the therapist. For instance, parents may be asked to show they argue with their sixteen-year-old about when he will do his schoolwork or clean his room. They are to continue the argument for the same amount of time it usually takes and to come up with the same impasses.
3. *Redefining* is attributing positive connotations to symptomatic or troublesome ac-tions. The idea is that symptoms have meaning for those who display them, whether such meaning is logical or not. In the case of an acting-out child, the therapist might redefine the child's behavior as an attempt to keep her parents together in the mar-riage by focusing their attention on her.

Mozdzierz et al. (1976) expand this list as they briefly describe 12 paradoxical tech-niques:

1. Making a *neutral response* to inflammatory comments when an angry or defensive response is expected.
2. Giving clients *permission* to maintain the symptom as necessary and, probably, de-sirable.
3. *Encouraging* clients to postpone their decision, thus delaying or prolonging the cri-sis situation.
4. *Forbidding* the clients to do what they already are not doing to avoid injury.
5. *Predicting* the return of the symptom.
6. *Exaggerating* the symptoms by taking them even more seriously than clients pre-sented them in their complaints.
7. *Championing the cause* for retaining the symptom.

8. *Redefining the symptom* from the negative to the positive.
9. Prescribing continuation of negative behavior, but under the direction, control, and cooperation of the therapist.
10. Encouraging the clients to *practice the symptom more* and work at improving their performance.
11. Treating the symptom as a valuable skill and requesting clients to *teach the symptom to the therapist.*
12. Provoking clients by *pairing a negative behavior of the client as the opposite of a behavior or trait about himself of which he is pleased* and proud. How could he do such a thing?

The use of paradox is powerful provided the therapist chooses the correct situation and proper time. Paradox always must be presented in a sincere manner to work effectively.

CREATING DIFFERENT BEHAVIOR

Most treatment begins by breaking up the patterns that support the problems. Once the patterns are disrupted the therapist needs to create new patterns. Often clients do not have the skills necessary to create or maintain new patterns. The therapist, therefore, needs to provide education to the client (Berger & Hannah, 1999; Carlson & Dinkmeyer, 2002).

Essentially the therapist needs to help the client to do something different. By changing the behavior and not the rules of the system the therapist has created what is called *first order* change. This means that the change has been on the surface. The therapist needs to create *second order* or permanent change. This involves an actual behavior change that changes the system itself and the rules that govern its operation. For example, it is possible to have a client share feelings that they have never before expressed and feel good about the catharsis. However, if the context does not continue to provide a safe place for expression it is unlikely that this level of expression will be maintained. In this case, first order change would be the catharsis and second order change would be the creation of an environment where honest expression was encouraged and supported.

Communication is often viewed as the fundamental source of problems or pathology. Faulty or unclear communication results in inaccurate or incomplete feedback so the system cannot self-correct (change its rules) and consequently overreacts or underreacts to change. Therapists need to teach clients effective communication as well as other skills that allow them to relate in a healthy fashion.

Teaching clients *communication* seems to be a core skill of most approaches to therapy. The instruction usually includes both the modeling and instruction of effective communication. Modeling is often the first step in teaching communication skills. The therapist must believe enough in the importance of communication to make it a part of their daily life. The therapist needs to model skills such as: listening, expressing a compliment, expressing appreciation, asking for help, giving feedback, and expressing affection. It is important to break each of these skills down into small, easy to follow steps. Each client will need very different skills. For example, some partners need to be quiet while others need to speak up; some need to listen while others need to talk; and, some need to assert themselves while others need to let them.

Learning to Resolve Conflict and Negotiate Problems

Central to the problem-solving process is to identify as many goals as possible. This process is based on the premise that there are many possible ways to handle a problem, people usually are aware of ways to solve a problem, and that generating solutions increases the chances that a good solution will be selected. Therapists know that clients who develop their own solutions are more likely to carry them out.

The basic strategy for creating possible solutions is brainstorming. The rules for brainstorming are that all solutions are accepted, solutions can be improved on, and as many solutions as possible should be generated. The therapist can use statements such as the following:

"Let's think of some ways that you can handle this situation."
"What ideas have you thought of that might be used?"
"Can you think of anything to add to the suggestion?"

The therapist needs to be very interested in what the client has tried so far and why they believe it did not work. The therapist works with the client to develop solutions that will reduce the severity of the problem. Problems need not be seen as signs of failure but rather can be viewed as feedback along the way to a successful solution. Sharing this philosophy with the client helps to normalize the problem.

Sometimes clients have a very difficult time seeing any solutions. Solution-oriented therapists help clients to identify any exceptions to the present pattern. The therapist helps the client look for times when the problem did not exist or was less severe. The assumption of this approach is that if there were times when they were problem-free they can learn how to create those situations again.

The therapist asks the client, "Was there ever a time when you didn't (state problem)?" The client usually can identify such a time even if it was many years before. The therapist helps the client to look at just how they behaved differently at that time. They specifically need to look at how they avoided the conflict/problem. From this discussion the client almost always can identify some behaviors that they can experiment with.

CHOICES AND PROBLEM SOLVING

Clients are always making choices. Some are conscious while others are unconscious. Not all choices are important and often people allow others to make choices for them. Oftentimes, clients get into trouble when they confuse what happens by choice with what happens by chance. Even when clients do realize that they have choices to make, they may find it very difficult making those choices.

Therapists need to help clients to understand the choice-making process (Glasser, 1998). Clients are often afraid and uncertain and fail to make choices that could shape and control their lives. It is important that clients realize that when they avoid making conscious choices that they are choosing to keep things as they are. Avoidance is acceptance. By not choosing they lose the opportunity for positive change.

The process of choice-making begins with awareness of the many areas in life in which we have opportunities to choose. Research indicates that what we say, how we feel, what we think, and how we act are all choices. It is actually hopeful for clients to realize that they *can* choose to be different.

It is important to be clear of the areas in which we can choose, as well as to learn to identify the instant when we can exercise our power to choose. If we are unaware of our moment of choice, we respond out of habit rather than as a result of having considered our options. Following every situation, or stimulus, there is an instant when we decide. By learning to identify the instant when a decision is possible, the client can begin to make choices that are in line with their goals. Many individuals are quick to believe they are unable to make instantaneous discriminations. They believe that "I can't control my anger" or that "I always panic in such situations." Therapists can help them to rethink this by asking them if they could control their anger at church or in front of a police officer. Once they can accept the fact that it is possible to identify the moment of choice they can begin to take control over the direction of their life.

Use the following choice-making guidelines when you need to develop new choices.

1. Learn to identify the instant when you have the possibility to choose.
2. Clearly identify what you want to achieve.
3. Identify your alternatives and assess the potential gains and drawbacks of each. Develop the habit of asking yourself, "What are my options? Are there any choices I might have overlooked?" Or, "If somebody offered me $1,000,000 to discover another solution, could I?"
4. Make choices that allow you to make maximum use of your strengths and abilities.
5. Become aware of how your choices affect others. How are your choices influenced by others? Will your choice be harmful or helpful to your relationships?
6. Make your choice and take responsibility for making the choice work.
7. Remember, a choice can be changed.

ASSIGNING TASKS

Tasks or homework can be assigned clients to change the sequence of interaction in their life. They may be used to help a client become more organized, establish operational boundaries, set rules, or establish family goals (Madanes, 1981). Tasks might include: (a) advice, (b) explanations or suggestions, or (c) directives to change the interactional sequence in the family (Papp, 1980). Tasks may be unsuccessful because clients may want to do something but do not know how to do it. Haley (1976) offers several suggestions to therapists for getting clients to follow their tasks or homework assignments:

1. Discuss everything the client has done to try to solve the problem. By this device the therapist can avoid making suggestions that already have been tried. The therapist

should lead the client to the conclusion that everything has been tried but nothing has worked. At this point the therapist is in a position to offer something different.

2. Ask the client to discuss the negative consequences if their problem is not handled now (i.e., "What will happen if the problem is not resolved?"). The potential consequences will be different for different people in the situation. Nevertheless examining the negative consequences for each person will emphasize the intensity of the problem.

3. Assign a task or homework that is reasonable and easily accomplished. To help the client complete the task outside of the session, practice it within the session. The therapist can coach the client and provide any missing directives.

4. Assign a task to fit the ability and performance level of the client. The task needs to be doable by the client.

5. Use authority to get the client to follow the homework assignment. There are times to ask the client what to do and times when the therapist uses their authority. The therapist is viewed as an expert by the client and they can state "From my experience. . . ." Or "From my vantage point, I think that. . . ."

6. Give clear instructions to the client. The responsibilities need to be spelled out clearly. The client needs to be asked if there is anything that might interfere with their completion of the task. Any concerns should be discussed and resolved.

By following these suggestions, therapists can help their clients to change both the structure and context of their lives.

SUMMARY

Systemic and structural techniques are very effective ways to disrupt ineffective behavioral patterns. The therapist uses these strategies to help the client create different views of reality and to develop new behavior patterns. The ideas often appear too simplistic, however this is deceptive. These are among the most powerful strategies in a therapist's repertoire of interventions.

REFERENCES

Berger, R. & Hannah, M. T. (1999). *Preventive approaches in couples therapy.* Philadelphia: Brunner/Mazel.

Carlson, J. & Dinkmeyer, D. (2002). *Time for a better marriage.* Atascadero, CA: Impact Publishers.

Glasser, W. (1998). *Choice theory: A new psychology of personal freedom.* New York: Harper Collins.

Haley, J. (1976). *Problem-solving therapy.* San Francisco: Jossey-Bass.

Hanna, S. M. & Brown, J. H. (1999). *The practice of family therapy: Key elements across models.* Pacific Grove, CA: Brooks Cole/Wadsworth.

Hoffman, L. (1981). *Foundations of family therapy.* New York: Basic Books

Madanes, C. (1981). *Strategic family therapy.* San Francisco: Jossey Bass.

Minuchin, S. (1974). *Families and family therapy.* Cambridge, MA: Harvard University Press.

Mozdzierz, G. J., Macchitelli, F. J., & Lisecki, J. (1976). The paradox in psychotherapy: An Adlerian perspective. *Journal of Individual Psychology, 32*(2), 169–184.

Papp, P. (1980). The use of fantasy in a couple's group. In M. Andolfi & I. Zwerling (Eds.). *Dimensions of family therapy* (pp. 73–90). New York: Guilford.

Piercy, F. & Sprenkle, D. (1986). *Family therapy sourcebook.* New York: Guilford.

Sherman, R. & Fredman, N. (1986). *Handbook of structured techniques in marriage and family therapy.* New York: Brunner/Mazel.

Sherman, R. & Dinkmeyer, D. (1987). *Systems of family therapy: An Adlerian integration.* New York: Brunner/Mazel.

■ ■ ■ ■ ■ ▬▬▬▬▬▬▬▬▬▬▬▬▬▬▬▬▬▬▬▬▬▬▬▬▬▬▬▬▬▬▬▬▬

CHAPTER 11

MAINTAINING CLINICAL GAINS, PREVENTING RELAPSE, AND TERMINATING TREATMENT

WHAT YOU WILL LEARN IN THIS CHAPTER

1. Strategies to maintain therapeutic change
2. What relapse prevention is and how to utilize it
3. How to effectively terminate and setup treatment follow up

Therapists are traditionally trained to identify, diagnose, and remediate a full spectrum of psychopathology (Sperry & Carlson, 1996). Although counselors and therapists are initially successful in helping clients improve their status, follow-up research shows that seldom do these gains maintain themselves. The degree to which clients follow through with, adhere to, or maintain the planned treatment change process is very low. Failure to adhere is a major obstacle to successful change, although counselors often deny or are very surprised that it is so common.

Therapists have had extensive treatment in frontloading the helping process by putting all their resources into identification, diagnosis, and remediation and very little into treatment adherence and relapse prevention. It is necessary for counselors to have a clear conception of not only how to help distressed clients but also how to maintain those gains once they are reached. It is becoming increasingly obvious that termination should not imply an end to treatment as much as it does a change in treatment intensity.

A great challenge for the therapist is to gain the ability to predict therapeutic success and maintenance. Some treatments seem to be likely to have long-term effectiveness while others are probably temporary, at best. What can therapists do to change the therapeutic conditions in order to increase long-term treatment success and prevent a relapse or return to previous levels of dysfunction? How long do effects last after successful intervention? What percentage of clients relapse after successful treatment? What distinguishes those who maintain treatment gains from those who relapse? What causes or creates relapse? Can relapses be prevented or minimized? This chapter addresses these questions and describes how therapists can create treatment adherence and reduce relapse and failure.

TREATMENT ADHERENCE/MAINTENANCE

No one set of adherence enhancement procedures will be successful across populations. More than 20 years ago, Epstein and Masek (1978) catalogued more than 30 different techniques designed to increase medical patient adherence. Examples of techniques that we have found helpful are:

1. Provide specific appointment times
2. Use reminders (mail, telephone)
3. Elicit and discuss reasons for previously missed appointments
4. Involve client in planning and implementation of the treatment program
5. Tailor the treatment plan
6. Simplify the treatment directives
7. Use psychoeducation and check for comprehension
8. Anticipate side effects
9. Process any negative feedback
10. Teach self-management skills
11. Use graduated regimen implementation
12. Involve significant others
13. Use role playing and paradoxical techniques when appropriate
14. Use a combination of approaches rather than single strategies

We have found it is essential to diagnose and assess each instance of nonadherence and to be flexible and tailor procedures to the specific circumstances and characteristics of the client. For example, a couple returns to therapy after one week indicating that the assigned homework of conducting a daily 10-minute dialogue was completed on only one day. The couple was asked to discuss their understanding as to why the assignment was not completed. After each person gave his or her explanation, a more detailed assignment was developed. A specific time was established, and a modified plan to meet every other day was agreed to. The couple was willing to conduct the activity, however, they needed assistance in changing present behavioral patterns.

TREATMENT ADHERENCES GUIDELINES

As we have previously discussed, the therapist needs to begin the treatment process with a comprehensive assessment. The therapist not only needs to diagnose the client's clinical condition but also needs to diagnose or assess the chances and reasons for nonadherence. The counselor must assess the client's adherence history, beliefs, expectations, and possible barriers or obstacles to adherence.

Once this has taken place, the following eight guidelines (adapted from Meichenbaum & Turk, 1987) will be useful.

1. Anticipate Nonadherence

Therapists need to begin to think about adherence at the beginning of treatment, often when information is provided by the referral source. The therapist must carefully weigh all data provided, especially those about treatment, length of problem, locus of responsibility, and extent of problem. Many clients are confused and misinformed about the process of therapy (that is, who does what). It is usually helpful to begin therapy by asking:

  a. Why have you come to treatment?
  b. What have you heard or been told about treatment?
  c. What do you expect to happen during treatment?
  d. What do you hope will be different after treatment?

The counselor also needs to assess factors that may facilitate or impede treatment such as rapport, readiness to learn or change, and willingness to accept responsibility.
Specifically, the therapist needs to assess factors such as:

  a. The client's expectation for treatment (if treatment is successful, how will you know? What will be different?)
  b. The beliefs and misconceptions about the cause, severity, and symptoms of the problem (would you give your explanation of the problem and describe how you believe it can be changed?)
  c. The goals of treatment (what do you want to accomplish in therapy?)
  d. The client's commitment to treatment (that is, how badly do you want to change?). (On a scale of 1 to 10 with 1 being low and 10 high, how important is it to you that change occurs?)
  e. The present level of skills
  f. The sense of helplessness and hopelessness versus resourcefulness, mastery and self-efficacy (how optimistic are you that the situation can be changed? Give a ranking on the 1 to 10 scale; have you ever brought about change in other aspects of your life?)
  g. Educational or physical limitations
  h. The life circumstances that may affect adherence (that is, limited time, limited financial resources) (what are some things that might get in the way of successful change?).

The preceding information is usually gathered directly using questions similar to the examples or indirectly in the initial interview. The information is used in tailoring the approach to deal with possible adherence problems. The therapist who anticipates nonadherence can usually make the corrections necessary to maximize treatment adherence.

2. Consider Treatment from the Client's Perspective

The therapist should not assume that his or her perception of events is the same as the clients. Clients come to treatment with certain attitudes, beliefs, expectations, and resources. The therapist should *join* the client (Minuchin, 1974). In this process the therapist adjusts to the communication style and perceptions of the client.

There are aspects of personality style conviction that guide a client's behaviors and habits. These beliefs form an explanatory model that aids the client in making sense of problems and events: how they respond, how they describe events, and how they cope with situations. This model also gives insight into the client's expectation for treatment, the outcome, and level of participation. The therapist needs to understand the client's explanatory model in order to develop a lasting intervention.

Additionally, the therapist must realize that clients have other commitments, demands, and life circumstances that may make the problem easier to maintain/support than its solutions. Clients live and have their problems supported within a social network. It *cannot be assumed* that just because someone has a problem and brings it to a therapist that they will adhere to change.

3. Facilitate a Collaborative Relationship that Is Based on Negotiation

A wise therapist knows how to avoid resistance by involving the client in the decisional process regarding their treatment: An acceptable treatment plan that is carried out appropriately is much better than an ideal one that is ignored. The therapist must be willing to negotiate within reason.

The therapist needs to use the client's words, ideas, and explanatory model in developing a treatment plan. The plan must flow from the client, using statements such as "It sounds like you want to . . ." or "It looks like you want . . . to happen in this way . . ." or "You seem to be in touch with the need to . . ."

4. Be Client Oriented (Understand the Client's Views/Explanatory Model)

What are the client's views, expectations, and knowledge concerning the problem and treatment? Do they believe they can successfully adhere to the treatment? Do they believe the treatment will actually work? How important do they feel the treatment is? What barriers does the client envision that will prevent or impede successful treatment? What does the client believe can be done to make adherence easier?

It is important to listen not only to what the client says but also to what they fail to say. The failure of the client to answer certain questions usually indicates that they are not collaborating and will not follow the treatment plan.

5. Tailor Treatment

As we have discussed, there is no standard treatment for any client. In considering a set of treatment recommendations, the therapist must consider, adjust, and modify treatment to fit each client.

As a general rule, treatment plans should be effective, simple, convenient, produce the fewest side effects, and require the least interference with normal daily activities. Whenever possible, connect adherence behaviors to normal daily routines such as meals, bedtime, time of awakening, and so on. Clients will need assistance in integrating new demands on their daily routines. For example, a suggestion of talking for 10 minutes each night at bedtime is more likely to be adhered to than talking during the day.

6. Enlist Family Support

Generally it is useful to make sure that the client and other significant people understand the treatment plan and goals in order to be allies. Therapists need to keep asking questions such as "Tell me again what you believe needs to be done and what exactly you are working on."

7. Provide a System of Continuity and Accessibility

Clients need to know that the therapist views the treatment process as lifelong and is therefore accessible at various stages in the client life cycle. The therapist needs to be an ally who is accessible, nonjudgmental, respectful, and sincere in the willingness to cooperate with them. The open-ended therapy model (Lebow, 1995) sees clients making use of treatment at various times in the life cycle.

8. Do Not Give Up

Many therapists write off nonadherence to system resistance. This allows them to blame the client and excuse themselves of any responsibility. However, skilled therapists must navigate the waters of resistance and develop tailored treatment plans. A well-designed plan will create cooperation and treatment adherence. It is this challenge that makes working with the client so rewarding.

WHAT IS RELAPSE PREVENTION?

Relapse prevention (RP) is a self-control program designed to teach clients who are trying to change their behavior how to anticipate and cope with the problem of relapse. In a very real sense, relapse refers to a breakdown or failure in a system's attempt to change or modify behaviors and adhere to treatment. Traditionally, based on the principles of social-learning theory (Bandura, 1977), RP is a psychoeducational program that combines behavioral skill-training procedures and cognitive intervention techniques with systems thinking.

The RP model was initially developed as a behavioral maintenance program for use in the treatment of addictive behaviors (Marlatt & Gordon, 1985). In the case of addiction, the typical goals of treatment are either to refrain totally from performing a target behavior (for example, to abstain from drug use) or to impose regulatory limits or controls over the occurrence of a behavior (for instance, to use diet as a means of controlling food intake).

The concept of RP has become a central focus of research and practice in health psychology and behavioral medicine. Because nonadherence, previously called noncompliance, with treatment is so high, ranging from 30 to 80 percent (Sperry, 1986), clinicians have sought ways to reverse this phenomenon. At the most general level, relapse is a return of a problem behavior following a problem-free period. The recent *Webster's New Collegiate Dictionary* refers to relapse as both an outcome and a process. The *outcome* is reflected in the use of the term *relapse* to denote "a recurrence of symptoms of a disease after a period of improvement," and the *process* is captured in the phrase "the act or instance of backsliding, worsening, or subsiding." The *process* implies that something has occurred that may or may not lead to a relapse.

Whether the process or outcome definition of relapse is chosen, it has obvious implications for the conceptualization, prevention, and treatment of relapse. Viewing relapse as a process, and not an outcome, implies that there are choice points in the process where the therapist and client can intervene (Ludgate, 1995). Marlatt and Gordon (1985) distinguish between lapse and relapse, arguing that a lapse implies a temporary state of affairs that might under some circumstances lead to a relapse. How a client responds to an initial lapse will determine whether a full relapse will occur. It is generally conceded that the prediction and prevention of relapses is desirable because the continuation of behavioral problems may reduce a client's quality of life and place limitations on the successful pursuit of goals. The understanding of relapse and the RP program can be used to ensure treatment adherence.

RELAPSE PREVENTION RESEARCH

Unfortunately, most research studies have been designed to measure outcome of treatment rather than long-term maintenance or effectiveness. Identification of RP properties in treatment is usually post hoc rather than a part of the original research plans. However, there is some research that can be useful in helping to understand the importance of RP.

Research by Bogner and Zielenbach-Coenen (1984) demonstrated that length in the intervals between the final therapy sessions does facilitate a couple's ability to benefit from marital therapy both initially and in the long term.

Whisman (1991) investigated the effectiveness of booster sessions on RP. This research used two mandatory booster sessions at three and six months after therapy and three optional sessions during the same six-month period. The results were not statistically significant. However, these findings seem to suggest that booster sessions deserve further attention and refinement; however, they do not unequivocally support booster session's efficacy. Whisman, however, outlined several ways the efficacy of booster sessions could have been improved, including using an experienced therapist, improving the booster session content, scheduling additional booster session during the first three post-therapy months, and extending the length of the maintenance component.

Truax and Jacobson (1992) felt that although no treatment differences can be supported at this time by research, there appears to be some treatment characteristics that emerge. These characteristics seem to support the use of matched and tailored treatment. The use of the traditional one-size-fits-all therapy does not seem to be supported by long-term maintenance assessments. Following are five treatment characteristics that emerged in their research:

1. Flexibility in Treatment Content

Despite many common themes among clients, each client is unique. The treatment must therefore be tailored carefully. The content of therapy may focus on thoughts, behavior, feelings, past, present, future, and so forth.

2. Flexibility in Treatment Format

Therapists need to structure the length and spacing of sessions according to the interaction and the purpose of the therapy. For example, traditional one-hour weekly sessions seldom work during the initial sessions of therapy or when skill training is needed.

3. Identifying and Modifying Salient Behaviors (Overt, Emotional, Cognitive)

It is important to gather a complete picture of the client's functioning. Often therapists and clients stop treatment after the presenting problem disappears only to resume treatment after a short passage of time.

4. Focusing on Reasonably Changeable Behaviors

Many behavioral changes may temporarily improve client satisfaction, but it is unlikely they all can be maintained. It is important to focus on behaviors that can be maintained. For example, if a client is guided to an interaction that leads to increased understanding and a spontaneous hug, this interaction is more likely to be repeated.

5. Effectively Generalizing from Therapy to the Client's World

This is perhaps the greatest challenge to relapse prevention. In addition to the ideas discussed in this book, the therapist must be able to design interventions that facilitate generalization from the therapeutic environment to the daily life of the client. Several steps have been recommended by Truax and Jacobson (1992) to improve generalization:

a. Maximizing the client's natural reinforcement potential
b. Assigning homework throughout therapy
c. Lengthen intervals between final sessions
d. Including booster sessions
e. Predicting stressful events (p. 315)

WHY CLIENTS RELAPSE

Essentially clients relapse because they are supposed to. Seldom does behavior permanently change, so that former behaviors never occur. However, relapse has often been seen as synonymous with treatment failure, a return to a previous behavior after a period of gain or change, and it is often viewed as an end state. This all-or-nothing perception fails to take into account that relapse is a common component of effective change. Mistakes and lapses are human and common in the change process. By allowing room in the treatment process for mistakes to occur (relapses), it is possible to avoid what has been called the *oscillation effect,* whereby a system is either in control or out of control. When relapse is expected and planned for, the affective and cognitive reactions to slips become significantly less intense, and the treatment program can be quickly reinstated. The length of the relapse period often depends on the personal expectations of the system involved. So, rather than a relapse being a dead end, it becomes a fork in the road with one path moving toward the old patterns and the other to the new ones.

Many people believe that quitting a pattern of behavior has to be all or nothing. Once a mistake has occurred they believe it is for all time and that intervention did not work. Many attribute the cause of relapse to a personal or family weakness or failure, such as the lack of willpower, weakness of character, or problematic family composition, rather than to difficulty of the tasks and the predictability of slips occurring during the course of change. The belief that total control is the only control needs to be challenged. People need to be taught how to view change on a continuum of where they are to where they hope to be.

Therapists must be aware that the combination of high-risk situations and no coping responses and negative expectancies increases the likelihood that relapse will occur. High-risk situations pose a threat to the system's sense of self-control and increases the risk of potential relapse. The three most common high-risk categories associated with a high relapse rate (Marlatt & Gordon, 1985) are (1) negative emotional state, (2) interpersonal conflict, and (3) social pressure. To this list we might add (4) highly charged anniversary dates. It is often helpful to work with clients to plan responses to these challenging situations. Simple discussion and the ability to be aware of high-risk situations are simple yet effective procedures.

If clients are taught a coping response in these high-risk situations, the likelihood of relapse can be decreased. This results in the development of a feeling of control or mastery similar to the concept of self-efficacy (Bandura, 1977). The client thereby develops feelings of confidence and knowledge that they can handle life's problems. Bandura's research indicates that if someone is successful in coping in one situation, this increases the likelihood that they will be successful in another.

Alfred Adler relates a striving for superiority to the achievement of mastery and overcoming feelings of helplessness. His approach to treatment is based on the client attempting to become more effective at controlling their environment. According to Adler, demoralized clients must be taken through "various devices to the point where they necessarily acquire faith in their own mental and physical powers . . . One must put tasks in their way which they can accomplish and from the accomplishment of which they gain faith in themselves" (Ansbacher & Ansbacher, 1956, p. 400). It is important for clients to feel empowered or encouraged if they are going to be able to maintain therapeutic gains.

A person usually acquires a sense of mastery through success experiences, although a cognitive framework that links a person's performance to their self-image is also necessary. In other words, the success experience must be meaningful and believable to the client. This meaningfulness, or link between performance and self-esteem, is governed by several variables including the client's background and current situation, task relevance, task difficulty, attribution of performance, and attitudes of significant others. This should not appear to be surprising as the primary goal of therapy is to help clients to acquire self-control and to change their image of someone who is overwhelmed by problems to one who can master them. Clients who have an increased sense of mastery over their behaviors, thoughts, and feelings are more willing to attempt to handle situations that they previously avoided. Through an increased sense of competence, a client develops more positive expectancies regarding their performance in difficult situations.

The client's belief or expectation that relapse will occur seems to be a powerful predictor of relapse. Thus, successful relapse prevention needs to address the belief structure of the client. Negative expectancies must be replaced with positive ones that serve as compelling goals. It is important to offer a new story or metaphor for the family that will prevent relapse (O'Hanlon, 1999).

RELAPSE PREVENTION

Relapse prevention is an intervention consisting of specific skills and cognitive strategies that prepare clients in advance to cope with inevitable slips or relapse in compliance to a change program (Marlatt & Gordon, 1985). Although the early work on RP was developed in alcohol and drug treatment programs, in which relapse and return to addictive substances is very high, RP principles have been applied to smoking cessation, pain control, weight management, sleep disorders, exercise adherence, and other health-promotion areas (Sperry, Lewis, Carlson, & Englar-Carlson, 2003).

Daley (1989) describes five different RP models, of which Marlatt and Gordon's (1985) is the most well-known and researched. This cognitive-behavioral model emphasizes the following points:

- Identification of individual high-risk situations
- Development of coping skills for high-risk situations

■ Practice in coping with potential lapses
■ Development of cognitive coping strategies for use immediately after relapse

Marlatt notes that the majority of relapses in adults occurs in response to stressful situations involving conflict or social pressure. He stresses that reframing the relapse as a mistake rather than a factual error or moral shortcoming is an important preventative measure that can help the individual get back on track and learn from the experience. RP helps the individual apply the brakes so that once a slip occurs it does not escalate into a full-blown relapse.

Wilson (1992) identified several different types of RP strategies that have been developed and evaluated to varying degrees with different types of problem behaviors. The techniques include:

1. Booster sessions
2. Treatment programs with RP strategies integrated into the initial treatment
3. Procedures that require minimal therapist contact such as periodic reminder letters (White & Epston, 1990), telephone calls, or the provision of therapy-related reading materials.

Problem behaviors are explained as a series of acquired habit patterns that are governed by cognitive and experimental processes in which antecedent events, beliefs, and expectations, previous learning history, and behavioral consequences play important roles. The maintenance stage of intervention must be considered as a period in which there is an opportunity for new learning to occur as the client is faced with situations, events, moods, and beliefs that might increase the risk of reinstatement of previous ineffective behavioral patterns.

According to Wilson (1992), relapse may occur because of a failure at any one of a number of points from initial treatment to maintenance; an effective treatment may not necessarily lead to perceived control or enhanced self-efficacy. Clients may fail to recognize and respond appropriately to high-risk situations. They may fail to develop adequate coping responses and may still have negative outcome expectancies about the use of effective strategies in future situations. Clients may use ineffective responses, or they may have positive expectancies about the effects of old coping strategies that in reality have failed in the past. They may also make incorrect attributions about the causes of lapse.

A major component of the RP program is the identification of high-risk situations for self-monitoring, self-efficacy ratings, and detailed analysis of past relapse episodes. The aim of these activities is to increase the therapist's knowledge of the factors that might lead to relapse and to increase the client's awareness of how these factors operate.

Throughout therapy, generalizations from therapy to daily life are facilitated through the weekly homework assignments and easing out the therapist reinforcement by increasingly drawing attention to natural reinforcers. By tailoring treatment, the therapist can use homework assignments that are unique to each client. To increase the likelihood that clients will continue active problem solving, the therapist must find a format that incorporates the client's natural problem-solving style. For example, some clients initially can be instructed to note problems by jotting them down. Other clients, however, may find it uncomfortable to wait and need to solve problems on the spot. Thus, it is important for the therapist to identify procedures that a client can use easily. Again, the success of therapy seems to be related to the careful analysis and tailoring of treatment.

CHANGE IN TREATMENT FOCUS

Traditional therapy strategies are much more effective at reducing negative behaviors than at increasing positive ones. Research continues to show that the differences between distressed and nondistressed clients is that distressed clients engage in more negative behaviors, while nondistressed clients exhibit more positive behaviors. Although these findings are not surprising they do not suggest that a simple reduction of negative behaviors without an increase in positive ones is probably not sufficient to help distressed clients to be genuinely happy.

Researchers (Baucom & Hoffman, 1986; Gottman, 1994a; Truax & Jacobson, 1992) believe that therapeutic durability can be improved by identification and creation of positive experiences. Unfortunately, most therapy seems to be focused on the elimination of negative behaviors.

The communication skills taught are generally aimed at problem solving. Thus, a number of destructive communications that interfere with the process often tend to be emphasized. To have meaning, many positive communications must be spontaneous, emerging from the person's internal thoughts and feelings about the partner or the topic (Baucom & Hoffman, 1986, p. 600).

Therefore, by changing the treatment focus to increasing positive behaviors, clients can learn to define progress based on realistic goals. It may be wise to help clients use the problem-solving process as a way to increase positive behaviors rather than to solve the problems themselves (which are often not reasonably solvable).

Research seems to support the notion that a client's ability to maintain therapeutic gains may well be affected by the discrepancy between their satisfaction levels (Whisman, 1991). Thus one client may focus attention on reasonable and maintainable behavioral changes. Unfortunately, therapists often bite off more than they can chew. When clients attempt to resolve conflicts that are not solvable, they may become more deeply entrenched in hopelessness. It is often more helpful for the therapist to first focus on helping clients understand their internal experiences without rushing to a conclusion. Therapists need to pay special attention to behaviors that are naturally reinforcing both in and out of sessions for the client.

A typical response to relapse is to increase the number of treatment interventions in order to create a more comprehensive broad-based package. This response seems to be based on the belief that more is better; the more treatment components, therefore, the longer the results will last. However, evidence suggests that the more techniques and procedures applied, the more difficult it becomes to maintain compliance. In addition, it seems that most intervention techniques are aimed at *initial* behavior change and not at the *maintenance* of the changed behavior. One of the main differences between initial and maintenance procedures is the initial techniques are usually administered by the therapist, while the maintenance procedures are mostly self-administered. (An obvious exception to this distinction is the use of booster sessions.)

OPEN-ENDED THERAPY

A useful perspective for the therapist is to think in terms of treating clients over a lifetime. The likelihood of one set of meetings putting a permanent end to problems throughout the lifespan is not great. It is much more helpful to view problems as occurring at different points in the lifespan and seeing therapy as a resource that can be used to resolve these difficulties. The therapist therefore becomes a resource, similar to the medical practitioner. Regarding therapy in this way establishes a direct manner of dealing with the deterioration that seems to occur after successful therapy.

At the beginning of therapy, the therapist presents the notion of termination with an open-ended viewpoint. The therapist discusses the benefits of having a planned termination; however, he or she also discusses the value of ongoing involvement. Working toward termination occurs throughout the therapeutic meetings.

Lebow (1995) highlights ten tasks that are central to ending most family therapy.

1. *Tracking progress in therapy to determine the appropriateness of ending.* This task involves regular assessment of how the client is progressing toward treatment goals.
2. *Reviewing the course of treatment.* The therapist provides time for the client to review the changes and events that occurred in the treatment process.
3. *Emphasizing the gains made and the client's role in the gains.* Often clients do not fully understand the extent of change nor their role in how change occurred. It is important to help the client realize the sense of competence and confidence that can occur by understanding one's role in successful change.
4. *Abstracting what has been learned from the treatment and how it may be applied later.* The therapist helps the client understand the behavioral, affective, and cognitive skills that have been developed and how they may be used as future problems occur.
5. *Internalizing the therapist.* The client needs to learn how to have the therapist remain with them, not as an active member or participant in their life but as an internalized member. Family members are often encouraged to develop skills by imaging what the therapist would say or suggest they do at a particular moment.
6. *Regarding the ending through the lens of other endings in life.* Therapists should develop an understanding of each client's unique history of endings. Some clients have a difficult time with endings while others find them comfortable.
7. *Saying good-bye with an opportunity to express gratitude and exchange feelings.*
8. *Discussing the conditions for returning to treatment.* Booster sessions may be used to promote the durability of change. These sessions are scheduled at regular intervals to renew skills and insights.
9. *Referring.* Sometimes ending work with one therapist opens the door to future work with another, such as moving on to some form of self-help group or educational

class. In some cases, the ending of treatment with one therapist occurs when a referral is made to another professional who has different skills.

10. *Defining post-treatment availability.*

STEPS TO RELAPSE PREVENTION

Relapse prevention has many potential applications for therapy. One of the most obvious involves providing therapy with clients in maintenance (that is, open-ended treatment) whereby the therapists will not only predict relapses but preventively intervene by preparing the client for them. There are five steps that can facilitate RP.

1. Create a Treatment Alliance

Effective intervention involves engaging the client in the therapy process, helping them to actively and collaboratively participate through complying with homework assignments. Success seems to be based on the client's level of involvement in and adherence to therapy. Researchers consistently discover that the level of client involvement is related to therapy outcome (Holtzworth-Munroe, Jacobson, DeKlyen, & Whisman, 1989). Active collaboration in the tasks appropriate to the treatment process may be conceptualized as treatment alliance.

2. Tailor Treatment

It appears that a high level of involvement or engagement needs to be sustained in the client relationship to produce effective long-term therapeutic change. How can this level of involvement be maintained to produce permanent change? The ability to engage a client effectively in the therapeutic process depends largely on the therapist's ability to provide highly structured treatment that is tailored to the needs of a particular client. In addition, as we also mentioned, matching intervention strategies to a particular client is an often neglected area of treatment. However, it is not surprising that the one size fits all therapies are not as durable as those that can directly address each client's specific concerns. The ability to match and tailor treatment according to how particular clients conceptualize their distress will greatly increase the maintenance of positive behaviors.

Although many therapists advocate the ideas of matching and tailoring in theory, practice shows that therapists tend to treat all clients with basically the same methods and approaches. The therapists act as if their ideas and intervention strategies are good for everyone. However, Jacobson, Schmaling, and Holtzworth-Munroe (1987) reported that individual tailoring of treatment plans and resultant idiographic flexibility can significantly reduce relapse.

3. Manage Stress

Another important consideration is the need to predict external stressors on the client. These stressors are often related to stages of life and are predictable. Research indicates that booster sessions and training in stress management (Sperry & Carlson, 1993) can be very helpful in this area. However, one should remember that just the use of booster sessions alone does not appear to be enough to prevent relapse. The therapist should initiate RP programming in the early stages of therapy and maintain it throughout treatment rather than wait for a relapse to occur.

4. Increase Positive Interaction and Encouragement

Satisfied people are in positive relationships. Researchers such as Gottman (1994a; 1994b) conclude that a ratio of five positives to each negative is crucial. The good moments of passion, humor, support, kindness, and generosity need to outweigh the bad moments of complaint, criticism, anger, disgust, contempt, defensiveness, and coldness. When clients learn the skills of encouragement (Dinkmeyer & Losoncy, 1980) they increase the likelihood of maintaining their gains.

5. Skill Training

Perhaps the most important determinant of relapse is whether effective skill training has occurred and whether these strategies were tailored to the client's needs in advance of stressful situations.

Perhaps the greatest challenge in promoting relapse prevention involves designing skills and interventions that facilitate generalization from the therapy to the client's daily life. Unless the client becomes self-sufficient and is able to often reinforce it, the therapy is likely to fail once the therapist has left. As mentioned previously, researchers have established several steps to improve generalization from treatment to home: (1) maximizing the client's natural reinforcement potential; (2) assigning homework through therapy; (3) lengthen intervals between final sessions; and, (4) predicting stressful life events (Truax & Jacobson, 1992).

TERMINATION

Each therapeutic approach has its unique approach to termination. The common feature is awareness on the part of both the client and therapist that the task has been more or less accomplished and further therapy is not needed. We do not, however, believe that therapy is ever *ended*. There really is no clear cut ending anyway. There is no need to continue therapy beyond its present usefulness, however, as long as you live you will have problems and hardships. Clients need to be encouraged to return to therapy whenever the need arises.

Sometimes therapists terminate treatment with a story or metaphor. One common one is that of having a broken leg. Imagine that someone has had leg problems and underwent surgery. The leg is now fixed, although it may be sensitive for years to come. Of course the client should live a normal life but be careful to avoid unnecessary risks or hazards. It is possible on certain days, such as when it rains, that the leg will experience pain or tenderness. The client will not need another surgery but it might be advisable to call the physician and go for a check-up. It is important to note that it is also possible to have another injury and need further surgery.

Types of Termination

1. *Suggested termination.* The therapist proposes to the client that from their viewpoint the client has made significant progress and is close to the goals of treatment. The therapist suggests that if further issues do not arrive in the next few weeks' therapy has been successful. The client is given an opportunity to see if their view corresponds to that of the therapist and to discuss whether termination is agreeable.
2. *Imposed termination.* The therapist believes that further treatment is against the client's best interest. The therapist might employ this type of termination when the client is deteriorating in treatment or seems to be incompatible with the therapist. This might also be utilized when clients are using therapy in place of life. Some clients substitute therapy for a real life relationship.
3. *Situational termination.* This type of termination happens when clients move due to employment or insurance plans no longer cover the therapist or further sessions. This type of termination is created by external situations rather than in the best interests of the client. This can create anger on the part of the client and guilt for the therapist. The therapist might find it helpful to assist the client to realize what was accomplished within the given circumstances and that most things in life have limits. The therapist should try to refer the client to another treatment source.
4. *Early termination.* This occurs when clients stop treatment prematurely, that is before the benefits of treatment were reached. Frequently clients drop out without giving any notice. That is without giving any formal notice. The effective therapist will notice signs of early termination such as noncompliance with homework, unwillingness to disclose in sessions or missed appointments. It is imperative for the therapist to attempt to contact the client and to determine what is going on and that the client is not being abandoned.

Methods and Process of Termination

The main methods of treatment involve gradually weaning or tapering off sessions, therapeutic vacations, and direct termination. Each can serve useful purposes. Tapering sessions can be done at whatever level the client and therapist are comfortable. Therapeutic vacations give the client a chance to be on their own without losing a formal connection. The use of direct termination depends a lot on the client and whether they can deal with an abrupt ending. The therapist carefully considers the most effective way for the client to leave therapy.

The therapist must consider questions like:

1. How will the termination impact the client?
2. What is the client's history of separations? Is the client likely to regress?

3. What is the client's reaction/opinion about termination? Can they see it as a positive step?

In conclusion, termination means that at a certain time, the client or therapist determines that the benefits of continuing in therapy are minimal or outweighed by the time, expense, or some other negative aspect of treatment. This should not be viewed as a sign that the client has been permanently healed or cured or that they will now be able to handle all of life's problems. It can often be viewed as a sign that the client can now use their own inner resources, friends, or other forms of help. The door needs to be left open.

SUMMARY

This chapter focused on maintaining the gains created in therapy, preventing relapse, and effectively terminating treatment. These steps are often overlooked in both training and treatment. There are specific steps that can be used that will increase the likelihood of the gains of effective treatment to be maintained. Therapists need to be aware of these strategies and use them in order to be a responsible treatment provider.

REFERENCES

Ansbacher, H. & Ansbacher, R. R. (Eds.) (1956). *The individual psychology of Alfred Adler.* New York: Basic Books.

Bandura, A. (1977). *Social learning theory.* Englewood Cliffs, NJ: Prentice-Hall.

Baucom, D. H. & Hoffman, J. A. (1986). The effectiveness of marital therapy: Current status and application to the clinical setting. In N. S. Jacobson & A. S. Gurman (Eds.). *Clinical handbook of marital therapy* (pp. 597–620). New York: Guilford Press.

Bognar, I. & Zielenbach-Coenen, H. (1984). On maintaining change in behavioral marital therapy. In K. Hahlweg & N. S. Jacobson (Eds). *Marital interaction: Analysis and modification* (pp. 27–35). New York: Guilford.

Daley, D. C. (1989). *Relapse prevention: Treatment alternatives and counseling aids.* Blaze Ridge Summit, PA: TAB Books.

Dinkmeyer, D. & Losoncy, L. (1980). *The encouragement book.* Englewood Cliffs, NJ: Prentice-Hall.

Epstein, L. H. & Masek, B. J. (1978). Behavioral control of medicine compliance. *Journal of Applied Behavioral Analysis, 11,* 1–9.

Gottman, J. (1994a). *What predicts divorce: The relationship between marital processes and marital outcomes.* Hillside, NJ: Lawrence Erlbaum Associates.

Gottman, J. (1994b). *Why marriages succeed or fail.* New York: Simon & Schuster.

Holtzworth-Munroe, A., Jacobson, N. S., DeKlyen, M. & Whisman, M. A. (1989). Relationship between behavioral marital therapy outcome and process variables. *Journal of Consulting and Clinical Psychology, 57(5),* 658–662.

Jacobson, N. S., Schmaling, K. B. & Holtzworth-Munroe, A. (1987). Component analysis of behavioral marital therapy: Two-year follow-up and prediction of relapse. *Journal of Marital and Family Therapy, 13,* 187–195.

Lebow, J. (1995). Open-ended therapy: Termination in marital and family therapy. In R. H. Mikesell, D. Lusterman, S. H. McDaniel (Eds.). *Integrating family therapy: Handbook of family psychology and systems theory* (pp. 73–86). Washington, D.C.: American Psychological Association.

Ludgate, J. W. (1995). *Maximizing psychotherapeutic gains and preventing relapse in emotionally distressed clients.* Sarasota, FL: Professional Resource Press.

Marlatt, G. A. & Gordon, J. R. (1985). *Relapse prevention: Maintenance and strategies in the treatment of addictive behaviors.* New York: Guilford Press.

Meichenbaum, D. & Turk, D. C. (1987). *Facilitating treatment adherence: A practitioner's guide.* New York: Plenum.

Minuchin, S. (1974). *Families and family therapy.* Cambridge, MA: Harvard University Press.

O'Hanlon, B. (1999). *Do one thing different.* New York: Morrow.

Sperry, L. (1986). Contemporary approaches to family therapy: A comparative and meta-analysis. *Journal of Individual Psychology, 42,* 591–601.

Sperry, L. & Carlson, J. (1993). *Basics of stress management.* Coral Springs, FL: CMTI Press.

Sperry, L. & Carlson, J. (1996). *Psychopathology and psychotherapy* (2nd ed.). Philadelphia: Taylor and Francis.

Sperry, L., Lewis, J., Carlson, J. & Englar-Carlson, M. (2003). *Health promotion and wellness counseling.* Boston: Allyn & Bacon.

Truax, P. & Jacobson, N. S. (1992). Marital distress. In P. H. Wilson (Ed.). *Principles and practice of relapse prevention* (pp. 290–321). New York: Guilford Press.

Whisman, M. A. (1991). The use of booster maintenance sessions in behavioral marital therapy. Unpublished doctoral dissertation. University of Washington, Seattle.

White, M. & Epston, D. (1990). *Narrative means to therapeutic ends.* New York: W.W. Norton.

Wilson, P. H. (Ed.) (1992). *Principles and practice of relapse prevention.* New York: Guilford Press.

PART VI

THE PRACTICE OF EFFECTIVE COUNSELING AND PSYCHOTHERAPY

...... ▬▬▬▬▬▬▬▬▬▬▬▬▬▬▬▬▬▬▬▬▬

CHAPTER 12

PRACTICAL ISSUES AND ETHICAL DILEMMAS

WHAT YOU WILL LEARN IN THIS CHAPTER

1. A suggested protocol for handling initial contact, intake, and a first session with a new client
2. Legal and ethical issues that frequently arise in counseling practice
3. Managing boundaries inside and outside of the session
4. Effective use of supervision, consultation, and referral resources
5. Using the Internet as a resource for counseling

PRACTICAL ISSUES AND ETHICAL DILEMMAS: OVERVIEW

What kind of information do I need to get from a new client? What do I do about a client who calls me almost every day? What kind of information can I share with a client's spouse? Should I be seeing kids if I have never taken a course in counseling children?

What if someone comes up to me at a party and wants to talk about a friend whom, she says, has told her she is seeing me in counseling? What if my supervisor tells me that I need to collect an unpaid balance from my client or terminate a client because of an unpaid bill? Will I still need supervision after I get my license?

New and experienced counselors face a number of practical and ethical issues in counseling. These issues range from pragmatic questions about what kind of information we need about our clients to how to handle financial issues, as well as issues around one's self-care and personal growth as a counselor. In this chapter, we address a number of these issues and provide some ideas about how you can go about finding answers to your own questions about practical and ethical issues in counseling. As you read this chapter, you will no doubt come to realize that we have a decisive bias toward continued growth and development for all counselors and therapists. Our hope is that you will see this as a beginning of a lifelong exploration and endeavor for excellence as a counseling professional.

One of the hallmarks of a profession is that members of the profession adhere to a code of ethics or professional conduct. Professional counselors are familiar with the ethical principles and codes of conduct in their field and keep current with legal and ethical issues as they arise. There are several resources available to counselors to help them maintain this currency. These include professional publications, participation in professional organizations, such as the American Counseling Association (ACA) and/or one or more of its divisions, taking advantage of professional development opportunities including national and state counseling association conferences and workshops, and participating in Internet-based information services or list serves specifically related to the counseling profession (to subscribe to ACAeNews, go to *http://www.counseling.org/*).

With the growth of the Internet, many professional groups including the ACA, the American Psychological Association (APA), the American School Counseling Association (ASCA), and the National Board for Certified Counselors (NBCC) have posted their ethics statements on the Web. These documents provide guidance for beginning and experienced counselors. In addition, the ACA and APA have developed standards of practice that apply ethics to counseling and research practice. With the growth of the Internet, both ACA and APA went further to develop standards or ethics statements concerning web counseling (Table 12.1).

Both practical and ethical issues are inherent in the counseling process. DePauw (1986) enumerates ethical considerations in three phases of counseling: the precounseling phase, the service provision phase, and the termination phase. He identifies three areas to consider in the initiation stage: precounseling considerations, service provision issues, and informed consent issues. A fourth and important consideration at this point is dangerousness or crises concerns including threats to self or others and child or elder abuse. In ongoing counseling, considerations include confidentiality, consultation and supervision, and record keeping. Two factors need to be considered in the termination phase, evaluation and the possible need for a referral.

PRECOUNSELING CONSIDERATIONS

One of the first precounseling considerations is how both the agency and individual counselors communicate with the public. Among the factors related to communicating

TABLE 12.1   Web-Based Resources for Ethics in Counseling Practice

ACA Ethics Statement	http://www.counseling.org/resources/codeofethics.htm
ACA Standards of Practice	http://www.counseling.org/resources/codeofethics.htm#sp
A Practical Guide for Ethical Decision Making	http://www.counseling.org/resources/pracguide.htm
Ethical Principles for Psychologists and Code of Conduct	http://www.apa.org/ethics/code.html
APA Statement on Services by Telephone, Teleconferencing, and Internet	http://www.apa.org/ethics/stmnt01.html
NBCC Ethics Statement	http://www.peoplehelpers.org/nbcc.html
NBCC Standards for Web Counseling	http://www.peoplehelpers.org/webethics.htm

with the public is the public image of the office or agency, the way clients are greeted either by phone or in person, and how the agency and individual counselors interact with the public.

Counselors who work in a busy school or agency setting may be too busy responding to student or client needs to be concerned with how someone hears about their services. However, whether working in a school, agency, or private practice, counselors need to assure that any advertising or public information is done in an ethical manner. There are several ways counselors can market their services. For example, counselors may seek referrals from other professionals, advertise their services through various media including the Internet, do targeted mailings, and offer talks for community groups or workshops for the public on various issues such as parenting or dealing with divorce. In their communications with the public, professional counselors take care to accurately represent their training and experience and to inform clients concerning their area of specialization as well as licensure, if applicable.

Counselors who work in private practice, as well as those who may work in more than one setting, such as a university and a private practice or counseling agency, must be careful not to abuse or misuse institutional affiliations.

> Sam, a counselor in private practice, was hired to teach a class in counseling theory at the local university as a substitute for a professor who became ill. In introducing himself to the class, he announced that he was in private practice and offered a reduced rate to any clients students referred to him.

While it is appropriate for Sam to tell students he is in private practice, and even be willing to respond to students' questions concerning the life of a private practitioner, it is not appropriate for Sam to use his role as instructor to solicit clients or to offer reduced rates as an incentive. What if Sam had offered extra credit for referrals?

It is important that clients have easy access to information about the credentials and areas of expertise of providers of mental health, counseling, or other psychological services. While there are several ways that counselors can communicate to the public concerning their services, counselors need to be aware of the ethical guidelines concerning advertising and public contact, and identification.

> Tom, who had an Ed.D. in school administration, returned to school after his retirement to get a Masters degree in counseling. He was routinely identified as Dr. Tom in the agency where he worked, leading clients to believe that he had a doctorate in counseling or psychology.

While there are no restrictions on advertising by counselors and, in most states, no restrictions on to whom licensed counselors can provide service, counselors need to be clear about their credentials and their range of expertise. Degrees not specific to counseling or those received from nonaccredited programs cannot be used in public contact or advertising related to counseling.

Counselors only offer services in areas where they have had training. Practicing counselors who wish to enlarge their scope of practice will do so only after taking the necessary course work and receiving supervision.

> Mary, who had recently passed her state licensure exam, decided to go into private practice. Although her training had focused specifically on individual counseling and she had not had any experience in working with children, she felt she would be too narrow if she did not offer a wide range of services. Therefore, she listed herself in the *Yellow Pages* as a therapist specializing in Marriage and Family, Child and Individual Therapy.

A satisfied client often refers other potential clients and a dissatisfied client can be a real detriment to recruiting additional clients. That, in itself, is probably a good reason for not attempting to provide services in areas where one has little training or experience.

Counselors are also, to a great extent, educators. One of the foundations of counseling is education and counselors can use their skills and knowledge as educators to offer workshops and training options for members of the community. For example, a parent training class, a marriage enrichment program, or a workshop concerning a particular issue in parenting, marriage, dating or any other number of subjects can provide a way for counselors to become better known in the community.

> Janet routinely offered an *Active Parenting* class as a service to her church. As a result of the class and the publicity it generated both in the church and the community, Janet's case load in family counseling maintained a steady growth.

INITIAL CONTACT, INTAKE, AND THE FIRST SESSION WITH A CLIENT

Initial client contact, intake, and the first session with a client are key factors in counseling outcomes. The manner in which the client is handled can either encourage or discourage the client's future participation in counseling. One of the factors contributing to a positive therapeutic outcome is client hope or expectancy (Lambert, 1992) and this expectancy can be influenced by any or all of the client's interactions with the agency or counseling office.

The decision to seek counseling may be based on any number of factors from a sense of dissatisfaction, anxiety, depression, a significant loss, or a sense of hopelessness. In some settings, the initial contact may be handled by a paraprofessional who elicits name, address, and phone number and schedules the potential client for an appointment with an intake worker. Whoever responds to a client's call also must be alert to the possibility of a crisis situation. There are three key factors to consider: 1) Why is the individual seeking counseling? 2) Why at this time? and, 3) Why this agency or this counselor?

As a counselor, you as well as other individuals in the agency or setting where you work begin building a relationship with the client at first contact whether on the phone or in person. When meeting someone new, we take in information concerning that person's appearance, what they say or do not say, as well as how they say what they do say, and how they behave toward us. If in your work setting, the client's initial contact is with an answering machine or a clerk, part of the client's perception of you as a counselor may be influenced by that contact. For example, a potential client who calls for an initial appointment and is put on hold for a long period of time may feel discounted. Put yourself in the client's place. If you were calling for an appointment, what would you want to know? Would you have concerns about parking or public transportation? Would it be important to know how long the initial intake session might take or at what times a counselor might be available? What about the cost of services?

During an initial face-to-face contact, it is important to be aware of both your behavior and the client's. What are the nonverbal messages that you give the client? What do you communicate to the client by your actions, expressions, or manner? How close are you sitting? Do you seem confident or hesitant? Anxious or relaxed? Bored or interested? What is your voice tone like? All of these behaviors can serve to influence the interaction between you and the client and, indeed, affect what the client says to you and how much the client is willing to share.

A critical task during the initial interview with clients is that of determining dangerousness and identifying crisis concerns. It is critically important that issues such as suicidal thoughts or behavior, substance abuse, concerns about personal safety, and sexual issues are addressed. In some cases, the presence of one or more crisis concerns may indicate the need for further evaluation or a referral to an alternate source of services.

Information to Give—Informed Consent

Clients need to know about the counseling process and what to expect in counseling. The nature of the information clients should receive prompts many counselors to choose to give this information in a written format. However, even when using a written statement, counselors also should spend some time at the beginning of counseling to provide this information verbally and assure the client's understanding. Some areas to be considered in providing clients information include:

1. The extent to which their privacy and confidentiality will be protected and the limits of confidentiality.
2. The expected number and frequency of counseling sessions.
3. What to do in case of an emergency.

4. Financial arrangements including fees, methods of payment, and insurance coverage.
5. How a missed appointment, cancellation, or late arrival for an appointment will be handled.
6. Their right to withdraw from counseling.
7. Their right to request a different therapist.
8. The training, experience, and theoretical approach of the therapist.
9. The nature of supervision and/or consultation the therapist would receive.
10. The potential benefits and risks of therapy.

Therapeutic Setting

When you think of a therapeutic setting, you might picture scenes from movies or television with comfortable chairs, possibly a couch, a desk, and dim lighting. However, a therapeutic setting is more and less than that. Karasu defines a therapeutic setting as "a sanctuary that is separate from everyday living" (1992, p. 33). While a quiet, comfortable place separated from the hustle and bustle of everyday life might be the ideal, the true nature of the sanctuary is in the relationship between the client and the counselor. It involves, on the counselor's part, the understanding of the client's concerns and needs, and an expectation that this process will work. This can occur in any setting, regardless of the seating arrangement, lighting, or how the area is decorated.

> A number of studies investigating the impact on outcome of the therapeutic alliance early in therapy have clearly established that the early alliance (i.e., the third to fifth sessions) is a significant predictor of final treatment outcome. . . . These findings indicate that the development of a positive therapist-client relationship may be critical from the onset of therapy. . . . Thus, therapists should be particularly attentive to the early relational climate, and work out any apparent difficulties in the client-therapist relationship in these first sessions. (Bachelor & Horvath, 1999, p. 139)

In building a therapeutic relationship, it is important to consider cultural factors as well as personal idiosyncracies. What visual cues can you use to help build a therapeutic relationship? For example, some individuals are uncomfortable if you stare at them, while others might consider you shifty if you do not look them in the eye. Your dress and grooming are also important. For some clients, a professional, business-like appearance is important. For others, informality may be the preferred look. Your own style and comfort are also important considerations. It is difficult to focus on a client when you are too warm or too cold or your clothing is uncomfortable.

By beginning the session as a conversation, treating the client as a person, a relationship of normality and caring can be established and can provide a way of holding the problem, of containing it together. This can be helpful and healing in itself. (McNeilly, p. 16)

What auditory cues or verbal greeting is most appropriate? What about voice tone? What about kinesthetic cues such as shaking hands or other forms of touching? While it is easy to develop a pattern of greeting, it is important to consider client differences and pay attention to the cues we receive from clients as we greet them.

The initial greeting also can give a message about the nature of the relationship that will develop between you and the client. Is this going to be a relationship between an expert and a novice? Are you planning to be friends for life? What do you want this relationship to be and how can you get off to a good start? When first meeting a client, greet the client by name and introduce yourself. If need be, indicate to the client where to sit. Before beginning the interview, briefly state the purpose of the interview and note the amount of time you expect it to take. If you plan to take notes, tell the client so and indicate the confidentiality of these notes. Finally, check to make sure that the client is comfortable.

When nearing the end of the initial session with the client, let the client know that the time is almost up. At this point, you may provide the client with a brief summary, suggest possible goals and outcomes for counseling, and negotiate an agreement for future sessions. Finally, ask the client if they have any questions of you.

ACTIVITY I: GREETING THE CLIENT

Practice various approaches to greeting. Consider eye contact, what you might say, and what you might do. What approach seems most comfortable to you as the counselor? As the client? Consider visual, auditory, and kinesthetic factors. How might preferences differ for individuals of different cultures? Do you respond differently based on age? Gender?

DECREASING ANXIETY

As a new counselor, you may feel a certain amount of anxiety as you prepare to meet with your client. It is important to remember that the client also comes with a level of anxiety. In fact, anxiety, based on a problem or concern, is often what brings the client to therapy.

"I'm worried about . . ."
"I'm having trouble with . . ."
"I'm afraid . . ."
"I wish I could . . ."
"It just doesn't seem to work when I . . ."
"I don't know what to do about . . ."
"I don't know what I want."

It is easy to pick up our clients' anxiety and add it to our own. Anxiety manifests itself in our physical well-being, our emotional state, and how we think. If you are worried that you will not be able to help the client, or that you will forget to get some important information, you will feel anxious and you might find that you have a bit of a headache or butterflies in your stomach. When this happens, the inexperienced counselor may feel the need to minimize the client's concerns or give the client advice.

The client who is experiencing unease about being in counseling might be thinking "This counselor is going to think I'm really stupid. This isn't really a big issue. Why did I come anyway? I'm feeling a bit queasy. Let's just get this over with." It is important to recognize the client's anxiety as well as your own and understand that it is a normal response because you want the client to feel that their issues and concerns are important. In order to do that effectively, we need to put aside our own anxiety and worries about doing well or remembering to get all the right information. One of the ways counselors can do this is to take time at the beginning of the session to get *centered*. For example, sit comfortably with both feet on the floor and pay attention to your breathing. Kottler (1986) describes the ideal therapist as one who:

> ". . . is comfortable with herself and appears warm, tolerant, sincere, serene, tranquil, and self-assured. This quiet confidence is balanced by a contagious zest for life. Passion. Excitement. Electricity. Enthusiasm. She radiates from body and soul." (p. 20)

Once you have some control over your own anxiety you can help the client deal with their anxiety. An approach that combines a professional stance with compassion and a nonjudgmental attitude can contribute to the client's sense of safety and allow for open communication. Simply stating the client's concern in words such as "This is really a worry for you" or "You want to figure out how to get this problem solved" can help the client realize that you recognize the client's concern.

BASIC INFORMATION NEEDS

There are varying opinions concerning amount and type of information one needs to get from a new client at the first session or during intake. Other than the basic information concerning name, address, phone number, best times available, and method of payment, it is important to know why the client is coming for therapy and what led to the client's decision to come at this particular time. To some extent, the therapist's theoretical orientation will influence the perceived need for specific types of information and what information the interviewer pays attention to. Thus, one interviewer may be particularly attuned to the client's body language while another may be more concerned about the details of a particular concern or symptom.

In some settings, a designated intake worker conducts an intake interview and then refers the client to a therapist for the first counseling session. However, in many cases, counselors may prefer to do their own intake interview. In either case, the intake interview, which involves gathering specific information, sets up expectations in the client's mind. For example, if the intake involves a series of closed-ended questions, the client may expect that the therapist will *do therapy* by asking questions. If the intake worker or therapist is hurried or distracted, clients may feel that the agency is not really interested in them.

Shea (1988) delineates six goals for the initial assessment interview:

1. To establish a sound engagement of the patient in a therapeutic alliance.
2. To collect a valid data base.
3. To develop an evolving and compassionate understanding of the patient.

4. To develop an assessment from which a tentative diagnosis can be made.
5. To develop an appropriate disposition and treatment plan.
6. To effect some decrease of anxiety in the patient. (pp. 6–7)

One of the problems beginning counselors often struggle with is that the client talks about the problem as being outside themself. The problem is the boss, the spouse, the mother-in-law, the children, and on and on. However, by selectively responding, the counselor can help the client focus on self and begin to build the necessary resources to make desired changes.

Compare the following two examples of client-counselor interchanges. The first is a made-up example and the second comes from an actual counseling session with John Krumboltz.

EXAMPLE 1

CL1:   I'm having problems with my mother. She just keeps getting on my case, wanting to know what I'm doing, where I'm going, how much money I spend. She has a key to my apartment and I know she comes in and snoops around when I'm not home. I don't want to get her mad at me but I have to do something.

TH1:   How old is your mother?

CL2:   Oh, she's not that old or anything, she just never had any interests except my dad and I know now with him gone, I guess she just doesn't know what to do. My dad was so good to her.

TH2:   When did your dad die?

CL3:   About two years ago. He was killed in a car accident. It wasn't his fault, just a lot of ice and snow and there was a big pile up. You might have read about it. Seven people were killed.

What do you see the therapist doing that keeps the client's focus off herself? What might have been a better response to the client's first statement?

EXAMPLE 2

CL 2:   (laughter) Well, I guess, I'm having trouble in, uh, relationships are complicated with people. Um, but I am having specific problems right now with my in-laws, and I know that that's common, that everybody, you know, you always hear all the mother-in-law jokes and things like that, but, um, uh, I'm having some real difficulty knowing what my boundaries are, how much should I give, how far should I bend, uh, (T H-Mhm) how much should I really care, should I let it bother me, should I not? Um . . .

TH 3:   It does bother you though.

CL 3:   It does.

TH 4:   Yeah.

CL 4:   It very much does.

TH 5:   I, I hear that.

In this excerpt, Krumboltz (Carlson & Kjos, 2000a) begins by responding to the concern Robin presents. Robin is heard and this allows her to go on and talk about how this problem affects her. Later, Krumboltz teaches her a way of responding to her mother-in-law and others with whom she might have boundary problems.

NOTE TAKING

Many counselors, particularly in the initial session, will want to take some notes to build a profile of the client and the client's problem. In the following interchange, Lenore Walker (Carlson & Kjos, 2000b) asks permission to take notes and, in so doing, begins building a base for a co-equal relationship with the client.

TH 12:   And if, you know, if, sometimes I'll take some notes or something if that's okay with you.

CL 12:   Oh, sure that's fine.

TH 13:   Just grab my pad [yeah] and sometimes I don't.

CL 13:   So I won't feel hurt if you don't take notes.

TH 14:   It does not mean I'm not listening.

CL 14:   Okay, all right, that's all right. That will be fine.

Notes, whether taken during the session, recorded shortly after the session, or both, serve a number of purposes. As part of a client's record, they provide a history of what has transpired in working with the client and can be reviewed prior to a session as a reminder of what has transpired in previous sessions. Notes are also helpful if, for some reason, the client is transferred or referred to another counselor. As counselors, notes can help us stay on track and be aware of how we are working with the client. Going back over a series of client notes may contribute to a clearer conceptualization of the case and the client's issues.

At the end of the first or intake session with a client, both the counselor and the client should have gathered some important information. As the counselor, you should have enough information to: (1) make a tentative diagnosis, (2) come to an agreement with the client as to what will be accomplished in your working together, (3) develop a treatment plan, and (4) estimate the number of sessions or length of time it will take to reach the client's goals.

The client should be informed about the counseling process and relationship. This includes, but is not limited to, (1) information about the length and frequency of sessions, (2) the client's rights concerning confidentiality, (3) the primary mode or modes of intervention that will be used (e.g., group, individual, family), (4) any supervision you might receive concerning the client's issues, and (5) the financial arrangements related to the provision of service. Finally, if you plan to audio- or videotape any sessions or have live observation for supervisory purposes the client will need to sign a release of information form.

Issues such as financial arrangements and donated services also need to be considered if you are working independently. Counselors may plan to do a certain amount of *pro-bono* work each year or accept clients for what their insurance pays rather than full fee. When considering a position with an agency, it is important to be aware of the fee structure and any financial arrangements available to clients. It also is important to determine what, if any, insurance coverage the client may have and inform the client of their options concerning insurance coverage. Not all health insurance policies cover counseling or psychotherapy. Many require a physician's referral and not all insurance companies recognize Master's level counselors. In some cases, it is necessary for the counselor to hold a license to be recognized by an insurance company. All but five states (California, Hawaii, Minnesota, Nevada, and New York) have counselor licensure.

When concluding an initial interview, the counselor will give the client a brief, accurate summary of what was discussed. In doing so, it is important to avoid jargon and speak at the client's level. At this point, the counselor might ask if the client has any questions or anything else they would like to say. Finally, the counselor offers a statement of appreciation.

What do you notice about in the following excerpt from the closing of Jill Sharff's interview (Carlson & Kjos, 2000d) with Phil?

TH 148: Okay well, we are about at the end of our interview here. [O.K., O.K.] Do you think that you've felt wary of letting me get too close to private areas of yourself?

CL 148: Today, yeah.

TH 149: Yes. Would you like to speculate about why?

CL 149: Um, it would have been easier just to talk about other things today.

TH 150: Because you are under stress.

CL 150: I don't know, just because that's always easier.

TH 151: Yeah, it's always easier, but underneath all that stress then maybe some, even though your life is going well, there may be some unhappiness that you might really want some help with, and as you go through these progressive interviews, you might be getting closer to a point where you wish you could open up a bit more, and you know, it's me today. Maybe next time you will feel more like doing it? I don't know.

CL 151: I do the best I can each time. [Yeah] And I know that like I'm here to try to get a little bit better, so I might reluctantly talk about stuff, but I talk about it or I don't. I didn't really hide anything from you.

TH 152: No, no I noticed that you told me things I didn't even ask. Yeah. But still there's a feeling of keeping me at bay just a little bit. Which you do in a very charming kind of way.

CL 152: Thank you. I don't know if that's a compliment or not. Probably not, but, a charming way. What do you mean by that?

TH 153: Well, you smile, and you're quite engaging, and you deal with the studio people in that same easy manner, yet when you meet with me, it's sort of a peculiar intimate situation. There is naturally some reluctance because, A. it's not really private, and B. you never see me again. But I'm just giving you the feedback that I sense something of that feeling of imminent intrusiveness or someone like me might get close to you. The next thing you get is a jab. Like I'm asking you about your awards, and in a very charming way you said, I don't really know what they are. Like you blow it off, and I now think it's so that I would not come in and say well, I knew you had it in you. Something nasty about it that you might expect from me, finding too much of how much pleasure you are actually taking in how far you've come. Things that you feel good about, but you don't want to be too boastful of them. It's almost as if you are still a bit surprised about where you're at, what you've done for yourself.

CL 153: Sometimes I am.

TH 154: Well, okay, we are going to finish I think. [O.K.] Thank you for talking to me.

CL 154: Thanks.

DEVELOPING A TREATMENT PLAN

A treatment plan is developed around the client's symptoms with goals and objectives related to these symptoms and treatment strategies linked to the goals. Clients have the right to participate in developing their counseling treatment plan including goals, treatment strategies, and anticipated outcomes. This is important for three reasons. The first is that what may seem to be a reasonable outcome for me may not look at all attractive, interesting, or even possible to you. The second, and more important, is that clients have the right to make their own choices. Finally, clients have ideas about what works and what does not work for them. Thus, a treatment strategy that calls for behaviors or actions that the client has tried and failed in the past may simply lead to another failure. When, as counselors, we attempt to set goals and treatment plans without the client's participation we can reasonably expect that counseling will not be successful. On the other hand, client goals are not always compatible with what might be accomplished through counseling and we may need to negotiate goals with the client. Many counselors find it helpful to review goals and outcomes with the clients at specific intervals and make adjustments as needed.

SERVICE PROVISION ISSUES

Jan, a counselor who offers career counseling gets a call from a prospective client concerning an appointment for career counseling. In talking with Tom on the phone, Jan learns that he has been suffering from anxiety related to a failing marriage and an unsettling work situation, and has been seeing a counselor for about three months concerning these issues. He is calling Jan on the advice of a friend who suggests that she can help him find a better job. How should Jan handle Tom's request? Should she agree to meet with Tom for career counseling?

Susan, a single woman, calls a mental health agency requesting an appointment with a counselor to deal with her feelings of depression and worthlessness. The agency has no openings at this time for individual counseling but does have a group starting for singles. How should the agency respond to Susan's request?

In providing services to clients, counselors look for the best service options to meet a client's needs. Would this client benefit most from individual counseling, group counseling, career counseling, or personal coaching? Would it be better to see this client in a couple or family counseling? What are the benefits or costs of putting a client in a group to wait for an opening for individual counseling? How does an agency handle an overflow of clients? What about a client who is already working with another therapist?

These are all questions that agencies and individual counselors and therapists need to deal with in their efforts to provide the best possible options for each client. In order to do this, individual counselors and agencies need to be aware of the resources in the community and maintain a network of referral sources. In addition, if a client cannot be accommodated within a reasonable time, they need to inform clients about the anticipated waiting time and provide a list of alternative services.

Professional counselors want to provide the best possible service to each client. Counselors can do this by being careful to stay within their own level of expertise and seek supervision when they find themselves stuck or floundering, by referring clients when a better service option is available, and by working cooperatively with other human service professionals. Most agencies have supervision sessions where counselors share cases and concerns. However, counselors also work in private practice settings and shared office arrangements. In these cases, it is important both for the client and the counselor's mental health to have adequate case supervision. A client seeking individual counseling may gain a greater benefit by participating in an alternate form of counseling such as marriage or family counseling, group counseling, or career counseling. Or, the client's problems may suggest the need of more than one form of counseling. In a situation where one of the issues between a couple is related to job dissatisfaction on the part of one of the couple, both marriage counseling and career counseling might be called for. Thus, one of the couple might work with two counselors concurrently. In these cases, both counselors will want to have permission from the client to share information so they can work cooperatively.

TRAINING AND SUPERVISION

While supervision is seen as a necessary part of counseling education, practicing counselors also need to be assured that they have or can access adequate supervision and consultation after graduation. Effective postgraduate supervision can serve to refine and enhance the counselor's skills, provide support and guidance for difficult cases, and prevent counselor burn out. Many counselors find that peer supervision or consultation is one way to enhance their effectiveness and promote professional growth. If supervision is by observation, audio or video tape, the client must give written consent.

In many cases, counselors are required to participate in continuing education activities to maintain licensure or certification. Even if this is not a requirement for licensure or certification, continuing education helps counselors maintain a fresh perspective and gain renewed energy and sense of purpose. A key source of continuing education opportunities is through professional organizations. The umbrella organization for counselors in the United States is the ACA which holds an annual conference in addition to on-line courses. ACA is made up of several divisions representing the different branches of counseling such as career, marriage and family, substance abuse, school, and group. Several of the divisions offer national conferences and/or other continuing education opportunities related to their particular issues. In addition, most states have branches of ACA and many of them hold regular conferences. Finally, groups of states may come together for a regional conference.

Information about the ACA and other professional organizations that offer opportunities for continuing education for counselors can be found on the Internet: *http:// www.counseling.org.*

DUAL RELATIONSHIPS

The relationship we have with our clients should be free of other interests. Therefore, a professional counselor or a counselor-in-training will want to avoid duel relationships. The Ethics Statements of counseling-related professional organizations have sections that refer to "dual relationships."[1] The ACA Code of Ethics states that:

> Counselors are aware of their influential positions with respect to clients, and they avoid exploiting the trust and dependency of clients. Counselors make every effort to avoid dual relationships with clients that could impair professional judgment or increase the risk of harm to clients. (Examples of such relationships include, but are not limited to, familial, social, financial, business, or close personal relationships with clients.) (ACA, 1995, Section A.6)

It may be a relief to know that it is not ethical for you to serve as a therapist for a relative, friend, supervisor, or fellow worker. As a counseling student, you may have had some interesting responses from friends and family members. Many students find that their friends and relatives think they are going to psychoanalyze them or can, somehow, magically read minds. You may have been asked for advice concerning personal problems. In fact, that may be one of the factors that motivated you to major in counseling. However, having had experience in giving advice to friends and family members does not necessarily mean that you will be a good counselor. Counseling and psychotherapy is more complicated than just giving someone advice or solutions. The counselor's goal is to help clients find their own solutions and then move on to make needed changes.

While the ethics statements define boundaries for whom we accept as clients, they also serve as a reminder that we take care when we happen to meet a past or current client in a social or business setting.

ACTIVITY II: A FORMER CLIENT

Jan's daughter Sue called to ask her to join her and a new friend for lunch. "I really want you to meet her, I know you will like her," Sue said. When Jan got to the restaurant,

---

[1]APA = Standard 1.17, ASCA = Standard A4, NBCC = B.9.

she noticed that one of her longtime clients, Marge, was just ahead of her. Jan had worked with Marge for some time concerning issues that arose from Marge being sexually abused as a child. Jan soon realized that Sue's new friend was Marge. How should she handle this?

CLOSING A SESSION

TH 146:   Our time's just about up. Anything you want to say?

CL 146:   Gosh, it goes fast.

TH 147:   Anything you'd like to say to me?

CL 147:   Thank you.

TH 148:   You're welcome, Ma'am.

CL 148:   Thank you because it, I needed to self-reflect, [TH Mhm] and I enjoy it.

TH 149:   Make time for Gina.

CL 149:   Yeah, to sort of just chill. Just sit back and think, add up, not really take a checklist, but . . .

TH 150:   No, more just like it turned out tonight. Just take, take time to listen.

CL 150:   Appreciate yourself. Yeah, to listen to myself, too. Because sometimes I do shut myself up. I do.

TH 151:   There go those faces.

CL 151:   I know, I know. (laughter)

TH 152:   That's all right. Maybe sometimes you ought to do it looking in the mirror.

CL 152:   I should, I should, because everybody sees them and I don't even know I'm doing it. Yeah. But no, I will reflect. [TH Good] That will be good. Thank you.

TH 153:   You're welcome, and very good fortune to you.

CL 153:   Thank you, thank you very much. (Carlson & Kjos, 2000c)

A counseling session can be very intense evoking strong emotions in the client. However, time eventually runs out, and the session is over. Some clients have difficulty closing and may even save a major issue or bomb for the last few minutes of a session. What do you do when your client has just presented a major issue or revelation and you know you have another client waiting? How do you handle a client who frequently has one more thing to tell you even after the session is over?

Part of the sense of security a client feels in counseling is based on the routine and limits that you, as the counselor, set. This includes the time, place, duration of the counseling session, and arrangements for the payment of fees if applicable. It is important for the counselor to address client behaviors such as habitually arriving late for sessions, demanding additional time for a session, or making frequent calls between sessions. Firm boundaries serve to provide a sense of safety and security for clients and those clients who challenge these boundaries are often the ones who feel the most insecure.

Termination and Follow-up

Ideally, termination occurs either when the goal or goals for counseling are met or when the therapist has completed the agreed upon number of sessions with the client. However, several factors can get in the way of an ideal termination and, in the case of premature termination, a number of issues may be involved including factors external to counseling as well as those within the counseling process itself. A key factor in persistence, as well as client change, lies in the client-counselor relationship. As in any relationship, the client may perceive the counselor on a continuum from distant and nonresponsive, to neutral, to warm and caring. At times, clients identify with characteristics in their counselor that mirror those of another such as a parent, teacher or sibling with whom they had a conflicted relationship. At other times, a client may look for the counselor to take on a role such as parent, friend, or lover, that goes beyond the boundaries of counseling.

In some cases the client may find that the issues are too overwhelming to face. Counselors need to be able to modulate the level of tension and emotion around difficult issues, allowing clients both the time and space to deal with sensitive issues at a pace that is comfortable for them. However, at times, clients may need to take a break from talking about a particular issue and focus on a tangential issue.

External issues also may play a part in a client's decision to stop out for a time or terminate counseling altogether. Among these are work or family pressures, the need to relocate, and physical illness, either of self or a family member. In some instances, the client may feel the need to prematurely terminate counseling because of limited mental health coverage or the lack sufficient financial resources to continue in counseling. However, no matter what the motivation or reason for termination, the counselor will want to give the client options to return if and as needed.

EVALUATION

One of the questions we might ask at the end of each session is "Did we accomplish what we wanted or planned to do in this session?" Clients who begin to feel that sessions are going nowhere and that they are accomplishing little in counseling are not apt to continue. Counselors who share those feeling are apt to be relieved when the client decides to terminate. Just as it is important to hear the client's concerns, share the treatment plan with the client, and work with the client's goals, it is important to check with the client from time to time to assure that the process of counseling is meeting the short- and long-term needs of the client. While ongoing evaluation is important, it is also important to consider client gains at the time of termination of therapy. Factors to be considered include:

- The client's ability to maintain the gains made in therapy.
- What resources the client has to handle situations that may threaten these gains.
- How the client's change affects family members and other individuals in his or her immediate world.

USING THE INTERNET AS A RESOURCE FOR COUNSELING

With the growth of the Internet, counselors have found a new and exciting source for information both for themselves and their clients. There are a number of web sites that serve the need of the profession and also may provide information useful to clients. This, in itself, can present a real challenge to you as a counselor, as a web savvy client may come armed with information that the counselor may not be aware of. However, as with any other information source, not every thing posted on the Internet is accurate and clients may misinterpret information, whether accurate or not.

Given this, counselors need to be cognizant of web-based information and able to use it effectively. See Table 12.2 for a list of web sites that provide links to sites that provide information that may be helpful to both the counselor and the client.

CONDUCTING A SEARCH

There are a number of search engines on the Internet and each provides instructions on how to format your search to get the results you are looking for. While search protocols are generally based on a common logic, there are differences in search engines. You may have already identified your favorite one, but it is interesting to try out others from time to time. The site *http://home.netscape.com/escapes/search/tips_general.html* provides general tips on how to search, and links to search tips for a number of search engines.

EVALUATING WEB PAGES

If you do a search simply using the word *counseling* you will find thousands of potential web sites. How do you know what sites will be useful to you or your clients? There are several factors to consider in evaluating a web site or web resources for counseling. These include the authority or credibility of the information provided, the purported purpose of the site, the objectivity of the materials presented, the currency of information provided, how useful information provided is in meeting you or your client's needs, and how easy it is to access the information.

TABLE 12.2   Selected Web Sites with Links to Counseling Resources

FOCUS	URL
School counseling, career counseling	*http://www.educationworld.com/counseling/*
Career counseling, career information	*http://ncda.org/membersonly/links.html*
Diagnosis, treatment	*http://www.mentalhealth.com/*

To determine whether the information provided on the site can be believed, we can look for information to answer the following questions. Who is the publisher and/or author? Does the publisher and/or author list their credentials or qualifications? Can I contact the publisher or author? If so, how easy is it to make that contact? What is the stated purpose of the site? How does this purpose fit my needs? Who is the sponsor or host for this web site? Sometimes the URL will provide information about the host. For example, a URL ending in "edu" indicates an educational institution while an ending in "gov" indicates a governmental agency. Can you determine the goals or objectives for this site? What sources are used? Is there enough information to check these sources? What opinions, if any, are expressed by the author or authors? Is this page a mask for advertising?

Once you have determined that the site has credibility, you may want to consider the currency of the information. When was the site last updated? Are the links current or updated regularly? If several of the links lead to dead ends, you might assume that the site has not been updated for some time.

Finally, how easy is the site to use? Can you find what you want? Can you move back and forth within the site with ease? Is there a clear plan or organization, an easily understood site map, and/or a table of contents? Can materials be downloaded or printed to a PDF file?

Because of the phenomenal growth of the Internet, new sites appear almost daily. Fortunately, there are groups that review web sites and provide links to sites that meet their criteria. Table 12.2 lists some sites that review and provide links to sites related to counseling.

REFERENCES

American Counseling Association. (1995). *Ethical standards.* Alexandria, VA: Author.

Bachelor, A. & Horvath, A. (1999). The therapeutic relationship. In M. A. Hubble, B. L. Duncan, & S. D. Miller (Eds.). *The heart and soul of change: What works in therapy* (pp. 133–178). Washington, DC: American Psychological Association.

Carlson, J. & Kjos, D. (2000a). *Cognitive therapy with Dr. John Krumboltz* (Reprint): Psychotherapy with the Experts Video. Boston: Allyn & Bacon.

Carlson, J. & Kjos, D. (2000b). *Cognitive-behavioral feminist therapy with Dr. Lenore Walker* (Reprint): Psychotherapy with the Experts Video. Boston: Allyn & Bacon.

Carlson, J. & Kjos, D. (2000c). *Existential-humanistic therapy with Dr. James Bugental* (Reprint): Psychotherapy with the Experts Video. Boston: Allyn & Bacon.

Carlson, J. & Kjos, D. (2000d). *Object relations therapy with Dr. Jill Savege Scharff* (Reprint): Psychotherapy with the Experts Video. Boston: Allyn & Bacon.

DePauw, M. E. (1986). Avoiding ethical violations: A time line perspective for individual counseling. *Journal of Counseling and Development, 64*(5), 303–305.

Karasu, T. B. (1992). *Wisdom in the practice of psychotherapy.* New York: Basic Books.

Kottler, J. A. (1986). *On being a therapist.* New York: Jossey Bass.

Lambert, M. J. (1992). Implications of outcome research for psychotherapy integration. In J. C. Norcross & M. R. Goldfried (Eds.). *Handbook of psychotherapy integration* (pp. 94–129). New York: Basic Books.

McNeilly, R. B. (2000). *Healing the whole person.* New York: John Wiley & Sons.

Shea, S. C. (1988). *Psychiatric interviewing: The art of understanding.* Philadelphia: W.B. Saunders.

CHAPTER 13

THE EFFECTIVE THERAPIST IN ACTION

WHAT YOU WILL LEARN IN THIS CHAPTER

1. What might be going on in a counselor's mind concerning a client
2. Factors a counselor might be considering in evaluating a case and determining a plan of action
3. How a case might proceed

AN OBSESSIVE CLIENT

May 8, Tuesday

Sylvia called this morning to warn me that she had referred an acquaintance, Janet, to me. Janet was someone she had met through scouting. Sylvia said that Janet is so obsessive that she drives her nuts. She tells me to be gentle with Janet because she is really reluctant to see me, or any therapist. I wonder if Janet will call? Should I have asked Sylvia for more information? What does Sylvia mean by obsessive? Maybe I should have asked for an example, but Sylvia isn't a counselor. Sometimes I wonder if she just knows enough about psychology and counseling to be somewhat dangerous. She took a class in abnormal psych last semester and has been giving labels to everyone. On the other hand, I am thankful that she refers potential clients to me—even if she thinks I am somewhat obsessive myself.

1. What does the word obsessive mean to you?
2. Do you think the counselor should have asked Sylvia for more information? Why or Why not?

Later Tuesday. —Well, Janet called and made an appointment (Monday 10 A.M.). I asked her a bit about herself—she is married, has a son, 12, and a daughter, 8. She says her husband is an entrepreneur, and has had about five different businesses since they married. She has a degree in education—specializing in early childhood, but hasn't worked except occasionally as a substitute teacher since her son was born. She didn't really talk about why she wanted to see me—just that Sylvia has given her my name. As I was about ready to hang up she said "Oh, just one more thing, I know it sounds silly, but is your office really in a safe place? I won't get attacked or anything, will I?" I assured her that the office was in a safe place and that I had never had any trouble with the location. Then she asked, "What time did you say?" I told her again. I am looking forward to meeting her. She sounds like an interesting, and possibly challenging, client. I will do a full intake at the first session.

May 14, Monday

Janet was on time, she was sitting in the waiting room reading a magazine when I ushered out my 9 A.M. client. First impression? She is a somewhat dowdy looking woman. About 5 feet 4 inches, a bit overweight. She had on a skirt and overblouse and the hem of the skirt was a bit crooked, as if part of it might be tucked into the waistband. She had on little or no makeup and her hair was pulled back in a rubber band. She looked as if she was very tired and, somehow, worried. However, she had a marvelous smile and a firm handshake. I liked her at once.

When we entered my office, she handed me the basic information form the receptionist had given her to complete. She took her time, looking around, moving to examine items on the wall and on my desk. She didn't touch anything, but she visually checked out each area. She even walked to the window and looked out. "Not much of a view," I said. She didn't respond. Finally she sat down in what I think of as the most uncomfortable chair in my office—a straight back, armless side chair. She sighed, looked down at her hands, and then at me.

3. Should the counselor have suggested where the client should sit?
4. What do you think was behind Janet's careful examination of the office?
5. Do you think there was any significance in the type chair she chose? Why or why not?
6. What, if anything, might be important about the way the client presents?

I briefly glanced at the intake form and then asked, "What brings you here?" Her response was "Well, Sylvia suggested I come." I tried again. "Why do you think Sylvia suggested you come?"

She sighed and tears welled up in her eyes. "Well," she paused, "my mother died about a year ago and I spend a lot of time thinking about that. I guess Sylvia thinks I'm obsessive. I guess I'm worse since my Mom died, but I've always been that way, but now . . . It's just that now, I feel so alone even when I'm with my family. I know I worry a lot and some nights I really have trouble sleeping because I'm just working things over and over in my mind."

"Can you give me an example?"

She looked around the room, then looked down at her hands. "Well, I drove by this building twice so I would be sure to know where it was. Then, I parked my car and came up to the door of your office earlier today so I would be sure I was in the right place. Is that obsessive? I have always been careful, but lately, I don't know, I just seem to be working so hard not to worry and still worrying so much." She sighed, "I'm not sleeping all that much, and I'm so tired and edgy or nervous all the time. If I'm not worrying about national security, I'm worrying about what to fix for dinner." She gave a wry laugh and looked down. All the time she was talking she was playing with her fingers, weaving them in and out.

I reflected that is sounded like it was affecting her life more and more and that was not a comfortable place for her to be. She agreed with me and went on to tell me how she kept trying to figure out ways to cope with it. I asked for some examples of how she had tried to cope. She responded by telling me about how she would try to talk herself down and then admitted that she had tried drinking a glass of wine whenever she began to feel really agitated but it did not seem to help that much and she felt that she might become an alcoholic the way her father had.

7. Do you think the counselor should have responded to the client's question about obsessive? Why?
8. How might you have handled the client's reference to the father being an alcoholic? Why?
9. What question or questions might you ask this client at this point? Why?

I made a mental note to explore her relationship with both her mother and father at a later date and asked her to tell me a bit more about herself. What kind of a person was she? She hesitated, looked around the room and sighed. "I guess I don't really know how to answer that," she said. "I'd like to think I was a good person, but sometimes I get so impatient and angry that I say things I really regret. And, I'm not a very good housekeeper. And, I yell at my kids way too much. I just worry about them all the time—maybe they will get run over on the way to school, maybe they'll get kidnapped or assaulted or something awful will happen to them and I won't be there. And, I do have a good education but I'm not really using it." At this point she was talking very fast. "And I know I should be more religious, but I hardly ever go to church, and it seems like my husband is angry at me all the time, and I get so down on myself. And I yell at my kids, and then worry that I'm being abusive or harming them somehow." She paused and I asked "What's that like, feeling so down on yourself?"

Again, a rush of words as she describes lying awake at night going over and over her faults and failures. She talks about watching other people's faces for looks of scorn or displeasure and not knowing just what she has said or done wrong but feeling that she has somehow caused them to be upset with her. She says she has really lost most of her friends because it's too much of an effort to go anywhere or have someone over. I begin to feel both a sense of sympathy for her and an impatience at her negativity.

10. Should the counselor have countered the client's negativity at this point? Why or why not? If she chose to do so, what might she have said?
11. Do Janet's complaints remind you of someone? Do you ever feel that way yourself?
12. Have you begun to formulate a diagnosis for Janet?
13. What might be the best way to work with Janet?
14. How would you feel about working with her?

I try to go for empathy over sympathy and reflect "It sounds like you've really been having a rough time." I remind myself that I need to probe for any dissociative or psychotic symptoms as well as suicidal ideation so I follow up with a question about unusual experiences or any thoughts of suicide. She looks puzzled. I loaded too much into that question. I go back, "Have you had any thoughts of suicide?" She responds with a definite "No." (Note to self: be more direct about the suicide thing.)

"What about unusual experiences or ideas?" She looks a bit puzzled and then shakes her head, "I don't think so," she replies. OK, I'm thinking—what have I missed—memory? "How's your memory been serving you?" I ask.

She again looks a bit puzzled, and appears to be thinking about how to answer. Finally, she sighs and responds with "I don't know if it's different. I do get confused at times, almost as if I need to remind myself who I am or what I should be doing." She went on to explain that she doesn't forget important things, just that at times she feels lost or out of place. I asked her what she does when she feels lost or out of place. She said she stops and tells herself to just calm down and that seems to work. She sighs and then says, "It's just so much work just to keep going."

15. Why do you think the counselor chose to use an empathic response at this time? What is the difference between an empathic response and a sympathetic response?
16. What import, if any, would you put on the client's feeling "lost and out of place" at times.

I need to learn something about her developmental history so I ask her to tell me about when she was growing up. She reports that she was the eldest of three with two brothers. Then she begins to talk about her youngest brother whom she describes as "all messed up—a junkie." I ask her how that affected her and she stops—then she says "I guess I think there for the grace of God, go I." I probe for more information and she talks about her fear of becoming addicted to alcohol or drugs. "And so, the wine . . ." I begin and she interrupts, "Yeah, I could be a real wino." She goes on to tell me that her father was an alcoholic who died in a car accident when she was eight years old. Another piece to the "Why now?", I note to myself.

I ask about her general health and she responds with a quick "I'm fine." I sense an impatience on her part, but I need to check this out further. I decide to do a quick checklist. She admits to diarrhea and frequent nausea, and adds that she must be allergic or something because she's been feeling "down," with little or no energy for some time. I ask if she's checked with her doctor and she replies that it isn't that serious. When asked how long she had been experiencing these feelings, she said she thought it had been going on for at least a year, maybe more.

I note that time is running out so I ask her if there is anything else that would be important for me to know about her. She doesn't answer right away, then she responds with "I don't know. I guess not." Then I ask her if she has any questions of me. She takes a deep breath and says "Do you think I'm crazy?" I never know quite what to say to that. What is crazy anyway? I tell her that I think she is a strong, capable woman who is facing some difficulties and that she has made a good decision to seek help at this time. I find I'm looking forward to working with Janet and suggest we meet once a week for the next six weeks with a plan to evaluate her status at that time. I also ask her to set up an appointment with her doctor for a physical and tell her that it is important that she tell the doctor about her problem sleeping and her edginess and nervousness. Finally, I suggest that she think about what goals she would have for therapy so we can discuss that the next time we meet.

I noted that we had about five minutes left, so I asked her if she would like to learn one quick way to help her gain some control over her anxiety. She agreed and I said, "Breathe." She looked puzzled, "Breathe?" I spent a few minutes helping her work on deep breathing and then recommended that she practice that three or four times a day, even if she wasn't feeling anxious. I went on to suggest that when she began to feel anxious, she could remember to breathe.

17. What, if any, important information did the counselor fail to get? What other questions might you have asked?
18. Do you have enough information to make a diagnosis for this client? If not, what other information would you like to have?
19. How might you have responded to her question about being crazy?
20. Why do you think the therapist told Janet to breathe?
21. What clues do you have that the counselor was engaging the client throughout this interview?
22. Following the guidelines in Chapter 5, develop a diagnostic formulation for this client.
23. Why do you think the counselor asked Janet to think about what goals she would have? Do you think that was a good idea?
24. What would your treatment goals be for Janet?
25. What, if anything, should the therapist be concerned about in her relationship with Janet.

May 21, Monday

The first thing Janet said when she walked into my office was "You're going to be mad at me, I didn't make an appointment with my doctor." I asked if it would help if I got mad at her. "No, I guess not," was the response. We spent some time dancing around this issue. I wondered what the payoff was for not seeing the doctor. Was she afraid of what the doctor would say? Or, was something else going on here? Finally, speaking very rapidly and almost gasping for breath, she told me that she was thinking I knew something she didn't—maybe she had some fatal disease or something and that was why I wanted her to see a doctor. She admitted that was irrational but still she was so worried that something was really wrong with her. We spent quite a bit of time just getting rational and it wasn't until about 30 minutes into the session that I was able to talk about a treatment plan and come to an agreement with her on how we would proceed. I think that one of the ways I will know I am being effective is by noting how she starts a session. I wonder if I should have acknowledged her honesty in telling me she hadn't called to make an appointment with the doctor.

We did get to one of my objectives—to talk about her goals for therapy. She reported she has had some difficulty with that—she just knew she wanted to not worry so much,

feel better about herself, and be able to do more things. (Reminder to self: Be more specific about this assignment; maybe a handout would help.) We spent some time defining
an acceptable amount of worrying, and what *better* and *more things* meant. She decided
that *better* would be that she wouldn't be so self-critical. I asked for more specificity and
she said she would spend less time berating herself. "How often do you berate yourself
now?" I asked.

"Every day, several times a day." was her response. I suggested she might want to
berate herself only a few times a day—maybe three or less. When we got to *more things,*
she had a better idea of what I was looking for and said she wanted to be comfortable going
to her son's soccer games.

I suggested that she might also want to be able to identify the source of her anxiety,
reduce the anxiety attacks, feel more in control of her life, and learn to manage stress better (Table 13.1).

We moved on to talk about what she says to herself when she feels the anxiety coming on and how effective that self-talk is. She says she doesn't talk to herself, she hears her
mother talking to her in her head. I ask her what her mother says. Her voice changes as she
says "Grow up." "Don't be silly." "Act like an adult." "You're being stupid again." "Baby,
baby, baby." "I'm sick of you."

Each statement is given with a sarcastic, or scolding tone. I find myself getting angry
at the mother and I say to Janet, "I don't think I'd get along with your mother very well."
She laughs at that and then sighs and tears begin to well up in her eyes. I wait a bit as she
grabs a tissue and wipes her eyes and then shakes her head. "My mom was a pretty unhappy person all the time I knew her."

"And probably pretty fearful, also." I respond. She is silent for a brief time and then
nods and gives a rueful laugh. "I guess I inherited it." I assure her that it is more likely that
she learned it and so she also could unlearn it. I go on to suggest each of the messages she
carries around in her head that holds her back may have one or more alternative message
that could help her go forward. I ask if she would like to look at one of the messages and
see if we could figure out an alternative. She looks a bit skeptical but agrees to try. I ask
her which message she would like to look at first. She chooses "Act like an adult." She
wonders what acting like an adult really is? I toss the question back to her. "What do you
think?" We play with that message—coming up with terms such as "Don't be playful." versus "Be playful." and "Don't be silly." versus "Take time to enjoy life." She gets into the
idea and decides she would like to spend some time this coming week developing coun-
terstatements to some of the negative messages she keeps struggling with. I suggest she

TABLE 13.1   Goals

MY GOALS FOR JANET	JANET'S GOALS
1. Identify source of anxiety.	1. Feel better
2. Reduce number of anxiety attacks.	2. Not worry so much
3. Feel more in control in her life.	3. Be able to do more things
4. Manage stress more effectively.	

start a notebook or diary and say I hope she will share some of her thoughts and ideas with me when we next meet in two weeks. She looked worried and asked, "Two weeks?" I reminded her about Memorial Day and noted that we could meet earlier on Tuesday the 29th if she wants to. She readily agreed. As she left, I again reminded her that she should make an appointment with her doctor.

Just as she was getting up to leave she stopped and said, "I remembered to breathe once—and I think it helped. Thanks."

26. How would you categorize the interventions the therapist used?
27. What other types of interventions might you have chosen to use at this point?
28. What evidence do you see that the client is engaged?
29. Was the counselor correct when she said anxiety was learned?

May 29, Tuesday

The first thing Janet told me after she got into my office was that she had made a doctor's appointment. "I don't know why I waited so long." she said. She went on to report that she had been trying to do the good messages but sometimes it just seems as if someone is screaming in her ears telling her how dumb, clumsy, and ugly she is. "It's so hard," she tells me. I ask if she would like to do some more practice in the session and she says she would. We spend the first half of the session reviewing and refining alternative messages. I am alert for *should* and *shouldn't* or *must* and *must not* statements and help her develop new statements by replacing should or must with "I would rather . . . ," "It would be better if . . ." or "It might not be a good idea if . . ."

Then I make a transition, asking her to tell me a bit more about her childhood. She said that she missed a lot of school because she was sickly. When I inquired into what she meant by sickly she says she doesn't really know—just that every morning her mother took her temperature and then decided whether or not she could go to school. She pauses for what seems like a long time and seems to be remembering or thinking something through. Then she asks me if I remember the saying "Step on a crack and you'll break your mother's back." I nod and she goes on to tell me about how she worried that something would happen to her mother and she would be an orphan. "I think I liked it that my mother took such good care of me. I was always afraid that something bad would happen and she wouldn't be there to save me."

"And, now she is no longer here." I respond. Tears well up in her eyes and she reaches for a tissue. I am thinking that she was no doubt taught to be anxious by what was most likely an anxious mother and that now I need to be aware of any feelings I might have of wanting to or trying to mother this client. I am also thinking about her children and how her anxiety must be affecting them. (Note: I learned later that she didn't make a real connection between her mothers's message and her own anxiety. I should have done an interpretive statement here.)

As we set up next week's appointment, I ask her to sign a release that will allow me to confer with her physician after she has seen him. I also remind her to continue to work on alternative messages and suggest that we again review them and their effectiveness the next time we meet.

30. Why do you think the counselor was concerned about how the alternative messages were worded? What is the difference between "I shouldn't . . ." and "It would be better if . . ."

31. What do you think the therapist is thinking when she looks for information about Janet's childhood?

32. Why do you think the therapist might be concerned about being caught in the trap of trying to mother the client?

33. What other issues do you see that might need to be addressed in future sessions?

34. Do you have a sense of the therapist's theoretical orientation?

June 4, Monday

Janet seemed somehow to have more energy this morning—not so dejected, I guess. She reported that she had seen her doctor and he had given a prescription for, as she expressed it, "something to calm me down when I start feeling anxious." So far she only had been taking the medication for three days and she reported that she was at least sleeping better even though she still worried about things. Then she said, "I have been thinking about this counter-message idea and I know I give my kids bad messages, too. Why do I do that? Is it the anxiety or is there more to it than that?" I paused to think of how to reply. Should I say "What do you think?" or tell her what my thoughts are. I took the easy way out and asked her what she thought.

She is quiet for a while then says "I think there is more to it than that." She pauses and then goes on "Something you said earlier—I just have been thinking a lot about when I was a kid." I encourage her to talk about what is going on with her right now and she begins to tear up. "I am so lonesome," she says and then goes on to talk about always feeling somehow different and inadequate around others. She talks about how her husband gets impatient with her worries, and how she keeps trying to be better but always seems to mess up. I respond with "And it would be nice if—or you would rather—be seen as adequate." She laughs. I make a note to get back to her relationship with her husband at a later time.

I ask her who says she messes up? She responds that she does—she just knows she has messed up. I probe for an example while thinking I would like to move toward developing some insight concerning early messages and how they affect her, but she continues to talk about the messages she gives herself. Finally, I ask her how she has learned to know when she has "messed up." She responds with "I just know" and I push a bit for more. "You just know?"

She is silent for a time but her face shows a range of emotions from puzzlement to sadness to disgust. Then she begins to talk in a low, almost childlike voice. "I've always been a scardy-cat—just worried about everything."

I am thinking that she has made several references to her mother—and I must admit, I am feeling some animosity toward that mother. But, what about her father? Would that be a place to go? In the meantime, Janet is still talking. She tells me about when she started school and how she was scared to go to school by herself, and so every morning her mother walked her to school. She tells about being taunted by the other kids because she is scared to cross the street by herself, scared to go down the big slide, or swing high on the swings.

She tells me, "Nothing is really safe, you know." I know I need to challenge that statement, so I simply say "Nothing?" and she responds with a short laugh and says, "I guess I am an all or nothing type of person." I want to go for the opening, but our time is about up so I ask her to look for examples of when all or nothing doesn't apply in her life and bring in a list next week. I suggest that she could ask her family to help her identify areas where some or a little bit might be safe or comfortable. She asked for an example. I mentioned her concern about keeping a perfect house. I note that time is running out and several things have come up that need attention. Lots to do next session.

35. Do you think the therapist should address the client's loneliness? Why or why not?
36. Why do you think the therapist gave the client an assignment that involved her family?
37. Should the therapist involve the client's family in the therapy process? If so, in what way might the family be involved?
38. What issues would you want to address at this point?

June 11, Monday

Janet started talking before she sat down. She said she was really surprised at how much difference the pills made and that even though the doctor had urged her to continue in therapy, she wondered if it would be worthwhile. We talked a bit about her goals concerning feeling better about herself and more in control of her life; and how her life might be different if she did feel more in control of her life. She agrees that she does need to work more on these issues. At this point, I am thinking about the homework I assigned last week, so I ask her if she had identified some areas where some or a little could be safe or comfortable.

She sighed and then responded "That was hard." She went on to say she had actually made a list and that didn't seem to work so her husband suggested that the bed didn't have to be made every morning and that she didn't need to start clearing the table the minute she finished eating. "I didn't know he noticed," she said. "So, I asked him to help me by reminding me when I was being obsessive."

I asked her what was on her mind at that point and she said she wanted to talk about her mother. She said she had been having dreams about her mother almost every night and kept hearing her words—mostly critical—in her head. "I'm really distracted," she reported. "I can't get her out of my head." She paused, then said, "Maybe that's because I'm not so busy being anxious about everything."

I asked her if she thought her mother had a message for her. She made a face and said that if her mother had a message it would be negative, such as telling her to be afraid, that she wouldn't get better, that this whole thing is a waste of time and money. "And would you agree?" I asked. She was quiet for some time, with her head down. Finally, she looked up and I could see tears. I handed her a tissue and waited. She took a couple of deep breaths, wiped her eyes and said, "I'm being difficult, aren't I?"

39. How would you respond? Why?

   a. Assure her that she is not difficult?
   b. Recognize that she is having a rough time?

   c. Ask her what she thinks?

   d. Ignore the question?

   e. Other?

40. Do you think the counselor should have responded differently to the client's tears. Why?

I waited a bit, then reflected that it sounded as if she had been doing some real work and asked if she would like to tell me more about that and how that had been for her. She told me that she had thought about her mother every day, that she had heard her mother's voice in her head. She went on to say that she had argued with her—even yelled at her. She said she knew her mother wasn't a happy woman, that she had been miserable most of the time. She said she searched her mind for a time when she and her mother had fun together. Then she said, "I guess I don't have much fun with my kids either. Isn't that awful? I don't want to be like my mother." Then she grinned and told me the assignment had been a way she could get her mother, so when she left the dishes on the table for an hour, she thought about how upset her mother would be if she saw that.

I debated about whether to ask about her father—she hasn't really talked about him at all, but instead, I probed to help her define fun and whether she felt bad about not having fun with her kids because she was supposed to have fun with her kids or because she really wanted to have fun with them. Her first response was that she wanted to have fun with her kids—then she paused and said "I guess I must think I'm supposed to because I even worry about that. Am I giving my kids the right kind of life? Am I playing with them enough? Am I teaching them the right things? What if they grow up to be failures or sick or crazy like me?"

I responded that it seemed that she put a lot of time and energy into worrying and criticizing herself for not doing the right things or not being good enough. She agreed. I asked "What would you do if you didn't devote all that time and energy to worrying and putting yourself down?" She was quiet for a while and then asked "What else can I do?"

I answered with "That's a good question. What would you do with all that time and energy?" Then I asked her whether she thought her children were being raised differently than she had been. Her response was, "Oh yeah, absolutely." At that point, we spent some time comparing the differences and I asked her to help me understand how these differences might affect her children. "I know one thing," she said "even as mixed up as I am, I'm having a lot more fun with my kids than my mother ever had with me." I reflected that she might find that she could have even more fun with her children, her husband, and even herself. She laughed and replied, "That would be good, really good."

June 18, Monday

Janet almost bounced in today. She reported that she is sleeping better and not worrying so much. She had spent most of the week housecleaning and, in doing so, threw out or gave away many of her mother's possessions. "I may regret that someday," she says, "but it felt so right and so good right now."

I said that I wondered if she felt like she was getting rid of some of her unpleasant memories and feelings. "I hadn't thought of it that way," she replied, "but I did feel somehow relieved and *clean,* if you know what I mean." I asked her to talk about *clean.* What did she mean? She paused and seemed to be thinking; I noticed color rising in her cheeks, then receding. "I'm not really sure," she said, "maybe I mean *free* in a way. I'm beginning to believe that I can put aside all that stuff and just *be* without being so caught in all that past." She goes on to tell me that she started to lay aside some pictures to bring in and show me but then she changed her mind and just put them in a box. I found myself primarily using empathy, reflecting feelings, and echoing back key words.

Later in the session, she began to talk about her father. As she did, she moved back and forth between anger and sorrow. She described him as not being around much of the time, and when he was, he often was drinking. She reported that he could be really mean and at times brutal, especially when he was drunk. During this time, her affect was flat and, at times, she spoke so quietly I would have to ask her to repeat herself because I couldn't hear what she was saying. I reflected that she might, in some sense, feel sorry for her mother. She looked at me with a how could you say that expression on her face and then responded "I never thought of that."

After Janet left, I thought about what we have been doing and where we were going. I went back and reviewed our original goals and made a note to review them with her next week. I have learned that, to some extent, each client calls on different parts of myself. Janet pulls on my empathy and I find that I need to be careful not to try to do too much for her—even as I admire her strength and determination.

41. How would you characterize the interventions the counselor is using?
42. What might the client's flat affect indicate?
43. What might you have done differently? Why?

June 25, Monday

Janet seemed almost to bounce into my office. She reported that she is feeling great and wondered if she really needed to keep coming to see me. I suggested that this was a good time to review the goals we had talked about a few weeks ago. I gave her a list of the goals I had made and those she had identified and asked her if she would rank them on a scale of 1 to 4 with 1 indicating little or no progress, 2 indicating some progress, 3 indicating significant progress, and 4 indicating goal met. I, in turn would rank both sets of goals and then we could compare our ranking (Tables 13.2 and 13.3).

We noted that I thought we had done more in terms of identifying the source of anxiety than she thought we had, and I admitted that she no doubt had met the goal of feeling better but I thought she could feel even better than better. We also disagreed on the worrying—she felt she was still worrying more than she wanted to.

I asked her which of the three areas that she rated a 2 would she like to start with. She chose source of anxiety, saying that she hadn't thought of that as being important. I responded that I had rated it higher because I thought she was telling me that she was anxious because she had been taught to be anxious. She looked puzzled, and then her face lit up. "Ah, my mother taught me to be anxious," she said "And you learned well." I responded. She laughed and retorted, "Well, she was a good teacher."

TABLE 13.2   My Rankings

MY GOALS FOR JANET	RATE	JANET'S GOALS	RATE
1. Identify source of anxiety.	3	1. Feel better	3
2. Reduce number of anxiety attacks.	3	2. Not worry so much	3
3. Feel more in control in her life.	3	3. Be able to do more things	3
4. Manage stress more effectively.	2		

"How does that change things, if you believe you learned to be anxious from your mother?" I asked. She was quiet for some time, seeming to be working on something. Then I noticed that her eyes were filling with tears. "I wonder what happened to her," she said. "She was so unhappy and so compulsive. I think that's why my dad was an alcoholic; she drove him to it. I don't know whether to feel sorry for her or to be angry with her. Maybe a bit of both."

"Are you ready to move on?" I ask. She nods so I ask her where she would like to go next. She chooses not worrying so much. I suggest that maybe some worrying is O.K., even normal. I ask her what it would it be like if she never worried about anything. She looks surprised. "Anything at all? Anything at all. Wow, I don't know." We spend some time talking about the concept of realistic anxiety or worry and some possible scenarios where a measure of anxiety might be a healthy response.

We've come to a point where the medication is working, the client has some idea about the underlying factors that contribute to her anxiety, and she has learned some ways to manage the anxiety. I believe she would benefit from some further work concerning her relationship with her mother, and probably her father, but I'm not sure if she will want to do that at this time. I realize that I, to some extent, invited her to discontinue therapy when I asked her if she was ready to move on. We set a follow-up appointment for two weeks later.

July 6, Friday

Janet called to cancel Monday's appointment. She said everything was going well, she was feeling really good right now. She said she knew she had some more work to do convinc-

TABLE 13.3   Janet's Rankings

MY GOALS FOR JANET	RATE	JANET'S GOALS	RATE
1. Identify source of anxiety.	2	1. Feel better	4
2. Reduce number of anxiety attacks.	3	2. Not worry so much	2
3. Feel more in control in her life.	3	3. Be able to do more things	3
4. Manage stress more effectively.	2		

ing her mother and probably, her father too, but she would like to take a break. I hope she returns for further work, but I know that with the medication, she has gotten some real relief. I really liked working with her and I think I did some good work.

44. Do you think that Janet has more work to do? If so, in what areas?
45. What factors might contribute to Janet's returning for additional counseling?
46. How would you work with Janet about issues concerning her mother and/or father?

BIBLIOGRAPHY

Gerzon, R. (1997). *Finding serenity in the age of anxiety.* New York: Bantam.

Johnson, S. (1997). *Therapist's guide to clinical interventions: The 1-2-3s of treatment planning.* San Diego, CA: Academic Press.

Wilson, R. R. (1996). *Don't panic: Taking control of anxiety attacks.* New York: Harper Collins. (See also *www.anxiety.com*)

INDEX

Accountability, 8–9
Active listening, 42
  minimal prompts in, 43
  reflection of content, 43–44
  reflection of feeling, 44–46
  silence in, 46
  suggested activities for, 45–46
Acute symptoms, 90–91
Adherence
  guidelines for, 161–163
  relapse prevention, 163–172
  techniques for, 160
Adler, Alfred, 77, 132, 149, 167
Adlerian formulation, 77
Anxiety
  allaying, 182–183
  psychodynamic view of, 5
  of therapist, 182
Assertiveness training, 107–108
Assessment, 16
  case study of, 94–95
  focused–functional, 56–57
  formal–diagnostic, 56–68
  of mental status, 59–60,
    63–64
  ongoing, 57
  purpose of, 55–56
  skill exercises for, 95–96
  traditional means of, 55
  See also Diagnostic assessment
Ataque, 29
Attending, 37–38
  internal, 38
  physical, 39–41
  suggested activities related to,
    38–39, 41
  verbal, 41–42
Attitude of patient, assessment of,
  60

Automatic thinking patterns,
  101–104

Bandler, Richard, 115
Beck, Aaron, 6, 99
Beck Depression Inventory (BDI),
  62–66
Behavior, changing, 154–155
Behavior rehearsal, 108–109
Behavioral interventions
  behavior rehearsal, 108–109
  cognitive restructuring, 100–101
  combating automatic thinking
    patterns, 101–104
  desensitization, 105–107
  four steps to happiness,
    104–105
  modeling, 108
  relaxation in, 106
  social skills training, 107–108
Behaviorism, 5
Berg, Insoo Kim, 32, 59, 116, 132
Biological formulation, 76–77
Blocking, 151
Body language, confronting,
  120–121
Boundaries
  marking of, 151
  restructuring of, 152–153
Brainstorming, 155
Buber, Martin, 37
Bugental, James, 38
Burns, David, 100

Case formulation, 85
  case study of, 80–83
  of clients and therapists, 72–73
  defined, 71
  skill exercise for, 83–85

types of, 71–72
Choice-making process, 155–156
Circular questions, 135, 136, 137
Clarifying, 115–116
  of deletions, 116
  of distortions, 116–117
  of generalizations, 117–118
Client
  case formulation of, 72–73
  cognitive status of, 60
  concerns of, 10
  cultural issues of, 29–31, 32
  financial issues regarding,
    185–186
  informed consent and, 180
  initial contact with, 179–180
  motivation of, 25–26
  orientation and attitude of, 60
  perceptual status of, 60
  personal expectations of, 31
  presentation of, 59
  presenting problem of, 58–59
  readiness for change of, 27–27
  resources of, 12–13, 60–61, 65
  rights of, 185
  safety issues regarding, 60
  skills training of, 172
  stress management of, 171–172
Client-centered therapy, 7
Clinical formulation, 71, 75–76
  development of, 78
  types of, 76–78
Clinical outcomes, 87
Cognitive interventions
  behavior rehearsal, 108–109
  cognitive restructuring, 100–101
  combating automatic thinking
    patterns, 101–104
  desensitization, 105–107

four steps to happiness,
104–105
modeling, 108
relaxation in, 106
social skills training, 107–108
Cognitive restructuring, 100–101
Cognitive status of patient, assessment of, 60
Cognitive-behavioral formulation, 76
Cognitive-behavioral therapy, 11
focus of, 5
therapeutic change in, 6
therapeutic relationship in, 6
Collaboration, 3
Collaborative empiricism, 6
Communication, importance of, 154
Communication skills, building, 108
Conflict resolution, 155
Confrontation
of body language, 120–121
of destructive behaviors, 122–123
of immediate behavior, 121–122
Continuing education, 188–189
Coping questions, 137, 144–145
Countertransference, dealing with, 125–128
Culture
and assessment, 61, 64–65
and case formulation, 80
influence on therapy, 32
Curative factors
client resources, 12–13
faith/hope/expectancy, 12
intervention strategies, 12, 13–14
relationships, 12

Deletions, combating, 116
Demoralization, 33
Desensitization, 3, 105–107
systematic, 6
Destructive behaviors, confronting, 122–123
Developmental history and dynamics assessment, 61

case study of, 64
Diagnostic assessment
DSM-III and, 55
presenting problem and context, 58–59
Diagnostic formulation, 71
development of, 74–75
DSM-IV and, 73–74
skill exercise for, 83–84
Diagnostic-linear questions, 134–135
Dietary supplements, assessing use of, 62
Disequilibrium, in systemic interventions, 150–151
Distortions, combating, 116–117
DSM-III, 55
DSM-IV TR, 73–74
Dual relationships, 189
suggested activity related to, 189–190

Effective Therapist Learning System
learning guide, 18
textbook, 17
using, 18
video, 17–18
Ego psychology, 3
Elaboration, 113–115
Emotional status of patient, assessment of, 60
Empathy, 26
importance of, 47
responding skills, 46–48
suggested activity related to, 48
Empowering questions, 137, 140–141
Enactment, 150–151
Encouragement
accentuating the positive, 50–51
marking behaviors, 49–50
Engagement, 15–16, 34
characteristics of, 24–26
empathy in, 26
skills involved in, 36–37
suggested activity regarding, 51
Ethical questions, 177
dual relationships, 189–190

at initial contact, 180–182
at precounseling stage, 178–179
range of, 176
in service provision, 187–188
Web resources related to, 177
Evaluation, of therapy, 191
Exception questions, 137, 142–143
Expectancy, 12, 14
Expectations
cultural, 32
personal, 31–32
Experiential therapy, 11
Explanatory models, 30–31
Externalizing questions, 137, 139–140
Eye movement desensitization and reprocessing (EMDR), 106–107

Faith, in therapy, 12, 14
Family dimension of life functioning, 93
Family Systems approach (Bowen), 7
First order change, 154
Focused-functional assessment, 56–57, 97–98
skill exercise for, 95–96
of symptoms, 90–91
Formal-diagnostic assessment, 56
components of, 58–63
of developmental history and dynamics, 61
importance of, 57, 58
interview format for, 66, 67–68
inventories, 65–66
of mental status, 59–60, 63–64
performance of, 66–68
presenting problem and context, 58–59
skill exercise for, 66, 68
Four steps to happiness, 104–105
Frank, Jerome, 33
Freudian model, 3
Functional outcomes, 87

Generalizations, combating, 117–118
Gentle commands, 114

Gestalt therapy, 6
Greeting, of client, 179–180
  suggested activity related to, 182
Grief, coping with, 106
Grinder, John, 115

Health dimension of life functioning, 93
Health history and behaviors, 62
  case study of, 65
Helping alliance, 4
Hispanics
  cultural issues regarding therapy of, 29
  linguistic issues regarding therapy of, 10
Hope, and therapy, 12, 14
Howard, Kenneth, 89
Humanistic therapies
  focus of, 6–7
  therapeutic change in, 7
  therapeutic relationship in, 7

Illness
  course of after intervention, 89–90
  natural course of, 88
Immediacy
  importance of, 127–128
  suggested activity for practicing, 128
Immediate behavior, confronting, 121–122
Informed consent, 180
Institutional affiliations, 178
Integrative formulation, 77
Integrative-multicultural-accountable perspective, 1
  background of, 8–10
  characteristics of, 11, 19–20
Internal attending, 38
Internet
  counseling resources on, 192
  ethics resources on, 177
  evaluating information on, 192–193
  searching on, 192
Interpretation

guidelines for, 124
levels of, 124–125
purposes of, 123–124
Interventions, 16–17
  cognitive and behavioral, 99–109
  psychodynamic, 110–130
  solution-focused, 131–147
  strategies and techniques for, 12
  systemic and psychoeducational, 148–158
Interventive interviewing, 131, 146–147
  diagnostic-linear questions, 134–135
  follow-up use of, 146
  history of, 132
  indications for, 145–146
  therapist intentionality in, 135
  types of questions in, 135–145
  value of, 133–134
Interview
  for assessment, 66, 67–68
  initial, 183–185
  interventive, 131–147
  psychodynamic, 111
Intimacy dimension of life functioning, 93

Joining skills, 37–38

Kohutian self–psychology, 4, 6, 7
Krumboltz, John, 44

Lambert, Michael, 10, 12–14
Life functioning
  assessment of, 92
  dimensions of, 93
Listening, active, 42–46

Madigan, Stephen, 41
Maintenance
  adherence guidelines, 161–163
  relapse prevention, 163–172
  techniques for, 160
Maintenance therapy, 17
Making connections, 118–120
  statements for, 119

suggested activity related to, 118
Managed behavioral health care, 8
  assessment use by, 56–57, 86–88
Marking behaviors, 49–50
Medical necessity, 87
Mental status assessment, 59–60
  case study of, 63–64
Miller, Scott, 132
Minimal prompts, 43
MMPI (Minnesota Multiphasic Personality Inventory), 55
Modeling, 108, 154
Mood of patient, assessment of, 60
Motivation, 25–26
  clinical implications of, 28–29
MRI interactional approach, 7
Multiculturalism, 9–10

Negotiation, 155
Neurosis, development of, 4–5
Nonverbal skills, suggested activity related to, 41
Note taking, 185–187

Ongoing assessment, 57, 96–97
  components of, 93
Open-ended therapy, 170–171
Orientation of patient, assessment of, 60
Oscillation effect, 166
Outcome questions, 137, 144
Outcomes revolution, 8
Over-the-counter (OTC) medications, assessing use of, 62

Paradoxes, 153
  techniques for using, 153–154
Participant observer, 4
Perceptions, altering, in systemic interventions, 151–154
Perceptual status of patient, assessment of, 60
Persistent symptoms, 91
Phase Theory model, 89
Phobias, removing, 106
Physical attending, 39–41
Placebo effect, 12, 14

Placebo effect *Continued*
  triggering and enhancement of, 34
Positive description questions, 137, 143
Positive thinking, 50–51
Practical issues
  closing a session, 190–191
  combating anxiety, 182–183
  evaluation of therapy, 191
  information gathering, 183–185
  at initial contact, 179–182
  note taking, 185–187
  at precounseling stage, 178–179
  range of, 176
  in service provision, 187–188
  training and supervision, 188–189
  treatment plan, 187
  using the Internet, 192–193
Prescribing, in therapy using paradoxes, 153
Prescription medications, assessing use of, 62
Presentation of patient, assessment of, 59–60
Presenting problem, 58–59
  case study of, 63
Problem-solving skills, 156
  training in, 108
Prompts, in active listening, 43
Psychodynamic formulation, 76
Psychodynamic interventions, 110–111
  clarifying, 115–118
  elaboration, 113–115
  interpretation skills in, 123–125
  interviewing, 111
  making connections, 118–120
  summarizing, 112–113
  therapeutic confrontation, 120–123
  transference and countertransference in, 125–128
Psychodynamic therapy, 11
  focus of, 3–4
  therapeutic change in, 4–5
  therapeutic relationship in, 4
Psychotherapists. *See* Therapists

Psychotherapy. *See* Therapy; Treatment
Punctuation, 152

Readiness for change, 27
  clinical implications of, 28–29, 30
  stages of, 27–28
Redefining, in therapy using paradoxes, 153
Reflecting
  content, 43–44
  feeling, 44–46
Reflexive questions, 135, 136, 137, 138
Reframing, 8, 151–152
Relabeling, 152
Relapse prevention
  models of, 163–164, 167–169
  reasons for relapse, 166–167, 168
  research on, 164–165
  steps in, 171–172
  techniques of, 168–169
Relaxation, 106
  techniques for, 182
Restraining, in therapy using paradoxes, 153
Rogers, Carl, 6, 7, 12, 13, 26, 37
Rorschach test, 55

Safety of patient, assessment of, 60–61
Satir approach, 7
Scaling questions, 137, 141–142
Scharff, Jill, 126, 186
Schemas, 3
  in cognitive-behavioral view, 5–6
  in psychodynamic view, 3, 5
Second order change, 154
Self-management, 93
Self-psychology, 4, 6, 7
Self-schemas, 4
Setting, therapeutic, 181–182
Shapiro, Francine, 106
Shazer, Steve de, 132
Silence, in active listening, 46

Social dimension of life functioning, 93
Social formulation, 77
Social history, and assessment, 61, 64–65
Social skills training, 107–108
Solution-focused intervention
  diagnostic-linear questions, 134–135
  follow-up use of, 146
  history of, 132
  indications for, 145–146
  therapist intentionality in, 135
  types of questions in, 135–145
  value of, 133–134
Strategic approach to therapy, 7
Strategic questions, 135, 137, 138–139
Structural approach to therapy, 7
Structural strategies, 149
  uses of, 150
Substance use, assessing use of, 62
Summarizing, 112–113
  suggested activity related to, 113
Symptoms, 90
  types of, 90–91
System perspective, 7–8
  characteristics of, 11
Systematic desensitization, 6, 105–106
Systemic interventions, 148–149
  assignment of tasks in, 156–157
  behavior changing, 154–155
  choice as focus of, 155–156
  disequilibrium in, 150–151
  perceptual alteration in, 151–154
  structural strategies, 149–150

TAT (Thematic Apperception Test), 55
Termination, of session, 190–191
Termination of therapy, 17, 191
  approaches to, 170–171
  methods and processes of, 173–174
  techniques in, 172–173
  types of, 173

Therapeutic alliance, 4
Therapeutic relationship, 171
  case study of, 105–207
  as curative factor, 12, 13
  establishment of, 36–53
Therapist
  active listening skills of, 42–46
  attending and joining skills of,
    37–41
  case formulation of, 72–73
  continuing education of,
    188–189
  diagnostic skills of, 57–58
  empathic responding by, 46–48
  encouragement skills of, 48–51
  engagement skills of, 36–37
  institutional affiliations of, 178
  interpretation skills of, 123–125
  licensure of, 186, 188
  marketing by, 178
  nonverbal skills of, 41
  scope of activities of, 179
  traditional focus of, 159–160
  training and supervision of,
    188–189
Therapy
  curative factors and dynamics
    in, 10–14

effectiveness of, 195–207
evaluation of, 191
focus and goals of, 33
future of, 1–2
initiation of, 23–35
integrative perspective on, 1, 11,
  8–10, 19–20
medical necessity and, 8–9
motivations for, 25–26
negotiation in, 73
open-ended, 170–171
paradigm shift in, 9–10
personalization of, 171
practical and ethical issues in,
  176–193
relapse prevention, 163–172
setting for, 181–182
stages in process of, 14–17
termination of, 172–174, 191
traditional perspectives on, 2–8
See also Interventions; Treatment
Tomm, Karl, 132
Transference, dealing with,
  125–128
Trauma, coping with, 106–107
Treatment
  adherence to, 160–163

assessment of necessity of, 87
changes in focus of, 169–170
desirable characteristics of,
  165–166
efficiency, 9
outcomes management, 88
outcomes measurement, 87
outcomes monitoring, 87
plan, 187
process, 90
See also Interventions; Therapy
Treatment formulation, 71–72
  development of, 79
  purposes of, 78–79
  skill exercise for, 84–85
Treatment plan, 187

Unbalancing, 152
Unconscious, psychodynamic view
  of, 5

Verbal attending, 41–42

Walker, Lenore, 43, 185
Warning symptoms, 91
Work dimension of life function-
  ing, 93
Working alliance, 4